Oxford Socio-Legal Studies

DIVORCE MEDIATION
AND THE
LEGAL PROCESS

GENERAL EDITORS   Max Atkinson   John C. Boal
Donald R. Harris   Keith Hawkins

Oxford Socio-Legal Studies is a series of books published for the Centre for Socio-Legal
Studies, Wolfson College, Oxford. The series is concerned generally with the
relationship between law and society, and is designed to reflect the increasing interest of
lawyers, social scientists and historians in this field.

Already Published (by Oxford University Press)

Genevra Richardson, with Anthony Ogus and Paul Burrows
   POLICING POLLUTION: A Study of Regulation and Enforcement
P. W. J. Bartrip and S. B. Burman
   THE WOUNDED SOLDIERS OF INDUSTRY Industrial Compensation Policy
   1833–1897
Donald Harris *et al*
   COMPENSATION AND SUPPORT FOR ILLNESS AND INJURY
Keith Hawkins
   ENVIRONMENT AND ENFORCEMENT Regulation and the Social Definition of
   Pollution
Robert Baldwin
   REGULATING THE AIRLINES Administrative Justice and Agency Discretion
John Eekelaar and Mavis Maclean
   MAINTENANCE AFTER DIVORCE
Paul Rock
   A VIEW FROM THE SHADOWS: The Ministry of the Solicitor General of
   Canada and the Justice for Victims of Crime Initiative
Bridget Hutter
   THE REASONABLE ARM OF THE LAW?: The Law Enforcement Procedures of
   Environmental Health Officers
Hazel Genn
   HARD BARGAINING: Out of Court Settlement in Personal Injury Actions
David Downes
   CONTRASTS IN TOLERANCE: Penal Policy in the Netherlands and England and
   Wales

DIVORCE MEDIATION AND THE LEGAL PROCESS

Edited by

ROBERT DINGWALL
and
JOHN EEKELAAR

CLARENDON PRESS·OXFORD
1988

Oxford University Press, Walton Street, Oxford OX2 6DP

Oxford New York Toronto
Delhi Bombay Calcutta Madras Karachi
Petaling Jaya Singapore Hong Kong Tokyo
Nairobi Dar es Salaam Cape Town
Melbourne Auckland

and associated companies in
Beirut Berlin Ibadan Nicosia

Oxford is a trade mark of Oxford University Press

Published in the United States
by Oxford University Press, New York

British Library Cataloguing in Publication Data
Divorce mediation and the legal process.—
(Oxford socio-legal studies).
1. Divorce--Law and legislation
I. Dingwall, Robert   II. Eeckelaar, John
346.01'66   K695
ISBN 0-19-825576-4

Library of Congress Cataloging in Publication Data
Divorce mediation and the legal process.
(Oxford socio-legal studies)
Bibliography: p.
Includes index.
1. Divorce mediation—Congresses. 2. Divorce
mediation—United States—Congresses. 3. Divorce
mediation—Great Britain—Congresses. I. Dingwall,
Robert.   II. Eekelaar, John.   III. Series.
K695.A55 1985   346.01'660269   87-28142
ISBN 0 19-825576-4

Typeset by Cotswold Typesetting Limited, Gloucester
Printed and bound in Great Britain by
Biddles Limited, Guildford and King's Lynn

Preface

The reform of divorce procedures has become one of the liveliest issues in family law and social policy throughout the English-speaking world. An increasing number of countries have, to a greater or lesser degree, replaced the traditional adversarial process by less formal alternatives, known variously as mediation or conciliation. These are intended to encourage divorcing couples to resolve disputes by agreement, rather than by adjudication.

In the autumn of 1985, the Centre for Socio-Legal Studies at Oxford University had the opportunity to play host to researchers from a number of countries with a common interest in the way legal systems deal with divorce cases. Their conversations revealed a shared dissatisfaction with the level of debate about the nature of the justice that was offered by conventional and 'alternative' processes and with the quality of the research evidence on which policy was being made. These conversations were formalized, first in a seminar and then in the present book, where other contributors were invited to join the core group in their reappraisal of divorce procedures.

The reader who is looking for confident policy prescriptions from this book is likely to be disappointed. There is no 'party line' and the editors have not sought to impose one. But that, in itself, is part of the significance of this volume, its attempt to demonstrate the genuine difficulty of the value issues involved in mediation and the lack of relevant data to inform discussion. Both of these remain compelling arguments against precipitate reform.

Certain themes do recur, however. Three of these are worth highlighting in this preface: the analysis of the values of the reform movement; the comparative perspective, which locates divorce procedures into a broader social context; and the emphasis on the study of process.

Much of the present literature on alternative means of dispute resolution in divorce cases has been produced by enthusiasts writing out of their clinical experience. These authors have made an important contribution to developing a body of theory and technique for the practice of mediation. But their work rests upon specific value premises which have often gone unrecognized. American writers, for instance, reflect major themes of their national culture in their description of mediation as a step towards a utopia of self-sufficient citizens defending their private interests by negotiation unaffected by state intervention. This view also has its adherents in Britain but the balance here tends to give more weight to a utopia of a harmonious and well-ordered society, which has replaced conflict with the adjustive efforts of a variety of social regulators. Several contributors address the consequences for practice in societies which incorporate major structural inequalities between men, women, and children, particularly if mediation ceases to be the preserve of self-critical pioneers and becomes part of a routine organization.

The dominance of narrowly focused programme evaluation studies has led to an underdevelopment of baseline research on how divorces are handled under traditional procedures. Yet without this, we cannot determine whether alternative methods of dispute processing really make any difference, let alone represent an improvement. We know, for example, from established socio-legal research that conflict over custody and access is rare when seen against the totality of divorce cases; that the legal profession generally tends to prefer settlement to trial in its handling of any dispute; and that traditional forms of social work intervention are associated with a fairly high level of dispute resolution already. The first part of this book, then, attempts to build up a picture of current practice from studies in both the UK and the USA.

In the second and third parts the focus shifts to studies of alternative dispute resolution systems in action. These, too, reject the programme evaluation tradition in its reliance on second-hand data. Records, self-reports, or client reports all bear a highly problematic relationship to the crucial face-to-face encounters between mediators and divorcing couples. While these interactions are treated as a 'black box', whose contents must remain invisible to the outside world, research and policy debate cannot progress. We can only speculate about how inputs and outcomes might be linked, we cannot establish the commensurability of different types of practice and we have only the bluntest of tools for improving the skills of practitioners or auditing the quality of their work. These papers do not pretend to have solved all those problems but they do attempt to give some indications of the means by which progress might be made.

The seminar on which this book is based was supported by funds from the Law Faculty of Oxford University. It benefited from the regular or occasional presence of a number of other participants including Mavis Maclean, Peter Manning, Rebecca Bailey-Harris, Regina Graycar, and Joy Hendry. In preparing this text, we have frequently been grateful for the advice of Lisa Parkinson and Thelma Fisher. The volume bibliography was compiled by Pam Watson and the whole typed by Linda Peterson and Jeanette Price.

Contents

Part I: Current Practices

1. The Development of Conciliation in England
   JOHN EEKELAAR *and* ROBERT DINGWALL   3

2. Negotiation Between Lawyer and Client in an American Divorce
   WILLIAM L. F. FELSTINER *and* AUSTIN SARAT   23

3. The Solicitor as Intermediary
   RICHARD INGLEBY   43

4. 'Civil Work' in the Probation Service
   ADRIAN JAMES   56

5. Divorce Mediation: An American Picture
   JESSICA PEARSON *and* NANCY THOENESS   71

Part II: Mediation on Court Premises

6. The Halls of Justice and Justice in the Halls
   GWYNN DAVIS   95

7. *Kaji Chotei:* Mediation in the Japanese Family Court
   SATOSHI MINAMIKATA   116

Part III: Mediation out of Court

8. Mediation, Conflict, and Social Inequality: Family Dispute Processing among the Bakwena
   ANNE GRIFFITHS   129

9. Three Models of Family Mediation
   SIMON ROBERTS   144

10. Empowerment or Enforcement? Some Questions about Power and Control in Divorce Mediation
    ROBERT DINGWALL   150

11. A Wider Vision?
    ROBERT DINGWALL *and* JOHN EEKELAAR   168

REFERENCES   183

LIST OF ACTS AND CASES   194

List of contributors

Robert Dingwall is a Research Fellow of Wolfson College and the Centre for Socio-Legal Studies, University of Oxford.

John Eekelaar is a Fellow of Pembroke College and Lecturer in Law, University of Oxford.

Gwynn Davis is a Research Associate at the Socio-Legal Centre for Family Studies, University of Bristol.

William Felstiner is Director of the American Bar Foundation, Chicago.

Anne Griffiths is a Lecturer in Scots Law at the University of Edinburgh.

Richard Ingleby is a Lecturer in Law at the University of Melbourne.

Adrian James is a Lecturer in Applied Social Studies at the University of Hull.

Satoshi Minamikata is an Assistant Professor in Law at Ibaraki University.

Jessica Pearson is Director of the Center for Policy Research, Denver.

Simon Roberts is a Professor of Law at the London School of Economics.

Austin Sarat is a Professor of Political Science at Amherst College.

Nancy Thoeness is a Research Associate at the Center for Policy Research, Denver.

PART I

Current practices

1. The Development of Conciliation in England

J. M. EEKELAAR AND R. DINGWALL

The term 'conciliation' has a surprisingly long history in English family law. Its use can easily be traced back into the nineteen thirties. The difficulty for any historical account, however, is that the meaning of the term has changed over the last fifty years. 'Conciliation' was originally used interchangeably with reconciliation. The distinction between intervention aimed at reducing conflict upon the breakdown of a marriage and intervention intended to repair a failing relationship was not clearly made until the nineteen seventies. Even then, the term 'conciliation' was used to describe a great variety of activities linked only by their claim to be pursuing the same objective. Nevertheless, it is useful to begin by tracing the history of this term in order to explore the interaction between family law and social policy that has shaped the context of current developments. We will, in particular, emphasize the relationship between changing ideas about conciliation or reconciliation, and the availability, cost, and acceptability of divorce. The process owes as much to concern for the public purse as it does to concern for public welfare.

Conciliation in the Thirties

To identify the earliest developments in conciliation, we need to go outside the official channels for obtaining a divorce and examine domestic proceedings in magistrates' courts. As McGregor *et al.* (1970) have shown, these, in effect, provided an alternative system for the legal termination of a relationship and the adjudication of financial and custody matters for those who could not afford the costs of a divorce through the High Court. By the early nineteen thirties magistrates' courts were making about 15,000 orders a year arising out of marriage breakdowns, while the High Court was granting fewer than 5,000 divorces.

In 1934, a Summary Jurisdiction (Domestic Procedure) Bill was introduced by Lord Listowel. This included a proposal for a 'special conciliation' summons which would allow either spouse to require the other to appear before a court which would then try to help them resolve their matrimonial difficulties. The idea of introducing this type of social work provision provoked some contention and it was shelved in favour of a departmental committee, whose report, *Social services in courts of summary jurisdiction*, was published in 1936. This showed that informal attempts at conciliation, mostly by probation officers but also by court officials and voluntary workers, were widespread. The committee felt that these should be officially encouraged but were concerned about the practice in many courts of allowing probation officers to see applicants before any hearing which, it was thought, could deny justice by obstructing access to the court. It recommended that all complainants should be seen by the court which would then decide which cases were suitable for referral to a probation officer.

In 1937, the Summary Procedure (Domestic Proceedings) Act extended the statutory duties of the probation service to give effect to these recommendations. In the same year, the Matrimonial Causes Act brought the first real extension of the grounds for divorce beyond adultery to include cruelty, desertion, and the insanity of the other spouse. The number of divorces granted annually immediately rose by almost 50 per cent. This may have contributed to the movement which led to the formation of the Marriage Guidance Council in 1938, but one should not overlook the widespread anxiety among social policy-makers during the thirties about the condition of the British family (Lewis 1980). Indeed it is probably more appropriate to analyse both the extension of court-based social work and the establishment of marriage guidance as part of that general concern than to relate them to specifically legal developments. The focus, then, was directed towards reconciliation, to patching up the breach in the family which had led them into litigation rather than in providing a less adversarial means of effecting a separation. Murch (1980), for example, stresses the Christian zeal of probation officers at this period and the 1936 departmental committee noted how conciliation may be 'activated by personal convictions as to the sanctity of the marriage tie' (p. 12).

The Experience of War

Most of these developments went into cold storage on the outbreak of war. The Marriage Guidance Council, for instance, suspended its activities and the number of divorces fell back from the peak year of 1938 when the new grounds came into operation. From 1941 onwards, however, the number of divorces began to rise sharply, reaching a peak of just over 47,000 in 1947. This was without any change in the grounds, although special wartime procedures did enable Service personnel to obtain divorces more cheaply and quickly than had previously been the case.

The official history of wartime social services was obliged to drop its plans to include a comprehensive study of the factors involved in the rising demand for divorce (Ferguson and Fitzgerald 1954: ix).[1] It is clear, however, that the authors regarded it as an important indicator of 'some malaise in the war-time family' (p. 21). The causes of these pressures on marriage were identified as the poverty of private soldiers' families, if there were small children and the wife was not working; the shortage of housing; the separations of overseas postings; and the enormous increase in the workforce participation of women, because of the physical stress of a double job in employment and housework, and the independence that economic activity made possible. As in other areas of social policy (Titmuss 1950), the demands of wartime led to major extensions in social services, both directly by the state and in partnership with voluntary organizations. The Marriage Guidance Council was reconstituted in 1943 to aid the civilian population, but the leading role was taken by the services' welfare associations. Their work was, of course, primarily motivated by questions of morale among the personnel of the armed forces and directed towards reconciliation. It was later claimed that this was successful in about 25 per cent of the divorce applications with which they were involved, although the veracity of this figure is impossible to establish (Denning Committee 1947: para. 18).

Nevertheless, the experience of wartime social services in dealing with divorce was to have an important effect on public policy. Ferguson and Fitzgerald (1954: 26) emphasized the general stability of the family under wartime conditions but also observed that the imprint of the war 'on the minds of men, women and children could not be erased by victory proclamations'. This comment may well reflect the post-war surge in divorces. The number quadrupled between 1944 and 1946.

Inevitably, this sudden upsurge in divorce suits placed great strain on the legal system. The response was to set up a Committee in June 1946 under the then Mr Justice Denning to 'consider and report upon what procedural reform ought to be introduced in the general interests of litigants, with specific reference to expediting the hearing of suits and reducing costs and to the courts in which such suits ought to proceed, and in particular whether any (and, if so, what) machinery should be made available for the purpose of attempting a reconciliation between the parties, either before or after proceedings have been commenced'. This

Committee's Final Report (Denning Committee 1947) paid considerable attention to the question of reconciliation. Its main strategy was to build on existing resources, especially the experience of the probation service in magistrates' courts since 1937. The Denning Committee (1947: para. 34 iii) thought that this role should be extended to divorce cases in the High Court, envisaging that a welfare officer would review every petition in cases involving children, with the power to investigate the position of the children and to attempt to reconcile their parents. Following this proposal, welfare officers were appointed to the divorce court in London in 1950. As Adrian James describes later, the work of the probation service in divorce cases has expanded steadily ever since.

For present purposes, however, the chief importance of the Denning Committee lies in the proposal put to it by Lord Merriman, then President of the Probate, Divorce, and Admiralty Division and senior 'divorce judge' (Denning Committee 1947: para. 23). He suggested that all undefended divorces should initially be referred to a tribunal responsible to a Commission of Conciliation and Enquiry. Each tribunal would consist of a lawyer and a welfare (or probation) officer. They would begin by exploring the chances of reconciliation. If this failed, the tribunal would make its own investigation of the facts and 'by consent of the parties, deal with' matters like custody and maintenance. Finally, the case would be referred to a court for the pronouncement of 'banns of divorce', which would automatically take effect unless someone objected to them.

Although this is clearly not a proposal for conciliation in the modern sense, the scheme does contain elements of that in an embryonic form. The 'justice' and 'welfare' aspects of divorce would be reflected in the personnel of the tribunal and it would be able to 'deal with' issues by consent in much the same way as the recent Booth Committee (1985) on divorce procedure recommended for 'initial hearings'. But the Denning Committee was still preoccupied with reconciliation and rejected the proposal. The Committee believed that it would introduce the attempt at reconciliation so late in the divorce process as to impair its chances of success and that these would be further undermined by the association of reconciliation with the authority of a tribunal.

Reconciliation: The Light that Failed

After the peak year of 1947, the number of divorces granted each year fell steadily throughout the fifties, with the exception of 1952 when there was a temporary rise resulting from easier access to legal aid. A similar decline occurred in separation orders. Nevertheless both remained at a higher level than in pre-war years and fears continued to be expressed about the stability of family life. The Royal Commission on Marriage and Divorce (1956: para. 39) thought that the incidence of divorce was still a 'matter of grave concern' and numerous similar comments are quoted in the introduction to Fletcher's (1962) spirited defence of the British family. As he points out (1968 edition: 142), in the nineteen fifties 93 per cent of marriages did not end in the divorce court.

Social policy debates are, however, rarely won or lost by reference to statistical evidence and the course of developments during the fifties can only be understood by reference to the tension between the desire to modernize the basic structure of English divorce law and the repeated claims of a Christian evangelical lobby, with important support in the education, health, and welfare professions, that the family was in decline as a social institution. In effect the price of rationalizing the divorce law was increased investment in attempts at reconciliation.

Until 1971, English divorce law was dominated by the theory of the matrimonial offence. This required the applicant for a divorce to establish that the other party had committed one of a short list of actions against them or their interests. The first attempt at reforming this came in a Private Member's Bill debated by the House of Commons in 1951, which would have allowed divorce to couples who had lived apart for seven years without either having to make an accusation of a matrimonial offence. The hostile reaction of the churches led to the establishment of the Royal Commission on Marriage and Divorce, which finally reported in 1956. The majority of the Commission rejected any movement toward no-fault divorce and emphasized the importance of further developing services for marriage guidance and reconciliation.

But this report failed to silence the critics of the matrimonial offence (e.g. McGregor 1957) and there was an important inconsistency in the traditionalists' position. The doctrine of the offence also required the applicant to show that it was that action which had motivated the suit. Thus the right to a divorce would be lost if the applicant had previously forgiven the other party for having committed the offence (condonation) or had colluded in its commission. Any attempt at reconciliation was likely to be inhibited by the possibility that apparent condonation could compromise the chance of a divorce if the attempt failed. This problem was eventually tackled by the Matrimonial Causes Act 1963, which explicitly allowed attempts at reconciliation to be disregarded by the court, although the actual effect of this was limited by restrictive judicial interpretation (*Brown* v. *Brown* [1967] P 105; *Godfrey* v. *Godfrey* [1965] AC 444).

The same Act also amended the provisions on collusion in ways which were intended to facilitate agreed solutions to divorce-related disputes. It is important to recognize the support given to negotiation throughout the post-war period. The High Court had declared in 1945 that agreements on matters like costs, maintenance, custody of children, and property rights did not constitute collusion (*Emanuel* v. *Emanuel* [1946] P 115). All that was forbidden was that the parties should 'concoct a false case . . . or create by arrangement between themselves the grounds for divorce' (Denning Committee 1947: para. 29 xi). Lord Merriman's proposals to the Denning Committee do not suggest that he saw any serious difficulties in linking agreements on ancillary matters with an offence-based approach to divorce itself. There was, of course, a risk that 'genuine' agreements could raise suspicions in the court's mind that the parties had arranged the presentation of the facts to satisfy the requirements of the offence theory and this may have constrained more cautious lawyers until the legislative changes of 1963 and the cases which confirmed that these provisions at least would be liberally interpreted (e.g. *Nash* v. *Nash* [1965] P 266; cf. Ingleby 1986*b*).

Even so, it seems highly questionable whether the typical experience of divorce in the post-war period has been of an aggressive adversarial contest. Critics such as Parkinson (1986*b*: 13) argue that 'legal rituals designed to achieve justice in criminal trials may not be appropriate in matrimonial and family law'. But this ignores the centrality of negotiation throughout the civil and criminal justice systems (cf. Melli *et al.* 1985, Erlanger *et al.* 1986). As Ross (1970: 3) observes for civil justice in the USA, 'the principal institution of the law in action is not trial: it is settlement out of court'. Baldwin and McConville (1977) and Genn (1987) make similar observations on criminal and civil justice in England. Indeed the existence of a divided legal profession may even accentuate this: solicitors have little to gain by getting cases into court. Thus, divorce law would be highly exceptional if its routine practice were dominated by trial.

Direct evidence is hard to find, although Melli *et al.* (1985): 41 n. 3) quote an important study from Maryland looking at divorce under a fault-based system in 1929. The authors estimated that there were genuine contests in no more than one case in every forty or fifty filed (Marshall and May 1932: 199–200). Parkinson (1986*b*: 13) quotes John Mortimer's (1982) autobiographical account of matrimonial practice in the nineteen fifties. But when the creator of Rumpole recalls the way in which barristers could make a good living out of fitting undefended divorces into one of the 'three immutable categories of adultery, cruelty and desertion', he is surely doing no more than endorsing the prevalence of unopposed applications and describing the traditional work of lawyers in fitting personal troubles into available legal categories (Cain 1983). As one contemporary lawyer observed,

Large incomes can be made at the Bar out of practices which consist almost entirely of undefended divorces. The hearing of an undefended suit commonly takes between ten and fifteen minutes, though much higher speeds are possible. Counsel are paid at an approximate rate of 12s. 6d. per minute for asking a string of leading questions. The paper work involved in settling documents, advising on evidence, and the like can be done by an experienced practitioner almost in his sleep. Some of it indeed can be mass produced; before the war one of the busiest members of the Probate and Divorce Bar used to settle a divorce petition simply by filling in half a dozen blanks in a mimeographed form from the stock which he carried in his chambers. Undefended divorces also provide useful initial training in court work for young men who are just starting at the Bar. (Harvey 1953: 133.)

We must clearly be cautious about the risk of erecting an alternative and equally unsupported stereotype to oppose the gladiatorial image of the divorce lawyer. Clearly some clients are, for a variety of reasons, likely to be more committed to litigating their matrimonial disputes to the bitter end and are likely to receive some encouragement from some lawyers. At the same time, there is no reason to suppose that the settlement-orientation reported in this volume by Richard Ingleby, and by William Felstiner and Austin Sarat, is an invention of the nineteen eighties and is not characteristic of the tradition of legal work in divorce cases (see also Burgoyne *et al.* 1987: 54).

Even so, there is still a significant difference between settlement-orientation and the promotion of reconciliation. The latter continued to preoccupy policy discussions. To secure the passage of the 1963 reforms, their promoter, Leo Abse MP, had to abandon his simultaneous attempt to revive the 1951 initiative for the introduction of a no-fault separation ground (Rheinstein 1972: 323). The debates on this legislation prompted the Archbishop of Canterbury to set up an advisory commission whose report was published in 1966 as *Putting asunder: a divorce law for contemporary society.* This was a rather less liberal document than has sometimes been proposed: its acceptance of the irrelevance of the matrimonial offence has a great deal to do with its recognition of the point made above, that it had engendered a great deal of *de facto* consent and collusion which tarnished the process of divorce with dishonesty and hypocrisy. Their proposals would have been based on a detailed investigation of the parties' relationship and its future potential carried out by a corps of 'forensic social workers'.

The publication of this report was followed almost immediately by the reference of divorce law to the newly established Law Commission. Their report, *The field of choice* (1966), rejected the Anglicans' proposals as administratively impractical and socially unacceptable. They observed that there was clearly a parliamentary majority for moving towards a no-fault approach and that the detailed inquiry envisaged was unworkable. But again, there is the concession to reconciliation as one of the four major problems to be faced in the reformed law (Law Commission 1966: 16–18). This remains a prominent element of the package agreed between members of the two commissions which formed the basis of the Divorce Reform Act 1969 (Lee 1974). Section 3 of that Act required solicitors to certify whether or not they had discussed with their clients the possibility of reconciliation and offered them referral to marriage counsellors. It also empowered the court to adjourn cases while attempts at reconciliation proceed, a power whose significance will become more apparent shortly.

But there was a sense in which all this concern was increasingly academic. Writing in 1962, Fletcher had suggested that the divorce rate was likely to continue declining in the absence of the special strains of war (1968 edition: 142). McGregor *et al.* (1970: 136) thought it had more to do with the erosion of Legal Aid by inflation, an interpretation which receives some support from the increase in divorce following the more generous provision of Legal Aid under the 1960 Act. This was, however, to prove more than temporary. The number of decrees granted annually rose steadily throughout the sixties and seventies. As Eekelaar (1984: 13–14) stresses, we should not automatically assume that this indicates a similar increase in marriage breakdowns. What is indisputable, though , is that it imposed great pressures on the legal system which, in turn, led to measures of procedural reform intended to ease these burdens and lower the direct cost to public funds. Arguably, this simplification and cheapening of the procedures also contributed to the rising demand on the system as some of the barriers to access were lowered. This is, of course, quite apart from the extension of the grounds by the 1969 Act, which made more marriage breakdowns eligible for divorce.

Whatever the Archbishop's Commission might envisage as an ideal divorce law, those concerned with the operation of the justice system seem to have been more concerned to find ways of containing costs. Undefended cases went out to the County Courts in 1968 and their powers were further extended by the Courts Act 1971 and the

Matrimonial Causes Act 1973. The Matrimonial Causes Rules were amended in 1973 to abolish hearings in some undefended cases and extended in 1975 and 1977 to cover all such cases (cf. Gibson 1980). Legal Aid has been restricted to 'ancillary disputes' over financial arrangements and the custody of children and is no longer available for the divorce process itself.

In the course of these developments, the provisions of the 1969 Act on reconciliation were an almost immediate dead letter. Indeed, the Law Commission (1966: para. 3) did not seem to have expected that they would have any effect beyond, perhaps, obliging solicitors to keep a note of the addresses of local marriage guidance agencies. The courts were too preoccupied with moving cases through to consider the kinds of investigation that might have prompted solicitors to take the duty seriously. Solicitors trying to keep within Legal Aid limits on fees would have no motive to spend time discussing reconciliation with clients who appeared to know their own mind. Reconciliation had played its part in making divorce law reform palatable: it was now to be discarded.

Conciliation: Counselling Ideals and Organizational Realities

Orthodox versions of the history of reconciliation in England give pride of place to the Report of the (Finer) Committee on One-Parent Families, published in 1974. The Committee's main concern was with income support for one-parent families but it set this within a general review of the relationship between this group of families and the state. A small part of the review covered the administration of family law. The Committee gave its blessing to the idea of reorganizing this into a single 'family court' providing the 'machinery and services . . . to deal realistically with the practical problems resulting from marriage breakdown' (Finer Committee 1974: para. 4.282). But this proposal was not born solely out of a desire for tidy administration: indeed, the report is extremely vague about how such a court would be organized. The Committee's emphasis lies much more heavily on the injection of a new spirit in the conduct of family law, hoping that the court would work 'in such a way as to provide the best possible facilities for *conciliation* between parties in matrimonial disputes' (Finer Committee 1974: para. 4.283 emphasis added). A few paragraphs later the report spells out a clear distinction between conciliation and reconciliation:

By 'reconciliation' we mean the reuniting of the spouses. By 'conciliation' we mean assisting the parties to deal with the consequences of the established breakdown of their marriage, whether resulting in a divorce or a separation, by reaching agreements or giving consents or reducing the area of conflict upon custody, support, access to and education of the children, financial provision, the disposition of the matrimonial home, lawyers' fees, and every other matter arising from the breakdown which calls for a decision on future arrangements (Finer Committee 1974: para. 4.288).

The main recommendations of the Finer Committee on income support fell victim to the loss of confidence in public welfare expenditure that has characterized British government policy since the mid-seventies. However, the Committee's broad vision made it attractive to many interest groups and commentators. In consequence, it has come to serve as an important symbolic legitimation for many proposed initiatives in family policy.

But the Finer Committee should be seen as reacting to ideas that were already current rather than as their originator or, at least, their importer. The actual differentiation of conciliation and reconciliation had been at least partially anticipated by a Practice Direction on Matrimonial Conciliation issued in 1971 by the President of the Family Division (Parkinson 1986*b*: 63–4). The Direction provided for courts to refer contested cases to probation officers for 'conciliation', a concept which was distinguished both from reconciliation and from an inquiry leading to a welfare report. It was the Family Division's response to the provision of section 3 of the Divorce Reform Act 1969, permitting courts to adjourn cases for attempts at reconciliation. But the Direction widens the scope of that provision to allow adjournment where 'conciliation might assist the parties to resolve their disputes or any part of them by agreement'. It must be said that there is no evidence that this initiative had any great effect. The Finer Committee do not refer directly to it and their approach owes more to accounts of overseas experience.

The real significance of the President's move, though, may be in the way it bridges the tradition of reconciliation and the new ideas of conciliation. It is tempting to infer that the judges of the High Court had come to share the widespread perception that the marriage-saving movement had failed (Murch 1980: 189). This disillusion is certainly marked in an important but neglected paper by Manchester and Whetton (1974), entitled 'Marital conciliation in England and Wales' and published about two months *before* the Finer Report.

The importance of Manchester and Whetton's paper lies in the way it straddles the shift from reconciliation to conciliation as the objective of the former 'marriage-savers'. By 1971, marriage guidance agencies were facing something of an organizational crisis. The demand for their services had remained static since 1966 against a sharply rising divorce rate. The 1969 Act raised their hopes and its implementation was 'warmly welcomed', but, but 1973, this had turned into a lament for its 'short-comings'. The National Marriage Guidance Council estimated that no more than 300 new referrals, an increase of about 1.5 per cent, had been generated by the Act's provisions.

Looking back from 1979, a Home Office Working Party noted the changing social conditions which had contributed to this crisis.

There were changes in the public attitude towards marriage and divorce, and in the divorce law itself. Legal aid, social and economic factors, including a wider liberty for women to support themselves by working outside the home, contributed to a growing incidence of marital breakdown. These and other changes reduced the pressure to 'keep couples together'. (Home Office 1979: para. 1.15).[2]

The marriage guidance movement responded by redefining its objectives. In the absence of any 'magic glue' for repairing broken relationships, it incorporated the newer ideologies of self-realization which were permeating personal social services during this period (cf. Dingwall *et al.* 1983).

Methods of casework were developed: for a generation they were the staple of practice and training in social work. They were designed to enable the client to understand more of himself and his problems, and, in understanding help himself. Out of this grew 'marital counselling' rather than 'marriage guidance'—a change of name denoting a sensitive shift of method and intent . . . the counsellor offers the client a relationship in which he may discover himself and find resources within himself—and within his marriage—by which to help himself and find his own way. In short, to enlarge his area of freedom and to move within it. The outcome may be in a marriage mended—or it may be a marriage ended, though with less hurt, perhaps less insult to the emotional and spiritual relationship, than otherwise there may have been. (Home Office 1979: paras. 1.15–1.16).

Manchester and Whetton argue that the legal system had failed to keep pace with these developments. The apparent weaknesses of the 1969 Act provisions resulted from the persistence of the idea that the objective of reconciliation services was the mending of marriages. By the time lawyers became involved this was an unlikely outcome and they would not see much value in referring clients for counselling. Lawyers, in Manchester and Whetton's view, needed to take a broader view of the possible contribution of marriage counselling to the dissolution of an unsatisfactory relationship. 'The suggested aim of a conciliation process is to reach fully considered decisions of all kinds, possibly including decisions on reconciliation, in an atmosphere of calm consideration rather than tension and hostility.' (Manchester and Whetton 1974: 358). Such a development would contribute to the well-being of children, the couple themselves, and the institution of marriage.

The marriage guidance services themselves have remained ambivalent about extending their work beyond counselling individuals in a way which is not committed to marriage-saving to the extent that it once was. But the developments identified by Manchester and Whetton are reflected in the 'out-of-court' or, as they now prefer, 'independent' conciliation services which have developed in England since 1975. The first of these was established in Bristol by a coalition of legal and social work agencies and accepted its first cases during 1978–9 under a pilot scheme supported by a funding from a charitable trust. This has continued to operate with a varying mixture of public and private funding and donations from clients and currently deals with about 350 cases per year. Although its finances have often been precarious, the Bristol services would generally be regarded as the best-established scheme and its structure and philosophy have had a wide influence. In contrast to the substantial fee-for-service sector in the US mediation movement, independent conciliation in England has been defined as something which should be provided as a freely available social service rather than as market-based economic activity. This locates it within the mainstream of English social services where there is no real tradition of client payment for counselling support. Even in its more radical modes, social work has been a paternalist or, perhaps, maternalist occupation with an idea that doing good in the world is compromised by the intervention of a cash nexus. The actual practice of an independent agency working in this tradition is discussed later by Robert Dingwall.

The influence of the Bristol experience has been emphasized by the articulacy of its former full-time co-ordinator Lisa Parkinson, who went on to occupy the key post of training officer for the National Family Conciliation Council, which was set up in 1981. This voluntary body had accredited thirty-four services by October 1986 and a further six were under review. The NFCC was in contact with another thirty-nine services. Parkinson's views are set out in something like ten articles and a book, but the most succinct expression of her arguments can be found in two articles on the pros and cons of mediation published by Family Law in 1983. She lists twenty positive features of conciliation which can be categorized into two major groups (cf. Dingwall 1986: 16–17). The first group stresses the benefits to the parties themselves. Conciliation enhances client's capacities for self-determination, encouraging people 'to take control of their own affairs and to work out their own solutions' (Parkinson 1983*a*: 23). Correctly done, it can lead to long-term personal growth. The second group identifies the benefits to children in mitigating the emotional impact of divorce and ensuring that their interests are recognized. Parkinson, herself, does not deal directly with the institution of marriage, although she later notes that this theme is evident in the writings of some advocates like the Society of Conservative Lawyers and the Order of Christian Unity, who still give more weight to the ideal of reconciliation (Parkinson 1986*b*: 71).

Part of the impetus behind the independent conciliation movement of the nineteen seventies can, then, be seen as a modernization of the concept of reconciliation. It might salvage something from the failure of marriage guidance to make any impact on the continuing rise in divorce numbers by reinterpreting its mission to fit a different social climate. To talk of a 'modernization' is not of course, to imply that the same individuals were involved. It is, in a way, more like the decay of late Victorian and Edwardian methods of voluntary philanthropy in the face of mass inter-war unemployment and the recognition that this was generated by social and economic structures which could only be influenced by state action. In a new generation, groups from whom volunteer social workers had been recruited became the source of lobbyists for public provision. Mass divorce was a product of social changes to which the conciliators were broadly sympathetic: greater social and economic opportunities for women; a welfare state which would prevent the total destitution of a mother and her children; and a diminished tolerance for family violence. There could be no question of trying to turn the clock back. It was, rather, a matter of finding ways to adjust conceptions of marriage.

This is a more complex shift than Murch (1980) and Davis (1983*a*) propose in suggesting that 'marriage-saving' gave way to 'child-saving'. One element of the case for conciliation certainly does speak to the protection of children. If they cannot be offered a model of marital stability, they could be given an example of parental co-operation in their interests. But conciliation could also preserve respect for the *institution* of marriage by particularizing the failures as a result of the conflict of each partner's personal aspirations. In the process it also affirms the moral worth of the parties: divorce is not a symptom of individual deficiency but a stage in their emotional growth from which lessons can be learned for future relationships.

But, during the nineteen eighties, further developments have occurred which reflect both changes in social work education and in the moral environment of practice. The combined effect has been to introduce a markedly more libertarian approach to family life and to reject the implicit paternalism of casework and counselling. Marriage is defined as a relationship which exists purely for the benefit of the spouses involved. If that benefit ceases, then its dissolution is not a matter for public concern. All that should be offered is a service to facilitate dispute resolution by helping the parties to identify the sources of conflict and providing an arena where violent emotions can be restrained in the interests of negotiation. If there are public issues, such as child protection, these should be referred by the concerned party to other agencies with a statutory duty to investigate and intervene.

This movement derives from community work and family systems approaches, which have become increasingly influential in social work curricula. These redefine social work as a means of 'empowerment', which explicitly contributes to its clients' capacities to act for themselves rather than encourage their dependency on agencies of the state or of philanthropy. In using these methods social workers and their clients become partners in a struggle for justice. The effectiveness of that struggle turns upon an ability to analyse a disturbed social situation and identify the sources of trouble where pressure can be applied. The level of analysis depends upon the nature of the problems. In community work it may focus on the local state, while in conciliation it focuses on a kinship network. What is important is the commitment to locating the problem in an interactive system rather than regarding its origins as psychodynamic. The most influential theoretical statements in the UK originate from the Milanese school of family therapy (Palazzoli *et al.* 1978; Palazzoli 1985), which theories have been widely adopted in less bureaucratized social work settings, particularly child guidance, probation, and some voluntary agencies which combine individual service with pressure group activity. Local authority social services departments seem to be less hospitable environments because of the organizational pressures of accountability.

The enthusiasm for family systems approaches in the probation service may seem, at first glance, unlikely. However, it may well reflect the comparative lack of management pressure on the civil work area, described later by Adrian James, and the willingness of local courts, if not the Family Division, not to ask too many questions of welfare officers who deliver settlements, as Gwynn Davis implies. It should be said, however, that it is not clear how far the full-blooded use of these methods in areas like Shropshire is actually being reproduced elsewhere. The language in which practice is described may change and new techniques be introduced in a rather ritualized fashion, without altering the substance of the work. But, in the absence of direct observations of practice, it is the language of justification which is important, particularly the way in which its radical communitarian anarchist roots leave it open to very different interpretations in a decade whose political vocabulary has been set by libertarian anarchists. Both traditions converge in an opposition to state intervention in family life (Dingwall and Eekelaar 1986).

But the influence of this sector should not be overstated. The biggest schemes at Bristol and Bromley deal with 300–400 cases per year: most deal with fewer than 100. At a generous estimate, it would be surprising if the independent schemes in total dealt with more than 2,000–3,000 cases in 1986. Their astute and well-connected lobbying has given the concept of conciliation a high public profile and stimulated defensive innovations in groups whose practice might be affected by any nationally funded developments. We have already questioned the extent of aggressively adversarial legal practice, but it is none the less true that it was only in 1982 that the Solicitors' Family Law Association was formed explicitly to advocate conciliatory approaches.[3] Some of the developments in probation work could also be analysed in these terms.

Nevertheless, if one is considering the practical effects on government policy and court practice then the truth for the nineteen seventies and eighties is much as it was for the sixties or even the forties: the dominant influence is neither marriage-saving nor child-saving but cost-saving. Again and again one is confronted by the struggle of civil servants, judges, and court administrators to cope with the pressure of a continuing rise in the demand for divorce. The result is a very different concept of conciliation.

The Managerial Version

We have already mentioned the series of attempts to contain the escalating costs of divorce to the legal system from about 1968 onwards. One of these was the initiative, also taken in Bristol, for 'in-court' conciliation. In 1976, the Presiding Judge of the Western Circuit convened a meeting of county court registrars to discuss ways of reducing the number of defended divorces scheduled for a High Court hearing. A Bristol registrar proposed the introduction of what came to be known as 'conciliation appointments' in such cases. The parties and their solicitors were asked to attend a meeting with the court registrar and a welfare officer in order to clarify the exact nature of the dispute. If there seemed some prospect of agreement the parties and the welfare officer would go to another room for private discussion, leaving the solicitors to explore possible legal arrangements. Should an agreement be reached, the registrar could make an order giving effect to it. Otherwise he would give directions for the trial of the dispute. The scheme succeeded in its objective of reducing court lists for defended divorces and was extended during 1978 to some custody and access disputes in undefended divorces (Parmiter 1981). Similar initiatives have since been taken in a number of county courts and at the Principal Divorce Registry in London.

Gwynn Davis's description of these sessions underlines their contrast with independent practice. The meetings are much shorter, on average 40–5 minutes per case where independent services would expect to allow several hours. There is an immediate threat, that failure to agree will impose further costs and delay. Finally, less attention seems to be given to the quality of settlements. Participants' statements are taken very much at face value. Davis (1982*c*), for example, observed a tendency to rely on children's statements about their preferences in custody or access disputes with little attempt to investigate the basis of these opinions, in the child's own judgment or in parental coaching. Indeed, Davis (1983*b*) has questioned whether such work can properly be called 'conciliation' at all.

Nevertheless, the two versions of conciliation were treated as fully equivalent by the Interdepartmental Committee on Conciliation (Robinson Committee) which reported in 1983. This committee had a specific brief to examine the cost-effectiveness of conciliation. It concluded that in-court conciliation could be justified on economic grounds while out-of-court conciliation could not. As its critics (e.g. Yates 1983*a*, 1983*b*; Bristol Trustees 1984; Westcott 1983; Davis and Westcott 1984) were swift to point out, this conclusion was predictable from the unquestioned assumptions of the Report's authors. There were three specific objections.

The first was the choice of outcome measure. The Robinson Committee measured success solely in terms of pre-court settlement achieved at the time of the meeting. The independent sector complained that this underestimated its contribution. In England, its members do not claim to tackle finance and property disputes, so that a low rate of achievement in these areas is not a sign of failure. Reconciliations were excluded from the Committee's calculations, although these should also be regarded as successes. Moreover, the independents argued, their work could also lay the foundation for agreements between conciliation and trial or for more durable settlements by creating a climate of co-operation which would allow custody and access arrangements to evolve with changes in the lives of parties and their children and avoid re-litigation.

The second criticism was the failure to allow for the slow build-up of case-loads in the independent schemes. Many of those studied by the Robinson Committee were relatively new and their fixed costs were averaged over a very small number of cases. Finally, the critics noted, the lack of information about the fixed overhead costs of the courts meant that no share of these was attributed to in-court conciliation. If the sectors were treated alike and compared only on variable costs, independent schemes appeared to come out 30–40 per cent cheaper, on the Report's own figures.

It would be wrong to imply that the Robinson Committee's work was consciously biased. Whatever its specific methodological weaknesses, we can see that, despite its interdepartmental membership, the Committee formulated its questions in terms of court and legal aid costs, thus dictating an accountant's approach and locating responsibility for a solution with the Lord Chancellor's Department. This, for example, may well explain the lack of attention to the growth of independent-style conciliation in the probation service, a Home Office responsibility, as an alternative to investigative welfare reporting in custody and access disputes. In terms of a national system for improving the quality of dispute resolution, this must represent a promising option because it appears to offer a more effective use of existing resources, without the need to create an agency network with new or redeployed funds. But the public resources involved are not within the budgets under pressure from the load of divorce work on the courts.

The dominance of these financial concerns continues to be reflected in the public statements of the Lord Chancellor's Department. When, in 1984, an invitation to tender was issued, for a project unit to carry out the more detailed programme evaluation studies recommended by the Robinson Committee, its task was defined as comparing modes of service provision

primarily with the view to assessing and comparing their costs and benefits—that is the balance of their cost against savings achieved for the legal aid fund, in the judicial and other costs of administering the courts, and in other aspects of public expenditure—but also with a view to attempting to assess and compare the non-financial benefits of different schemes particularly for the parties and their families. [Emphasis added.]

Fully two-thirds of the discussion of items to be investigated related to cost factors. At the time of writing (1986), this work is under way at the University of Newcastle-upon-Tyne. Even before its completion, however, the Lord Chancellor's Department has returned to the cost-cutting theme. The *Legal Aid efficiency scrutiny* (1986) presents conciliation, in an unspecified form, as a means of saving 'possibly' £5 million each year in divorce litigation.

The only partial exception to the dominance of financial consider-ations lies in the Report of the Matrimonial Causes Procedure Committee (1985) chaired by Mrs Justice Booth from the Family Division. This Committee, significantly, was dominated by lawyers rather than civil servants.[4] It had begun work in 1982, following a review by the Law Commission of the substantive law relating to financial provision on divorce (Law Commission 1981). A number of recommendations were made with a view to encouraging the self-sufficiency of the divorced spouses and a 'clean break' in their financial relationships. But the Commission also thought that this would be better achieved through conciliation and that the procedural law should be examined with the object of removing unnecessary obstacles to agreement.

The result was the Booth Committee, which was asked to investigate the 'procedure and practice' of the High Court and County Court and to make recommendations to 'mitigate the intensity of disputes; encourage settlements; and to provide further for the welfare of the children of the family'. But again the cost-saving theme recurred as all these recommen-dations should also have regard 'to the desirability of achieving greater simplification and the saving of costs'. At first sight, the Committee appear to have endorsed the social work version of conciliation.

It is of the essence of conciliation that the responsibility remains at all times with the parties themselves to identify and seek agreement on the issues arising from the breakdown of the relationship. The conciliator's role is to assist the parties in the process. He should be neutral not only in the sense that he does not take sides as between the parties, but also in the sense that he does not have a preconceived solution to any particular problem. (Booth Committee 1985: para. 3.10).

But the organization proposed by the Committee owes much more to the in-court model. All cases which involved children or were to be defended would be set down for a preliminary hearing by a registrar. The registrar would have power to make orders, by consent or otherwise, about most matters potentially in dispute and to attempt to promote agreement where possible. The actual conciliation however, would still be referred to a court welfare officer from the probation service. In its initial Consultation Paper (1983), the Committee clearly imagined that this interview would occur on the same day in the same court premises with the possibility of an immediate return to the registrar. There was some retreat from this in the final report, but the Committee still appear wedded to the notion that longer adjournments should be the exception rather than the rule.

The Booth proposals will be discussed more evaluatively in the Conclusion to this volume. For the present, however, they may serve to underline the confusion which currently bedevils English policy debates. On the one hand can be found the quasi-therapeutic ideals of the independent movement where the concept of conciliation forms part of a wider, if not always explicit, programme of responding to individual pain and promoting social betterment. On the other lie the organizational concerns of civil servants and court administrators faced with a deluge of cases and the political denial of matching resources. It is important not to be dismissive about the importance of value-for-money analyses in public expenditure: resources are not infinite and their use should always be carefully scrutinized. But the emphasis on indicators of performance can lead to organizational practices designed to generate good figures rather than to improve the service (Rein 1983). It can also narrow the focus to those costs borne by a particular organization or budget head to the neglect of their total social impact. Does a transfer from public to private ordering necessarily reduce the social costs of matrimonial dispute resolution or does it actually introduce a new range of transaction costs for the parties involved that diminish net social welfare?

More importantly, when the language of accountancy becomes the only language of policy argument, other possible social objectives like equity and justice may be neglected. One danger in the present situation is that the caring ideals of the independent sector may be appropriated to provide a fig-leaf for crude retrenchment in the public services. But, as we have indicated, there are problems with the basis of the independent conciliators' arguments, given the lack of data on past or current 'normal legal practice'. And questions can and have been raised about the relationship between the ideals of the voluntary movement and the experience of its clients in their encounters with conciliation.

The approach of the Robinson Committee and the dominant tradition of programme evaluation studies rests upon shaky assumptions about the equivalence of a great variety of social forms which all happen to share the same name. It is hoped that the essays in this volume will prompt more fundamental investigations of the nature of these different types of organization and social interaction and provide a more informed understanding of the complex moral issues that any choice entails.

Notes

1. This was the result of illness and pressure of other work on Richard Titmuss, who had been expected to contribute that analysis.
2. A detailed discussion of the interaction of macro- and micro-factors in the decision to divorce can be found in Hart (1976: 59–102).
3. The foundation of this Association also needs to be considered in the context of structural changes occurring within the English legal professions as a result of the loss of the monopoly on property conveyancing, which had been solicitors' staple income. These have been reflected in movements towards specialization and product innovation in an attempt to lower costs or generate new income.
4. There were two non-lawyer members: the Lay Observer (the Law Society official responsible for the final review of complaints against solicitors) and the Chairman of the Domestic Courts Committee of the Magistrates' Association.

2. Negotiation Between Lawyer and Client in an American Divorce

WILLIAM L. F. FELSTINER AND AUSTIN SARAT

Traditionally, the sociology of the legal profession has portrayed lawyers as important intermediaries between clients and the legal system (Brandeis 1933; Parsons 1954); many more people see lawyers than have direct contact with formal legal institutions (Curran 1977; Miller and Sarat 1981). Lawyers serve clients as important sources of information about legal rights, help clients relate legal rules to individual problems, and introduce clients to the way the legal process works. But, despite the importance of the discourse between lawyers and their clients, we know very little about what actually goes on in the lawyer's office. Our understanding of lawyer–client interaction has a very shallow basis in systematic empirical research (for an exception in the United States, see Hosticka 1979; for examples in other countries, see Berends 1981 (Holland); Bogoch and Danet 1984 (Israel); Caesar-Wolf 1984 (Germany); Cain 1983 (England)). Legal sociologists are, in this respect, far behind sociologists of medicine, who have over many years conducted numerous studies of doctors and patients (see, for example, McIntosh 1974). Researchers have been frustrated by norms of confidentiality, the routines of busy professionals, and an inability to convince lawyers of the need for research on lawyer–client communications (see Danet *et al.* 1980). Yet without direct knowledge of such communications, it is difficult to pose or answer major questions about the content, form, and effects of legal services.

The Research, the Case, and the Conference

In the research from which this paper is derived we observed divorce cases over a period of thirty-three months in two American sites, one in Massachusetts and one in California. This effort consisted in following one side of forty cases, ideally from the first lawyer–client interview until the divorce was final. We followed these cases by observing and tape-recording lawyer–client sessions, attending court and mediation hearings and trials, and interviewing both lawyers and clients about those events. Approximately 115 lawyer–client conferences were tape-recorded (Sarat and Felstiner 1986). In this paper we focus on one lawyer–client conference to explore the ways in which lawyers and clients negotiate their differing views of law and the legal process and how that negotiation influences decisions about preferred paths to disposition.

The client and her husband in this case were in their late thirties and had no children. Their marriage had been stormy, involving both substantial separations and infidelity by the husband. Both had graduate degrees and worked full time; financial support was not an issue. They owned a house, bank stocks, several limited partnerships in real estate, his retirement benefits, and personal property. The house was their major asset. It was an unconventional building to which the husband was especially attached. Housing in the area is very expensive. This divorce was the client's second; there were no children in the first marriage either. She had received extensive psychological counselling prior to and during the case which we observed.

The parties in this divorce initially tried to dissolve their marriage by engaging a mediator, who was an established divorce lawyer with substantial experience in divorce mediation. At the first substantive session, the mediator stated that he did not think that further progress could be made if both the spouses continued to live in the house. Although she considered it to be a major sacrifice, the wife said that she had moved out of the house to facilitate mediation after her husband absolutely refused to leave. The client reported that she was careful to warn her husband whenever she intended to visit.

Over time, however, this arrangement upset her husband. Rather than raise the problem at a mediation session, he hired a lawyer and secured an ex-parte order restraining the client from entering the property at any time for any reason. This ended any prospects for mediation and the client, on the advice of the mediator and another lawyer, hired the lawyer involved in this conference.

Subsequently, a hearing about the propriety of the ex-parte order was held by a second judge. The issues at this hearing were whether the order should be governed by a general or a divorce-specific injunction statute, what status quo the order was intended to maintain, and whether the husband's attempt to secure the order violated a moral obligation undertaken when the client agreed to move out of the house. The second judge decided against the client on the first two issues, but left consideration of the bad faith question open to further argument. The client's therapist attended the hearing and the lawyer–client conference that immediately followed. At that conference the therapist stressed that contesting the restraining order further might not be in the client's long-term interest even if it corrected the legal wrong.

The Legal Process of Divorce

Clients look to lawyers to explain how the legal system works and to interpret the actions and decisions of legal officials. Despite their lack of knowledge about and contact with the law, clients are likely to have some general notions that the law works as a formally rational legal order, one that is rule governed, impersonal, impartial, predictable, and relatively error free. How do lawyers respond to this picture?

In this conference the lawyer presents the legal process of divorce largely in response to questions or remarks by the client: the client repeatedly enquires about both the legal system's procedures and rules. While most of her questions concern the details of her own case, several are general. Thus, she invites her lawyer to explain the way that the legal process operates as well as to justify its operation in her case. At no point does the lawyer deliver a monologue on how it works. His comments are interspersed in the discussion of major substantive issues, particularly concerning what to do about the restraining order and how to proceed with settlement negotiations. Throughout the conference the client persists in focusing on the restraining order until finally she asks:

CLIENT. How often does a case like this come along—a restraining order of this nature?

LAWYER. Very common.

CLIENT. It's a very common thing. So how many other people are getting the same kind of treatment I am? With what, I presume, is very sloppily handled orders that are passed out.

LAWYER. Yeah, you know, I did talk to someone in the know—I won't go any further than that—who said that this one could have been signed purely by accident. I mean, that the judge could have—if he looked at it now—said, I would not sign that, knowing what it was, and it could have been signed by accident, and I said well, then how does that happen? And he said, well, you've got all this stuff going; you come back to your office, and there's a stack of documents that need signatures. He says, you can do one of two things: you can postpone signing them until you have time, but then it may be the end of the day; the clerk's office is closing, and people who really need this stuff aren't going to get the orders, because there's someone else that needs your attention, so you go through them, and one of the main things you look for is the law firm or lawyer who is proposing them. And you tend to rely on them.

The lawyer thus states that a legal order of immense consequence to this woman may have been handled in a way that in several respects is inconsistent with the formalist image of a rational system: it may have been signed by accident. Moreover, the lawyer claims that he has received this information from 'someone in the know', someone he refuses to identify. By this refusal, he implies that the information was given improperly, in breach of confidence. Furthermore, the lawyer's description of how judges handle court orders suggest a high level of inattention and routinization. Judges sign orders without reading them to satisfy 'people who really need this stuff'. While the judge is said to ignore the substance of the order, he does pay attention to the lawyer or law firm who requests it. The legal process is thereby portrayed as responding more to reputation than to substantive merit. Thus, the client is introduced to a system that is hurried, routinized, personalistic, and accident prone. A lawyer's capacity to protect his client's interests depends in part on his special access to the system's functionaries who will react to who he is rather than what he represents.

Later in the conference the relationship of law to values like fairness and justice is discussed more explicitly. At that point the client muses about her goals and hopes about the legal process of divorce.

CLIENT. Well, I mean, I'm a liberal. Right? A liberal dream is that you will find social justice, and so here was this statement that it was possible to fight injustice, and you were going to protect me from horrible things like judicial abuse. So that's uh, it was really nice.

To the client, 'justice' demands that the error of the restraining order be righted. For the lawyer that kind of justice simply gets in the way of what for him is the real business of divorce: to reach a property settlement, not to right wrongs or vindicate justice. There is, if you will, a particular kind of justice that the law provides, but it is not broad enough to include the kind that the client seeks. For her, justice requires some compensation, or at least an acknowledgement that she has 'been treated unjustly'. When she finally gets the lawyer to speak in terms of justice, he admits that it cannot be secured through the legal process.

CLIENT. But as you say, if you want justice in this society, you look somewhere other than court. I believe that's what you were saying to Bob [her financial consultant].
LAWYER. Yeah, that's what I said. Ultimate justice, that is.

Legal justice is thus juxtaposed to ultimate justice. The person seeking such a final accounting is clearly out of place in a system that focuses much more narrowly. To fit into the system the client must reduce her conception of justice to what the law can provide.[1] But perhaps the language of justice serves, for this client, a purpose that is neither as abstract nor as disinterested as her language suggests. This client identifies justice as the vindication of her own position. She never refers to a more general standard. Thus the failure of law to provide justice is, for her, a failure to validate her position. The language of justice also serves to bolster her image of herself as an innocent, rather gracious victim of an evil husband and his untrustworthy lawyer. Tendencies toward self-exculpation and blaming are quite common in the divorces in our sample, although the use of the language of justice toward such ends is not. This language also serves to exert moral pressure on this lawyer to validate the client's sense of herself even as he attempts to explain the limits of the legal process.

In total, the lawyer's description of the legal process involves an open acknowledgement of human frailties, contradictions between appearance and reality, carelessness, incoherence, accident, and built-in limitations.

To Fight or Settle?

Given such a legal process, how should divorce disputes be managed? This concern is central in most of the cases that we observed, and it is an issue that may recur as lawyer and client discuss each of the major controversies in a divorce case. Generally the question is whether the client should attempt to negotiate a settlement or insist on resolution before a judge. This question is sometimes posed issue by issue and sometimes across many issues.

While many clients think of the legal process as an arena for a full adversarial contest, most divorce disputes are not resolved in this manner. Although not all lawyers are equally dedicated to reaching negotiated agreements, most of those we observed advised their clients to try to settle the full range of issues in this case. This is not to say that these divorces were free of conflict, for the negotiations themselves were often quite contentious. Although some of our lawyers occasionally advised clients to ask for more than the client had originally contemplated or to refuse to concede on a major issue when the client was inclined to do so, most seemed to believe that it is generally better to settle than contest divorce disputes. Thus, we are interested in the ways in which lawyers get their clients to see settlement as the preferred alternative.

The conference we are examining revolves around two major issues:

(1) whether to ignore or contest the restraining order; and (2) what position to take concerning disposition of the family residence. Both issues force the lawyer and client to decide whether they will retain control of the case by engaging in negotiations or cede control to the court for hearing and decision. The lawyer definitely favours negotiations.

LAWYER. Okay. What I would like your permission to do then is to meet with Foster [spouse's lawyer], see if I can come up with or negotiate a settlement with him that, before he leaves . . . I leave his office or he leaves my office, he says, we've got something here that I can recommend to my client, and I can say, I've got something here that I can recommend to my client. My feeling is, Jane, that if we reach that point, both lawyers are prepared to make a recommendation on settlement to their respective clients, if either of the clients, either you or Norb [husband], find something terribly disagreeable with the proposal that we have, the lawyers have come to between themselves, then the case just either can't be settled or it's not ripe for settlement. But we would have given it our best shot.

The major ingredient of this settlement system is the primacy of the lawyers. They produce the deals while the clients are limited to initial instructions and after-the-fact ratification. The phrase 'we would have given it our best shot' is crucial. The 'we' seems to refer to the lawyers. Indeed, their efforts could come to nothing if either client backs out at the last minute. The settlement process as described thus has two dimensions—a lawyer to lawyer phase, in which an arrangement is worked out, and a lawyers versus clients phase, in which the opposing lawyers join together to sell the deal to their clients (see Blumberg 1967). If the clients do not accept the settlement as a package, the only alternative is to go to trial. Furthermore, if the professionals are content with the agreement they have devised, dissatisfied clients not only have nothing to contribute but also had perhaps better seek psychotherapy:

LAWYER. I'll say, [client] Jane, if we're going to court over what turns out to be one percentage point, go talk to Irene [therapist] some more.

The client in this case is reluctant to begin settlement negotiations until some attention is paid to the restraining order. While she acknowledges that she wants a reasonable property settlement, she reminds her lawyer that that is not her exclusive concern.

CLIENT. Yes, there is no question in my mind that that [a property settlement] is my first goal. However, that doesn't mean it's my only goal. It's just my first one. And I have done a lot of thinking about this and so it's all this kind of running around in my head at this point. I've been looking very carefully at the parts of me that want to fight and the parts of me that don't want to fight. And I'm not sure that any of that ought to get messed up in the property settlement.

The lawyer responds by acknowledging that he considers the restraining order to be legally wrong and that he believes it could be litigated. Thus, he confirms his client's position and inclination on legal grounds. Yet he dissents from her position and opposes her inclination to fight on other grounds. First, he states that the restraining order, although legally wrong, is 'not necessarily . . . completely wrong' because it might prevent violence between spouses. This complicated position is a clear example of a tactic frequently used by lawyers in divorce cases—the rhetorical 'yes . . .but'. The lawyers we observed often appeared to be endorsing the adversarial pursuit of one of the client's objectives only to remind the client of a variety of negative consequences associated with it. In this way lawyers present themselves as both an ally and an adviser embracing the wisdom of a long-term perspective.

Second, the lawyer is worried that an effort to fight the restraining order would interfere with the resolution of the case, that is, of the outstanding property issues. Although the lawyer considers the restraining order to be a legal mistake, its effect would end upon final disposition of the house. In the meantime, the client can either live with the order or pay for additional hearings. He believes that it would be unwise for her to fight further not only because the contest would be costly but also because it would postpone or derail entirely negotiations about the house and other tangible assets. Thus when the client asks whether the issue of the restraining order has been raised with her husband's lawyer, her lawyer says:

LAWYER. Well, I've talked to him. My feelings are . . . that what has been done is illegal, that I want to take it to the Supreme Court. I told Foster off. I basically told him the contents of the letter. I said that I think that Judge Cohen is dead wrong, and I would very much like to litigate the thing. On the other hand, I have to be mindful of what Irene said, which is absolutely correct, does that move us toward or away from the ultimate goal, which is the resolution of the case.

The lawyer's position in this case can be interpreted as a preference for negotiations over litigation based on his determination that this client has more to lose than gain by fighting the restraining order and for the house. In this view the lawyer is neutral about settlement in general and swayed by the cost–benefit calculation of specific cases. Thus there is a conflict between the client's desire for vindication on what the lawyer perceives to be a peripheral issue and the lawyer's interest in reaching a satisfactory disposition on what for him is a much more important issue. Time and again in our study we observed lawyers attempting to focus their client's attention on the issues the lawyers thought to be major while the clients often concentrated on matters that the lawyers considered secondary. While the disposition of the house in this case will have long-term consequences for the client, the restraining order, as unjust as the lawyer understands it to be, is in his view a temporary nuisance. His sense of justice and of the long-term best interests of his client lead him to try to transform this dispute from a battle over the legality and morality of the restraining order to a negotiation over the more narrow and tangible issue of the ultimate disposition of the house and other assets, which he believes can and should be settled.

In attempting this transformation, the lawyer allies himself with the therapist.

LAWYER. I agree with Irene that that [fighting the restraining order] is not the best way. . . . It's probably the worst way. This [negotiating] hopefully is the best way.

This lawyer, and most of those we observed, construct an image of the appropriate mode of disposition of a case that is at odds with the conventional view in which lawyers are alleged to induce competition and hostility, transform non-contentious clients into combatants, and promulgate a 'fight theory of justice' (Felstiner, Abel, and Sarat 1981; Frank 1950; Mather and Yngvesson 1981; Simon 1978).

The client's own ambivalence toward settlement continues throughout the conference. In discussing a letter that her lawyer had prepared to send to the other lawyer outlining their position on the restraining order, she says:

CLIENT. So it was an important letter, and I didn't realize how much I wanted to continue fighting until I read the first portion of this letter. . . . It kind of let me feel that finally . . . I'd found a knight in shining armour.

To which the lawyer responds:

LAWYER. Ouch.

The transference reflected in her reference to a 'knight in shining armour', a female client's substitution of her male lawyer for her failed husband, may not be unusual in divorce cases, but nowhere in our sample is it as explicit as it is here.

However, as they move further into the discussion of whether to fight or settle, the client begins to interpret settlement as a capitulation and to reiterate her own ambivalence about how to proceed.

CLIENT. And I think I feel some level of fear about this process of negotiation and how much more I'm going to have to give up. I don't feel tremen-, you know, there's a part of me that does not feel very satisfied with having capitulated repeatedly, and now we're simply doing it with a property settlement. . . . I mean, I don't want to fight and I do want to fight, right? That's exactly what it comes down to.

LAWYER. Yes you're ambiguous.

CLIENT. Oh, boy, am I ever. And I have to live with it.

She may have to live with her ambivalence, but her lawyer needs a resolution of this issue. The lawyer seeks this resolution by allying himself with the 'don't fight' side of the struggle. Her advocate, her 'knight', has thus become the enemy of adversariness. Through him the legal system becomes the champion of settlement. Ironically, the client's ambivalence serves to validate the lawyer's earlier suggestion that he might be wasting his time and her money trying to settle this case because she might refuse a deal at the last minute.

The conference reaches closure on the fight/settle issue when the lawyer again asks whether he has her authority to negotiate on the terms they had discussed and repeats his earlier warning that this may be their last chance for a settlement:

LAWYER. Well, then I will make a . . . my best effort—we are now coming full circle to where we were this morning, which is fine, which is where we should be. I will make my best effort to effect settlement with Foster along the lines that you and I have discussed and the specific terms of which I can say to you, Jane, I recommend that you sign this. The decision, of course, is yours. If you don't want to sign it, we're going to go ahead with the litigation on the restraining order and probably a trial. Things can change. We can effect a settlement before the restraining order, which is highly unlikely, or between the time the restraining order issue is resolved and the actual time of trial, maybe there will be another settlement.

The lawyer's reference to 'coming full circle' reflects both the centrality of the dispositional question and the amount of time spent talking about issues the lawyer considers to be peripheral. Having invested that time the lawyer secures what he wanted, both an authorization to negotiate and an agreement on the goals that he will pursue. The client, on the other hand, has aired her ambivalence and resolved to try to end this dispute without a legal contest. Both her ambivalence and her eventual acceptance of settlement are typical of the clients we observed.

The Legal Construction of the Client

To get the clients in divorce cases to move toward accepting settlement as well as to carry out the terms of such agreements, lawyers may have to try to cool them out when they are at least partially inclined toward contest. In divorce as in criminal cases, the lawyer must help redefine the client's orientation toward the legal process (Blumberg 1967). In the criminal case this means that lawyers must help the client come to terms with dropping the pretence of innocence; in divorce work this means that lawyers must help their clients view the emotional process of dissolving an intimate relationship in instrumental terms. In both instances, lawyers and clients struggle, although rarely explicitly, with the issue of what part of the client's personality is relevant to the legal process. Thus, the discussion of whether to fight or settle is more than a conversation about the most appropriate way to dispose of the case. Contained within the discourse about negotiation is the construction of a legal picture of the client, a picture through which a self acceptable to the legal process is negotiated and validated (Gabel 1980; Unger 1975). This construction is necessary because the legal process will not or cannot deal with many aspects of the disputes that are brought to it. Legal professionals behave as if it were natural and inevitable that a litigant's problems be divided up in the manner that the legal process prescribes. Lawyers thus legitimate some parts of human experience and deny the relevance of others, but they do not explicitly state what is required of the client. Rather, the approved form of the legal self is built up from a set of oppositions and priorities among these oppositions.

The negotiation of the legal self in this case begins by focusing on the relative importance of emotions engaged by the legal process and the symbolic aspects of the divorce as opposed to its financial and material dimensions. Throughout this conference the lawyer warns his client not to confuse the realms of emotion and finance and instructs her that she can expect the legal process to work well only if emotional material is excluded from her deliberations.[2]

The emotional material is rather complex and difficult for both lawyer and client to sort out. The client is, in the first instance, eager to let her lawyer know that she feels both anger and mistrust toward many participants in the legal process.

CLIENT. One of the things I'm feeling is a tremendous discontent that some form of negotiation is going to now begin without any act from Norb that establishes trust (. . .) Ahh. It doesn't seem that I have a lot of options. I simply will have to accept that, and I guess I will have to live with that pain . . . I think it's dreadfully unfair. But it doesn't seem that I can get any satisfaction, so I'll have to.

LAWYER. That's not entirely true. You can litigate. Strongly we can litigate.

CLIENT. Well, I think the only question then is whether or not an overture then is even possible before litigation. I'm not sure. I mean, yes, I have these things separated in my mind, but how can I trust this human being to do anything? I don't know if I can. I feel that pretty strongly.

Because she feels betrayed by her husband, the client wants 'some gesture from him' as a means of establishing the basis for negotiations. Moreover, she feels that she is already two points down *vis-à-vis* her husband. First, he has the house and has denied her any access to it, although her departure was an act of generosity done for the good of the marital community. Second, she 'knows' that he is going to get the house and that she will at best get half its market value. She repeatedly asks the lawyer about gestures or concessions to even this score:

CLIENT. So I wrote this as a draft to send to Norb. . . . And obviously I'm still waffling . . . I mean, I don't know exactly how to give up this hearing. Part of me says, it's real clear and I ought to. But I want some gesture from him.

CLIENT. This is the problem for me. I feel that, even to get to this point, I have given up a substantial amount. One thing that I've given up is the home in Pacificola. I don't give a fuck how much cash Norb gives me, I'm not going to be able to recreate that scene, and that's just a fact of real estate in Pacificola. I want the negotiation to begin there. I want some attention to be paid to what I have already conceded to even get to this point.

CLIENT. I just think that's a very, very big concession, and I think if I'm to take another kind of settlement, then that is the first thing that ought to be seen. Now, that's a very good faith negotiation thing for me to do, say okay, Norb has this tremendous emotional investment in the house; I'm willing to let go of mine.

The lawyer virtually turns his back on this part of the client's emotional agenda, on this effort to define those parts of herself that are legally relevant. There is no substantive response to the question of trust and the need for a gesture, perhaps because the lawyer feared that further exploration might complicate his efforts to have his client focus on reaching an acceptable division of property. There can be little doubt that this objective governed his thinking.

LAWYER. Okay, now, that disagreement—or, it wasn't even a disagreement—that—where we weren't on the same wave-length—was really a matter of style than of end result. Right?

CLIENT. You mean, what part?

LAWYER. Where you said that you wanted me to start these negotiations by making it clear that major concession was being made at the outset and it was being made by you.

CLIENT. Yes.

LAWYER. Okay, I understand that now. Let's come back to the end of it. . . . What am I shooting for? Okay, I agree. That's the way it ought to be begun, and that point ought to—during my conversations, I ought to keep coming back to that, if I have to use it. Just make that strongly. But what am I shooting for? What's the end result? Is it what I was talking about initially?

CLIENT. Sure. I mean, that's as much as can be expected, I believe. Am I right in that?

The lawyer proposes to turn the client's demand for concessions into an opening statement and implies that an equal division of assets is the only possible legal settlement. The client, on the other hand, appears to believe that it is dangerous to trade values with someone that you do not trust for both the chance that they will take advantage of you in making the deal and the probability that they will fail to do what they promise are increased. The lawyer is, and can afford to be, uninterested in trust. Protection of his client does not lie in fostering good will and mutual respect between the spouses but rather in the terms of the bargain and in its enforcement powers. His duty is to see that the settlement agreement is fair to his client, whatever the motives or morals of the other side may be, and that the structure of the agreement guarantees that his client gets what she bargained for or its substitute, or at least the best approximation available.

By playing down the question of trust the lawyer is telling the client that the emotional self must be separated from the legal self. Gestures and symbolic acknowledgement of wrongs suffered belong to some realm other than law. He is, in addition, defending himself against a kind of emotional transference. Much of the emotion talk in this conference involves the lawyer himself, directly or indirectly. In the discussion of trust the client makes the lawyer into a kind of husband substitute ('a major trust relationship has ended. And then . . . I'm supposed to entrust somebody else . . .'). The client described him as her 'knight in shining armour', an image of protection and romance; she acknowledges having sexual fantasies about him and she speaks of her expectation that he would protect her from 'judicial abuse'. These demands on her lawyer typify the kind of environment in which divorce lawyers work. Moreover, the discussion of trust and its betrayal signals to her lawyer the need for an elevated watchfulness. He may, like her earlier source of protection and romance, not be fully trusted. The gesture implicitly demanded of him is an embrace of her sense of justice and of what that implies in practical terms.

By downplaying emotions and signalling the limited relevance of gestures, the lawyer defends himself against both the transference and the test. He must find a way to be on his client's side (for example, repeatedly acknowledging the legal error of the restraining order) and, at the same time, to keep some distance from her (for example, responding 'Ouch' to the image of the knight). Achieving this precarious balance is a peculiar, although not unique, difficulty of divorce practice (for a similar discussion in the criminal context, see Blumberg 1967).

To maintain this balance the lawyer acknowledges the difficulty of separating emotional and property issues, but continually reminds the client of its necessity if they are going to reach what he calls a 'satisfactory disposition' of the case. The notion of satisfactory disposition, however, is itself problematic. The lawyer's definition of 'satisfactory' tends to exclude the part of the client's personality that is angry or frustrated. Satisfactory dispositions are financial. The question of who is satisfied is left unasked. Moreover, the responsibility for finding ways to keep emotions under control is assigned to the client. The lawyer offers no help in this task even as he acknowledges its relevance for this client and for the practice of divorce law. If no settlement is reached it will, at least as far as their side is concerned, be because of a failure on the part of the client.

Throughout this conference the lawyer stresses the need for two parallel separations: the separation of the emotional issues from the legal and the separation of the client and her husband.

LAWYER. . . . I'd say the ambiguity goes even deeper than the issue of fighting and not fighting It's how . . . The ambiguity is what Irene talked about and that is—it's the real hard one—it's terminating the entire relationship. You do and you don't, and the termination . . . I mean, you're angry; you're pissed off. You've said that. And are you ready to call a halt to the anger and I'm not so sure that that's humanly possible. Can your rational mind say, okay, Jane, there has been enough anger expended on this; it is time to get on with your life. If you are able to do that, great. But I don't know.

As the lawyer sees it, the client will only be able to make an adequate arrangement with her husband when she can contemplate their relationship unemotionally. As the client sees it, the second separation seems impossible if the first is carried out. She cannot become free of her husband if she thinks about legal problems in material terms only—if she fails to take her feelings into account she will continue to be affected by them. Thus, the programme the lawyer presents to the client appropriates her marriage to the realm of property and defines her connection to her husband exclusively in those terms. She, on the other hand, sees property issues embedded in a broader context. The client speaks about the separation of the emotional and financial issues as being difficult to effect because it is unnatural. The market does not exhaust her realm of values, and she has difficulty assigning governing priority to it. Yet this is what the lawyer indicates the law requires.[3]

Nevertheless, the separation of emotional and economic matters may benefit the client. While it does exact an emotional toll, concentrating on the instrumental, tangible aspects of the divorce may produce a more satisfactory disposition than focusing on the emotional concerns. The lawyer may be trying to explain to his client that in the long run she is going to be more interested in the economics of the settlement than in the vindication of her immediate emotional needs. In his view, legal justice, although narrow, is justice none the less, and his job is to secure for her the best that can be achieved given the legal process as he knows it.

Putting emotional matters aside may also serve the interests of lawyers untrained in dealing with emotional problems and unwilling to find ways to cope with them. It allows lawyers to sidestep what is clearly one of the most difficult and least rewarding aspects of divorce practice. In so doing they are able to avoid assuming a sense of responsibility for the human consequences of being unresponsive to emotion. In this conference, for example, the lawyer suggests that the legal process works best for those who can control their emotions and concentrate on the instrumental, the calculating, the pecuniary. The client's uncertainty about the possibility of such a separation of issues is met by a certainty expressed by the lawyer. But the lawyer's certainty is not that the client can effect the required separation but rather that the separation is an imperative of the legal process without which the system cannot efficiently deliver its goods. Having expressed this imperative, the lawyer is thus relieved of any responsibility for helping his client come to terms with the anger and frustration that condition her feelings about property issues. Ultimately, it seems that the client gets the message. As she says, 'The extraneous factors, which are every bit as important as the rest of it, are not going to be paid attention to at all.'

Conclusion

Lawyer–client interaction involves attempts to negotiate acceptable resolutions of problems in which lawyers and clients usually have different agendas, expectations, and senses of justice. As in any negotiation, the parties possess different information and have different needs to fulfil. Clients know their histories and goals, lawyers must learn about them. Lawyers know the law and the legal process, clients must find out about them. Every conference is thus to some extent competitive: the participants set out to fulfil their own agenda and generally only provide what the other wants on demand (Griffiths 1986).

Competition and accommodation between the lawyer and client shape the course of divorce litigation—when negotiations are initiated, how they are conducted, what is asked for and offered, and whether a case is settled. Moreover, the manner in which the contest over agendas and expectations is resolved may also have a powerful effect on the way clients feel at the end of the process, on their levels of satisfaction, and on their views of the legitimacy of law.

Lawyer–client interaction: the lawyer's perspective

Clients bring to their encounters with lawyers an expectation that the justice system will impartially sort the facts in dispute to provide a deductive reading of the 'truth'. They expect the legal process to take their problems seriously, and they usually seek vindication of the positions that they have adopted. They expect the legal process to follow its own rules, to proceed in an orderly manner, and to be fair and error free.

To some extent, it is the job of lawyers to bring these expectations and images of law and legal justice closer to the reality that they have experienced. For them legal justice is situational and outcomes are often unpredictable. The legal process provides an arena where compromises are explored, settlements are reached, and, if money is at issue, assets are divided. Lawyers are intimately familiar with the human dimensions of the legal process. They know that in most instances the process is not rule governed, that there is widespread use of discretion, and that decisions are influenced by matters extraneous to legal doctrine. Moreover, they believe that most clients cannot afford or would not want to pay the cost of a full adversarial contest. They may conclude, therefore, based on experience, that the client who demands vindication today will want both a larger financial settlement and a smaller lawyer's bill tomorrow.

Because lawyers' experience is so much more extensive than that of clients, lawyers attempt to 'teach' their clients about the requirements of the legal process and to socialize them into the role of the client. Some of the client's problems and needs will be translated into legal categories (Cain 1983) and many more will have legal labels attached to them. The client in contact with a lawyer and the legal process must frequently be talked into a frame of mind appropriate to the needs of legal business. Lawyers serve the legal system by helping clients 'redefine . . . [their] situation and restructure . . . [their] perceptions' to facilitate a reconciliation between the client's objectives and the needs of legal institutions

(Blumberg 1967: 20). In the lawyer's office the client is likely to be introduced to a system of negotiations in which formal hearings are rare, rights are no guarantee of remedies, unfamiliar rules of relevance are asserted, and the nature of their own disputes and objectives are transformed (see Felstiner *et al.* 1981; Macaulay 1979; Mather and Yngvesson 1981; but see Cain 1983).

In fact, the range of client expectations with which lawyers must come to terms cover almost everything that is involved in a divorce—the distribution of property, the level of support, the rights to custody, the speed with which things are done, the wisdom of the rules and the judges, the roles that lawyers are willing to play, the times at which they are available, and the fees that they charge. Moreover, the clients that we studied expect their lawyers to tell them about their rights and obligations and to predict how they will fare in contests over houses, retirement benefits, visitation rights, support payments, and the like. Whatever their reservations about lawyers as a group and litigation as a means of resolving disputes, they expect their lawyers to navigate them through troubled waters. They want to believe that charts exist, that shoals are marked, and that channels to safe harbours are defined. But lawyers present a different picture: where clients want predictions and certainty, lawyers introduce them to the frequently unpredictable reality of divorce. While not every client is mistaken about all of these matters many divorce lawyers understandably feel that they must constantly be on their guard against clients who seek what cannot be delivered. A major professional function therefore is to attempt to limit clients' expectations to realistic levels.

A heavy dose of cynicism helps lawyers accomplish this goal. The cynic chips away at the legal façade until the client realizes that she is enmeshed in a system ridden with hazards, surprises, and people who are out to get her. By focusing on the mistakes, the irrationality, or intransigence of the other side, the lawyer creates an inventory of explanations that puts some distance between himself and responsibility for any eventual disappointment. Yet at the same time that he creates doubts about the legal process, the lawyer must give the client some reason to rely on him. The lawyer's emphasis on his insider status is one means of doing this. Nothing is guaranteed, the lawyer acknowledges, but the best chance for success rests with those who are familiar with local practice and who have a working relationship with officials who wield local power. This formula is repeatedly presented to clients by the lawyers in our sample.

By stressing the importance of being an outsider, the lawyer is not necessarily suggesting that the system is corrupt. He is not promising that he has an illegal way to deal with an illegal system, but rather he is creating an atmosphere in which the client will feel that she is being helped to attain a reachable goal despite being trapped in a system laced with uncertainties. The interests of the legal professional in this instance depart from the interests of the legal system. This lawyer constructs a picture of the legal process that fixes the client's dependency on him as it jeopardizes her trust in any other part of the system. The consequences of this for the client's view of law in general or participation in its legitimation rituals seems quite remote from his concerns. His talk, the image of the legal process that he constructs, is the talk of a cynical realist. The legal process he presents inspires neither respect nor allegiance.

Lawyer–client interaction: the client's perspective

Because divorce clients may not direct their litigation does not mean that they play no part in it. Because clients may acquiesce in the end to the lawyer's agenda does not mean that they do not make demands on their lawyer during the process. Clients may insist that lawyers attend to issues beyond those that are technically relevant and with which lawyers do not feel particularly comfortable; they may persist in bringing these matters into the conversation even after lawyers think that they have been settled. Clients may, in addition, resist recommendations that a lawyer believes are obviously in the client's interest. They may press lawyers to explain and justify advice given, actions taken, and results produced. Finally, clients may insist that lawyers interpret and account for the actions of others particularly their spouse, their spouse's lawyer, and judges, and that lawyers justify these actions in light of the client's sense of what is appropriate and fair. In these ways, clients transform the agendas of lawyers as well as their preferred professional style.

   In addition, this conference provided the client with an opportunity to work through conflicting goals: she did not want to capitulate to her husband but she did want to put an end to the fighting between them. Like many of the clients we have observed, she is uncertain about what she really wants. The wisdom of a negotiated settlement is clear to the lawyer, but for her it is fraught with ambiguity and difficulty. She insists that her lawyer concede, at least to her, that her need for a symbolic 'gesture' is comprehensible and legitimate. In so doing she secures some acknowledgement of her self-conceived victimization and some limited vindication. This drama, in which clients insist that their lawyers validate their partial and biased understandings, is a routine part of the divorce process. Lawyers, especially experienced divorce lawyers, understand this and provide such validation even when, as in this case, they attempt to discourage their clients from seeking it in the courtroom.

The consequences of the two perspectives

The competing perspectives of lawyer and client and the manner in which they are articulated establish the boundaries within which the strategy and tactics of divorce litigation develop. When the client feels betrayed and victimized, the lawyer may have to spend a significant amount of time and energy in selling negotiation as the means of resolving the case. This effort may affect the timing as well as the style and success of settlement efforts. Most of the lawyers we observed invest considerable effort in these client-management activities. In our sample it is the exceptional lawyer who fans the flames of the client's anger or accepts uncritically the client's version of events without reminding the client of the difficulties and costs of acting out of emotion.

Moreover, when divorce clients demand to know about the legal rules that will be applied, the probabilities of achieving various results, the costs they will incur, the pace at which various things will happen, and the roles that different actors will play, there are no standard answers that lawyers can give. What the client is asking for is a distillation of the lawyer's experience as it is relevant to cases like hers. What the lawyer can provide is not a *corpus juris* learned in law school or available in any texts but rather a personal view of how the legal system actually works in the community in which he is practising.

The lawyer's emphasis on the uncertain and personalistic nature of that process may have three effects. First, the extent to which the lawyer's picture of the legal system is at variance with the image that the client brings to her contact with the law may help to explain the common finding that experience with the legal process often results in dissatisfaction and a lower level of respect for law, regardless of substantive outcome (see Sarat 1977). Clients are brought face to face with the law's shortcomings by the testimony of their own lawyers (Sarat and Felstiner 1986) as well as the results that they experience.

Second, this characterization of the legal process may increase the client's dependence on the lawyer. People in the midst of divorce frequently feel a reduced sense of control over their lives. Their former lover and friend has become an enemy. They cannot live where and as they did, they must relate to their children in new ways, they may face new jobs and major economic threats, and their relations with family and friends may be strained, sometimes to the breaking point. When lawyers then introduce clients to an uncontrollable and unpredictable legal system, their sense of reduced control over their lives may become even stronger. They are, in essence, further threatened by a system that they had expected would reintroduce structure and predictability into their lives. In this situation the lawyer's services become more essential and the lawyer himself more indispensable (see Illich 1977).

Finally, the lawyer's emphasis on the client's need to separate emotional and instrumental issues may help to construct or reflect a vision of law in which particular parts of the self are valued while others are denied or left for others to validate. In the legal realm, lawyers insist that the rational and instrumental are to govern. While this lawyer clearly recognizes the human consequence of this opposition and hierarchy, he never questions it but instead treats it as both necessary and inevitable (Gabel 1980; Gordon 1982). Throughout this conference the lawyer encourages the client to be clear headed and to grant priority to monetary issues. By defining the ultimate goal as the resolution of the case and resolution in terms of the division of property, and by seeking to exclude the emotional focus that the client continues to provide, he expresses the indifference of the law to those parts of the self that might be most salient at the time of the divorce.

Notes

Acknowledgements: The research on which this paper is based was supported in part by two grants from the US National Science Foundation (SES 8119483 and 8510422). An expanded version of this paper appeared as 'Law and Strategy in the Divorce Lawyer's Office, *Law and Society Review*, 20.

1. No-fault divorce law incorporates this conception of the role of the legal process by eliminating the kind of moral accounting that had been required as part of the divorce process. 'Under no-fault both "good" spouses and "bad" spouses are treated equally when it comes to dividing marital property. . . . The implicit message of no-fault divorce is that one's moral behaviour during marriage has become a matter of choice rather than a matter of law' (Weitzman 1984: 12). There is thus no longer any need to force 'the parties to label their behaviour in moral terms' (ibid., 21). In fault divorce, lawyers were required to attend to the client's sense of injustice and even to encourage its expression. Under no-fault, the law retreats from moral issues and focuses instead on reaching agreements. Divorce settlements no longer lead to final vindication, the kind of official judgment of good and bad motives and behaviour that clients could once obtain through formal adjudication.

2. Although most lawyers we studied tried to avoid discussion of their clients'

emotional problems, this conference is not characteristic of the sample in two respects. First, there is more explicit talk about emotions than one would typically find. For this client, the discussion of her emotions seems to satisfy a need in and of itself. Second, some lawyers clearly encourage clients to link their feelings to the divorce process, primarily when the lawyer feels that the client may otherwise be willing to surrender too much too quickly or when the lawyer seeks to use the client's 'agitated state' as a bargaining ploy.

3. If the intent of no-fault reforms was to reduce the tendency of legal process to encourage acrimony between otherwise friendly divorcing spouses (Weitzman 1984), its effect may also be to make the legal process more alien for those whose divorce is angry and bitter and who confront a legal process inhospitable to those aspects of their divorce that may seem most important to them.

3. The Solicitor as Intermediary

RICHARD INGLEBY

Advocates of mediation have often characterized lawyers' behaviour in divorce cases as adversarial and disputatious. But studies of legal dispute processing over a wide variety of areas suggest that litigation tends to be a 'last resort' rather than the norm (e.g. Skolnick 1966; Hawkins 1983; Dingwall *et al.* 1983). In matrimonial proceedings parties have long been encouraged to resolve their disputes outside the courtroom (Ingleby 1986*b*) and empirical evidence to support the notion that divorce lawyers are routinely adversarial is notably lacking. Even Parkinson (1986*b*: 25), the leading British writer on mediation practice, acknowledges that studies of divorce lawyers' attitudes and their clients' perception show '. . . solicitors do not necessarily take a sharply adversarial stance in matrimonial proceedings . . . they often restrain their clients from litigation'. The actual behaviour of divorce lawyers in practice has not, however, so far been the direct object of empirical investigation in Britain.

The research reported in this chapter was intended to fill that gap. It is based on a longitudinal study of the management of sixty cases, twelve from each of five solicitors practising in a large English city, examining their records at quarterly intervals over a period of one year. Within the access and resources available to a doctoral student, these practices were selected to reflect as wide a range as possible of size, organization, and market conditions. It will be argued that the data demonstrate that solicitors do not necessarily behave in an adversarial fashion but may prefer a conciliatory style of representation and that there are characteristics of English divorces which may make out-of-court negotiations between solicitors more suitable than mediation as a mode of dispute resolution. Solicitors, then, should not be discouraged from continuing to perform this role in the future.

The Behaviour of Solicitors

There are two possible sources of evidence to test the conventional wisdom that solicitors tend to behave in an adversarial and litigious manner when handling divorce cases. One would be to examine the extent to which disputes are actually brought to court. The problem with this is that the *Judicial Statistics* provide an incomplete picture of the way the courts are used. In the 1985 edition, for instance, Table 4.11 shows that 14,786 applications were made for maintenance pending suit (interim support payments), but does not indicate how many were withdrawn or were repeated applications in the same case. A more satisfactory picture can only be built up from the direct examination of solicitors' activities in the course of matrimonial disputes. The present paper takes the arrangement of financial support for the client as an example of these, since it is often the first task a solicitor has to perform on becoming involved with the case. In the following discussion names and identifying details of the cases have been changed.

Support payments were made between the spouses in only twenty-five of the sixty cases studied. The remainder fell into three categories: 'no resources', where both parties were unemployed or on low wages; 'no need', where both parties were economically self-sufficient; and 'no relationship', where the parties were living in different countries.

In sixteen of the cases where payments were made, the parties themselves had come to an agreement before the solicitor became involved. There was no evidence of solicitors seeking to disrupt these agreements and intensifying or taking control of the dispute. The Solicitors' Family Law Association advises its members: 'Your new client may arrive having already reached broad financial agreement. Be very reluctant to overturn this . . . your goal is . . . arrangements with which your client will feel comfortable.' (Solicitors' Family Law Association 1986: 42.) Whether members or not, the solicitors in this study adopted this line.[1] The solicitor who noted that a husband's offer 'to pay on the home until sale and £200 per month' as 'generous' was typical of the sample.

If there was no existing agreement and the main source of support was likely to be the husband's earning capacity, a solicitor representing a wife with child-care obligations would normally begin by writing to the husband suggesting that he should seek legal advice so that the relationship between the parties could be formalized. Analyses which concentrate on the bargaining between solicitors need to recognize that a negotiation framework must be established before such bargaining can begin. It is analogous to the mediator's first state of 'creating structure and trust' (Folberg and Taylor 1984: 38) or 'preparing for negotiation' (Haynes 1981: 5). For example, one of the solicitors in this study was contacted by a client, Mr Smith, who had received a letter from his wife's solicitors suggesting he should contact his own. The solicitor's first action was to telephone the solicitors who had sent the letter. The call was noted with the comment that they 'wished to deal with the matter amicably'. This was confirmed in a letter of the same date, where the solicitors 'agreed to put the affairs on a more formal basis'. In reply to this letter the wife's solicitors said that they were 'much obliged' for the contact having been made. An agreement about support was soon arrived at and adhered to without problems. By such means agreement was reached quickly and non-contentiously in six cases.

An application to the court was only threatened in three cases. In all of these it followed letters expressing the desirability of agreement and the duty of a father to maintain his children. The main intention was to bring pressure to reach agreement rather than to get the case into court. In the one case where the threat had to be carried through, an agreement was reached at the door of the court and put into an agreed order. The solicitor representing the wife wrote, enclosing a copy of this order, that she was 'happy the decision came from him [i.e. the husband] rather than from the judge'.

In the present sample, there were court hearings dealing with applications to establish interim support payments in only four cases out of the thirty-five where no payments were being made. All of these arose where the wife's sole source of income was social security payments and in no case was any payment actually made by the husband despite the existence of an order. It seems likely that the applications arose from a desire by the social security authorities to enforce the obligations of a 'liable person' and that the court was being used in the context of a dispute between the husband and the DHSS rather than between spouses. Although DHSS staff are not now supposed to bring pressure on claimants to enforce 'liable person' obligations as a condition of receiving social security payments (Cretney 1984: 936), it is not clear that the official guidelines are invariably followed in practice (Hoggett and Pearl 1983: 604), as some of the solicitors in this sample confirmed. The entanglement of the welfare state in matrimonial disputes will be examined more fully later.

The main source of problems during the performance of agreements which the parties have made is that the terms are often uncertain (Griffiths 1986). Does an agreement to pay for the running of a car include all the repair bills, or only the MOT roadworthiness test and the insurance? Does an agreement to cover the 'household bills' cover a telephone bill which is much larger than usual? Although disputes such as these are not infrequent, the means by which they are resolved are consistent with the discussion above. The solicitors negotiate over what was intended in the agreement, appealing to the agreement, rather than to the court or to the husband's legal obligations.

Thus, in a case where there was some dispute at the time of the first conference as to whether the husband was threatening to stop paying support according to the agreement which had been made at the time of the recent separation, the wife's solicitor telephoned the husband's solicitor and asked her to speak to the husband to ask him to 'cool it'. The husband's solicitor reminded her client that 'it was not in his interests to inflame the situation', and the payments continued to be made. It seems clear that the solicitors value the agreements their clients have made, try to establish agreements where none have been made, and appeal to the fact of the agreement rather than the threat of court proceedings if problems arise in its performance.

The cases where the existence of the agreement does not preclude later court-based proceedings are those where the dispute is about the level of support in the agreement or its complete non-performance. Mrs Jones had come to an arrangement with her husband that he would pay £20 per week to her for the care of her two children. A few months after the separation she told her solicitor that she was finding it very difficult to make ends meet, and her solicitor asked her husband's solicitor to increase the level of the payments. The request was refused. Mrs Jones's solicitor pointed out that the money paid was not enough to support the children according to the standard of living before the marriage. In the absence of any agreement on the part of the husband, an application to the court for an interim order was threatened, and made when this met with no response. At the hearing Mr Jones was ordered to pay £40 per week for the children. Although this case did result in a court hearing, it seems clear that the use of the court was because the other options had been exhausted, rather than because of any litigiousness on the part of the solicitor.

As Sarat and Felstiner (1986: 113) concluded, in discussing their study of American divorce lawyers, 'most of those [lawyers] we observed, construct an image of the appropriate mode of disposition of a case that is at odds with the conventional view in which lawyers are alleged to induce competition and hostility' (cf. Griffiths 1986). Nevertheless, the infrequent resort to court should not lead to the conclusion that its availability is unimportant. It is impossible to say how many clients would come to agreements if they thought that there was no possibility of court proceedings. However, as Robert Dingwall shows later, the avilability of a court hearing can also be a significant factor in the work of mediators. It is not a basis for differentiating the two approaches.

The Advantages of Non-adversarial Behaviour

The fact is that a non-adversarial approach to divorce work by solicitors carries both economic and strategic advantages. This may appear to conflict with the conclusions of those who have examined the negotiations of personal injury claims (Ross 1970; Genn 1987). The difference may well be attributable to the fact that in matrimonial disputes, goodwill and co-operation are necessary both to achieve and perform an agreement, whereas 'hard bargaining' is necessary where the transaction costs are unequally distributed between an individual plaintiff and a corporate defendant and there is no 'continuing relationship' between the disputants. Although the relationship between a husband and a wife is not a completely equal one, the comparatively greater equality and the need to maintain the relationship between the parties if the settlement is to be workable mean that a non-adversarial approach is more suitable.

This, of course, is particularly marked in child-care disputes where the goodwill of both parties is clearly essential if access arrangements are to be successful. The data on these bring out the strategic advantages of a conciliatory approach. One solicitor regarded the following requests for greater access as much harder to refuse than a threat of a court application.

thank you for your offer . . . would you be prepared to consider a modest extension of access on other occasions . . .

we are of the impression that your client may be agreeable to overnight access on alternate weekends . . . please let us know if this is the case.

We understand access is proceeding very satisfactorily and our client is most grateful, in particular for the additional access on Christmas Day . . . in view of the success, would your client consider some limited holiday access during the summer.

The material on this case also brings out the way in which the parties can use the lawyers to re-establish their relationship and regain control of the dispute. The solicitor's notes of her meeting with the wife after the last of these requests recorded that 'she agreed to holiday access but would prefer him to ask her rather than us'. The solicitor then wrote to the husband's solicitors, saying that her client was 'happy for access during the summer holidays, amenable to any reasonable proposals your client puts forward and happy to speak to him direct'.

The belief that agreements which the parties have made themselves are more likely to be observed than court orders seemed to be one of the main considerations which led the solicitors to favour negotiated agreements. Quite apart from the avoidance of further dispute and possible litigation, the solicitors also tried to minimize possible obstruction and delay in the legal process. For example, in the case of Mr Smith, cited earlier, his solicitor wrote that they would 'welcome the opportunity of discussing the grounds before the petition is issued'. Although it is not always possible for the divorce petition to be agreed, especially if all the proceedings have to be dealt with under the rules for public legal assistance, the 'Green Form' scheme, it is clear from the data that solicitors prefer to discuss the petition before it is presented. This makes it less likely that the petition will provoke disagreement and the complications of a defended action.

It is often suggested that it is in lawyers' interests to intensify dispute, as they will benefit from the greater costs which are incurred on behalf of their client. The idea that it is in lawyers' interests to litigate rather than negotiate is even less plausible in England than in the United States. Since the profession is divided between barristers and solicitors, much of the profits of litigation (if any such exist) will accrue to the barrister rather than the solicitor. Moreover, the greater costs incurred by contentious negotiations are not necessarily reflected by greater profits. Less contentious cases take up less time and are less demanding on the solicitor. 'Client satisfaction' seems influenced to some extent by the amicability of the negotiations, and a satisfied client is more likely to pay the bill promptly.

To summarize thus far, if we use Parkinson's definition of conciliation as,

a structured process in which both parties to a dispute meet voluntarily with one or more impartial third parties (conciliators) to help them to explore possibilities of reaching agreement, without having the power to impose a settlement on them or the responsibility to advise either party individually

the data suggest that the process of out-of-court negotiation by solicitors may well comprehend at least those aspects of the definition which relate to the desirability of agreement. This suggests that the only way in which solicitors may not be functioning as conciliators is in the 'partiality' involved in advising of their clients. As Galanter (1984: 268) has suggested,

the negotiation of disputes is not an alternative to litigation. It is only a slight exaggeration to say that it *is* litigation. There are not two distinct processes, negotiation and litigation; there is a single process of disputing in the vicinity of official tribunals that we might call *litigotiation*, that is, the strategic pursuit of a settlement through mobilizing the court process.

Indeed, we may do better to think of mediation and negotiation with lawyers as varieties of 'litigotiation' than as polar opposites.

The Peculiar Characteristics of Matrimonial Disputes

Any analysis of the policy implications of these findings must also take account of the distinctive features of disputes relating to divorce. Four of these appear to be particularly relevant: the multi-party nature of the dispute; the changeable nature of the facts; the evolutionary character of the parties' knowledge of the issues and their preferences; and the emotional charge inherent in the breakdown of a marriage.

The multipartite nature of divorce

One of the most influential discussions of dispute resolution in divorce cases has been that offered by Mnookin and Kornhauser (1979). But their characterization of divorces as essentially two-party disputes which are potentially susceptible to out-of-court settlement by 'private ordering' has limited relevance to the United Kingdom and even to other areas of the United States (cf. Melli *et al.* 1985; Griffiths 1986). Wherever there is a developed welfare state, it is likely to assume a significant third-party role in many divorces. The situation of a Californian couple deciding on the distribution of their entitlements to shares in the equity of the former matrimonial home is very different from that of an English couple trying to disentangle a joint tenancy in public housing without prejudicing their access to that sector. The housing authority, and other welfare agencies, have powers, duties, and interests which constrain the possibilities for any party-controlled settlement. This is reflected both in reported case-law and the data from this study.

The question of litigation being prompted by social security authorities was raised earlier. A leading case on this is *Hulley* v. *Thompson* ([1981] 1 WLR 159; cf. Cretney 1984: 934). Mr Thompson had agreed to transfer his share in the matrimonial home to his wife, while she agreed not to seek support for either herself or their two children. This agreement was incorporated into a consent order when the couple were divorced. The Supplementary Benefits Commission then sought to recover payment from Mr Thompson for the money that they were paying to Mrs Thompson, while he argued that he had fulfilled his obligations by performing the agreement embodied in the consent order. The High Court held that the presence of the consent order did not remove Mr Thompson's duty to maintain his children under section 17(1) of the Supplementary Benefits Act 1976. The implication of this decision is that the financial issues in the Thompson divorce were as much between Mr

Thompson and the DHSS as they were between Mr and Mrs Thompson themselves. In the present research, another 'Mr Thompson' was under pressure from the social security authorities to pay more than the £5 per week per child which had been agreed by both spouses and their solicitors.

Local authority housing provides other examples of the way divorces involve outside parties, even where the couple are not already in public sector accommodation. The duties of local authorities to provide housing, under the Housing (Homeless Persons) Act 1977, do not apply where the reason for the housing need is that the applicant is 'intentionally homeless' (ss. 4(4), 4(5) cf. Bryan 1984; Robson and Watchman 1981). A person is defined as intentionally homeless 'if he deliberately does or fails to do anything in consequence of which he ceases to occupy accommodation which is available for his occupation and which it would have been reasonable for him to occupy' (s. 17(1)). In the present study, for example, one of the solicitors was advised in a letter from the relevant housing department that, 'if your client was to voluntarily sell her share of the home she may be considered to be intentionally homeless and not considered for council accommodation for three years'. The situation here is clearly analogous to the Thompson case, in that the dispute is as much between the client and the local housing authority as it is between the client and her spouse.

The need to include third parties' decisions in many dispute resolutions means that it will often be impossible to resolve the dispute at a meeting between the divorcing parties alone. Further, awareness of the need for such third-party decision may only arise after consideration of other options, and the decision of the third party may well take time to emerge. The point is not confined to those cases where the third party is an agency of the state. Where the matrimonial home is privately owned, but mortgaged, it will be necessary for the mortgagee, usually a building society, to consent to any transfer of title from joint to sole ownership. The conditions which the building society may wish to be fulfilled before consenting to such a transfer may well involve complex financial negotiations. Nor is it a problem confined to the poor. Similar considerations can also affect more affluent households trying to secure the most favourable treatment of the divorce from tax authorities (cf. Mnookin and Kornhauser 1979: 962). Two recent cases, *Morley-Clarke* v. *Jones (Inspector of Taxes)* ([1986] Ch 311] and *Sherdley* v. *Sherdley* ([1986] 1 WLR 732), have examined the use of maintenance orders for tax avoidance and the constraints introduced by the first of these decisions significantly affected one of the cases in this study. In such circumstances, the possibility of private ordering and a dispute resolution process which focuses almost exclusively on the two parties involved seems seriously misconceived.

The changeable facts of matrimonial disputes

Much of the mediation literature draws a distinction between fact-finding and the exploration of settlement options in matrimonial disputes (e.g. Folberg and Taylor 1984: 26). This study suggests that these topics cannot be so easily separated.

One of the 'facts' of the dispute will be the preferences of the parties for different outcomes. These are particularly susceptible to change, in a situation where 'emotional pressures are high and judgement apt to be clouded' (*Edgar* v. *Edgar* [1980] 1 WLR 1410). The parties' needs and resources are also liable to change. In this study, there are cases where the husband is employed at the time of the first contact with the solicitor but becomes unemployed during the negotiations, and where parties who choose to remain in the matrimonial home in the period immediately following the separation cannot keep up the outgoings of the house. Children's needs may alter more quickly than those of their parents, introducing a further element of uncertainty (Wallerstein and Kelly 1980: 302).

This is not to say that mediation cannot take account of such changes but it is unlikely that this would be possible in the kind of brief, one-off meeting envisaged by the Booth Committee and discussed elsewhere in this volume.

The emergence of parties' knowledge

Booth-style in-court mediation also seems likely to encounter problems with the parties' imperfect knowledge of the resources which will need to be reallocated. The question is not exclusively one of the honesty or dishonesty of the parties but simply that the relevance of certain facts may not initially be apparent and may only be recognized during or even after the negotiating process. As Folberg and Taylor (1984: 47) recognize, 'Before good decisions can be reached, both participants must have equal information and both must fully understand what these issues are'. But even under the present English system, this ideal has been hard to achieve and the courts have been asked to set aside agreements based on inadequate knowledge or understanding (Ingleby 1984, 1985). In legal proceedings, these have led to more stringent rules about disclosure being imposed on parties before a consent order will be granted (SI 1984/1511; SI 1985/1315). It is far from clear how mediation can deal with this issue. Certainly the Booth Committee's rejection of advance disclosure, on the grounds that 'financial affidavits are likely to contain contentious matters which would not be conducive to a settlement' (para. 4. 156), seems to be another example of the attempt to pursue agreement solely to save court costs and without regard to the quality of the outcome.

The bitterness and violence of matrimonial disputes

The final reason why negotiation by solicitors may be preferable to an intensive mediation process relates to the emotional charge of the dispute. The length of time necessary for divorcing people to adjust to their new status is a major theme in a number of studies (e.g. Wallerstein and Kelly 1980; Hart 1976). Out-of-court negotiations take place over a longer period of time than most mediations, at a pace controlled by the parties rather than the court or the mediator. This allows time for the facts to stabilize and the parties to come to terms with their situation. The process is well-illustrated by the access dispute discussed earlier. The mother was clearly more confident about allowing access after she realized that her position with the child would not be threatened and she had adjusted to the separation. A precipitate attempt at conciliation might well have hardened attitudes in such a case.

A physical distance between the parties may also defuse some of the tensions surrounding the breakdown of the relationship which are often manifested in violence. Atkins and Hoggett (1984: 124) estimate that, 'something between one-third and two-fifths of all divorcing couples have experienced violence in their relationship'. In the writer's sample there is violence reported by the clients in twenty-eight of the sixty cases, nearly half of the sample. That not all of these clients used the fact of the violence on the divorce documents is one reason why this figure is slightly higher than those obtained from studies of petitions. It is difficult to sustain the argument that the allegations of violence brought by spouses are fabrications in order to secure advantages under the domestic violence legislation. The solicitors in the study often sought confirmation of the injuries from general practitioners or hospital casualty departments, and frequently saw the bruisings and lacerations for themselves.

The nature of the violence was as frightening as its extent. Most of the violence reported constituted beatings but there were even more serious incidents in a significant number of cases. One client had been kicked in the stomach when she was pregnant. Another had to have sixteen stitches inserted in a facial would caused by her husband attacking her with a knife. One client's husband was so outraged at her having had an IUCD inserted that he beat her onto the bed and tried to remove it by inserting a bottle into her vagina. When one client fled the matrimonial home, the solicitor had to protect not only her client, but also her client's mother, whom the client's husband threatened with a six-inch knife so that she might divulge her daughter's whereabouts.

The level of violence tolerated by women before they visit a solicitor has been discussed elsewhere, as has the inadequacy of the legal regime for dealing with the problem (Pahl 1985; Borkowski *et al.* 1983). In the present context, it is sufficient to suggest only that the background of violence in nearly half the cases in the sample means that parties may feel better able to negotiate at arms' length, rather than be confronted with each other in the same room, a problem which is acknowledged by some advocates of mediation, (e.g. Folberg and Taylor 1984; 38–47) but perhaps underestimated by others. If Haynes's suggestion to 'bring out a bottle to give the participants a symbolic way of closing the mediation process' (Haynes 1981: 76) was followed in every case there is a danger that one of the participants would smash the bottle on the table and push it in the other's face.

Some Advantages of Partiality and Formalism

The claim that conciliators are necessarily impartial has been severely criticized. Freeman's (1984: 19) concerns about the dangers of 'rampant interventionism, a system of indirect controls and pervasive reliance on professional expertise' appear to be borne out by attitudes like those of Haynes (1981: 135) who acknowledges the mediator's power 'to influence the couple in any given direction'. Dingwall (1986: 22) has reported elsewhere that 'conciliators do apply various sorts of pressures to achieve or obstruct certain possible outcomes', although his contribution to the present volume shows that these may not always immediately be successful.

The other problem, which Anne Griffiths also discusses, is that impartiality in an unequal dispute can merely reinforce those inequalities. Divorce disputes may be characterized by inequality in the power to control income, the power to reject, and the power to resist a settlement (Haynes 1981: 49–52). Settlements which reflect and reinforce that pattern are seen to be undesirable from most points of view; yet none of the advocates of conciliation seem to have shown how conciliators can compensate for the effects of such inequalities without falling foul of the objections on the ground of interventionism (Ingleby 1986*a*: 67).

If we consider as an example of inequality the knowledge of the extent of the parties' financial resources, the expectation that parties will voluntarily disclose all their assets on a 'financial worksheet' (Folberg and Taylor 1984: 48; Haynes 1981: 154–6) seems over-optimistic in the light of the 'non-disclosure' cases which dogged the English courts in the late seventies. In these cases, agreements were negotiated on the basis of incomplete information and then sought to be set aside when more complete knowledge of the parties' resources came to light. The solution adopted by the Matrimonial Causes Rules Committee was to provide that the court could only approve agreements which were supported by evidence of the parties' income and capital (Ingleby 1984).

The duty on parties to provide the court with such information, and the power of solicitors to request it, would appear to be important safeguards in the negotiation process, and prerequisites both for the redress of inequalities and for informed consent to agreements reached through negotiation. This makes the comments of the Booth Committee about the disadvantages of affidavit evidence even more surprising. The absence of such evidence leads to less satisfactory agreements, not only in terms of the amount of information on which the agreement is based, but also in terms of the inequalities in the amount of information possessed by each of the parties. The assumption that there was less need for disclosure when the parties were agreed was one of the reasons for the absence of compulsory disclosure provisions in relation to consent orders before 1984 (Ingleby 1986*a*: 64). The absence of such provisions was responsible for many problems which arose after the agreements were made.

The idea that matrimonial disputes are between the divorcing parties alone is difficult to sustain. Divorcing parties' legal representatives seem better placed than conciliators to act as intermediaries between the various third parties whose agreement will be necessary for the dispute to be resolved. It appears reasonable to conclude that divorcing parties are best protected against the potential injustices of informal settlement by the 'formalism and rule of law which . . . provide a measure of protection to the powerless' (Freeman 1984: 16). The data discussed in this chapter suggest that the portrayal of lawyers as behaving adversarially may be a misrepresentation, and that there may well be advantages in a form of dispute resolution which provides for the various agencies involved in the dispute to participate in its resolution through a process better suited to the parties' emotional needs. Perhaps the criticisms of lawyers by the advocates of mediation are motivated by the need to create a distinct identity for mediation, in order to attract government funds in Britain or to draw clients away from lawyers and therapists in the United States. A more considered appreciation of the role of solicitors suggests that the advocates of conciliation have set up the wrong skittle, and it is their portrayal of the lawyers, rather than the role of lawyers itself, which should be knocked down.

Notes

1. Only one of the solicitors was known to be a member of the SFLA, although another was considering joining.

4. 'Civil Work' in the Probation Service

ADRIAN JAMES

The probation service has been identified with social work support to the criminal courts since the end of the nineteenth century. Its involvement with matrimonial disputes in the civil courts is, however, much less widely recognized, although of almost equal antiquity. As a proportion of the service's work, the welfare role is relatively small. This has tended to result in its neglect by writers on probation and to a periodic debate, within the service itself and outside, about whether it should be hived off. Recent policy developments have assumed that the service will continue to undertake civil work for the immediate future. As the following discussion will show, some uncertainty remains about its long-term prospects in the probation service. Nevertheless, as the major social work involvement in divorce in England, an understanding of these activities is surely central to any sensible debate on future policy and provision. In their contributions to this book, Richard Ingleby, and William Felstiner and Austin Sarat have suggested that the antithesis between mediation and legal processing may have been overdrawn: it is at least arguable that the same is true about the alleged opposition between mediation and custody investigation.

The Growth of 'Civil Work'

Robert Dingwall and John Eekelaar have described above the first recognition of the scope of informal work in domestic magistrates' courts during the nineteen thirties and its endorsement by statute in 1937. The Denning Committee (1947) resisted proposals to establish comprehensive family welfare provision within the probation service, partly because of the stigma associated with its criminal work (Bochel 1976: 195). Nevertheless, it did recommend the extension of court welfare appointments to the High Court, with powers to advise and guide, as well as to investigate, parents on the care of their children. The issue was considered again by the Royal Commission on Marriage and Divorce (1956), which discussed the possibility of seeking welfare reports in every divorce application involving children. This was rejected as both impractical and undesirable. Parents, it was thought, should have impressed upon them their continuing responsibility for taking decisions about the welfare of their own children, rather than leaving this to the court [Bochel 1976: 199). The legislation following this report restated the duties of the probation service and required the provision of welfare officers at High Court sittings outside London. When divorce work was delegated to County Courts in 1968, welfare officer appointments were also required. With the greater availability of personnel and the increase in divorce, the number of reports prepared for Divorce and Magistrates' Courts increased dramatically: from 3,370 in 1961 (Home Office 1966) to 12,916 in 1971 (Home Office 1972).

In the early nineteen seventies, however, the resources of the probation service came under increased pressure from the criminal justice system. The demand for reports in criminal proceedings had risen from 109,032 in 1961 (Home Office 1966) to 204,699 by 1971 (Home Office 1972), a proportionally smaller but numerically much larger increase than in work for the civil courts. At the same time, the overcrowding of prisons led to a series of diversionary proposals involving probation staff, many of which were introduced by the Criminal Justice Act 1972.

One response to these developments was a policy debate about the future direction of the probation service. Should it aim to offer a broadly based social work contribution to the whole court system or should it become much more specifically focused on its role in the criminal justice field. The service received conflicting messages. The loss of work with delinquent juveniles and their families following the Children and Young Persons Act 1969 to local authority social services seemed to be shifting the service in the direction of work with adult offenders. The House of Commons Expenditure Committee (1972: ix) saw matrimonial work as a 'natural candidate for removal'. The Home Office identified the provision of alternatives to custody as 'a strategy for the service . . . for the next twenty years or so' (Haxby 1978: 23–4) and the Finer Committee (1974) regarded the association with offenders as disqualifying the probation service from work in the family court.

Against this, it could be argued that the relationship between marital breakdown and criminal behaviour (cf. Rutter and Giller 1983) meant civil work could have a valuable preventive function. Moreover, while the loss of this work might free resources in the service for its criminal justice functions, it would still mean that resources would have to be found elsewhere for some other agency to do it. Certainly the continuing growth in demand for court welfare services meant that there could be no serious question of simply withdrawing them. Requests for reports more than doubled again between 1971 (Home Office 1976) and 1983 while matrimonial supervision work, following up children whose parents were divorced, had risen from 9,457 cases in 1971 (Home Office 1976) to 15,290 in 1982. The most recent statistics are given in Tables 1 and 2. Thus, although the number of referrals for attempts at matrimonial reconciliation fell drastically, and there were changes in the types of report requested (Table 1), the overall involvement of the service in civil work continued to increase.

This decade of uncertainty appears to have been at least temporarily resolved by the recent *Statement of national objectives and priorities for the probation service in England and Wales*, published by the Home Office in 1984. This gives a clear, if limited, commitment to the continued involvement of the service in the civil courts. The debate has now shifted to one over the aims and methods of that work, particularly the extent to which techniques of mediation or conciliation can be used as an alternative to the traditional process.

The Current Situation

The main duties of the probation service in civil work lie in the provision of information to the courts on matters relating to the welfare of children. Divorce courts have substantial powers to request reports: in advance of a hearing; to enable a judge to declare his satisfaction with consensual arrangements for custody; to provide information where custody and access are disputed; or in cases where an interim custody order is being sought. The service may also become involved in proceedings for separation, affiliation, wardship, adoption, guardianship, and custodianship, either through the provision of reports or, in some instances, as a supervisor of arrangements for the children.

Tables 1 and 2 show that civil work accounts for just under 10 per cent of the 285,880 court reports written in 1982 (Home Office 1984a) and about 7 per cent of the 147,160 persons under supervision at the end of 1984 (Home Office 1986). Home Office calculations assume that about 8 per cent of expenditure on the probation service is allocated to civil work, although local areas vary considerably around this figure (Hall and Martin 1983). In commenting on the slight decline in civil work shown in Tables 1 and 2, the Home Office regard this as 'in line with the expectation of the Statement of National Objectives and Priorities . . . that the proportion of resources allocated to civil work would be

TABLE 1.   Reports for the Civil Courts

	1979	1980	1981	1982	1983[a]
Inquiries concerning custody of and access to children:					
Magistrates' Courts	4,600	4,980	5,490	6,300	6,400
High/County Courts	12,990	13,410	14,300	15,440	16,000
Satisfaction reports	2,290	2,100	2,080	1,910	1,500
Guardian ad litem Inquiries:					
Adoption proceedings	2,790	2,940	3,060	3,120	2,900
Other proceedings	420	450	520	570	800
County Court Inquiries	900	990	760	930	
TOTAL	23,990	24,870	26,210	28,270	27,600

[a] Figures compiled by Association of Chief Officers of Probation; Home Office figures for 1983 not available.

Source: Probation Statistics, England and Wales, 1983.

TABLE 2.   Children Subject to Civil Court Supervision Orders (at Year End)

	1979	1980	1981	1982	1984[a]
Matrimonial proceedings	14,740	15,130	14,930	14,520	10,790
Wardship supervision	180	200	210	210	200
Guardianship supervision	600	590	610	510	350
Children Act 1975 supervision	60	60	40	50	40
TOTAL	15,580	15,980	15,790	15,290	11,380

[a] Home Office figures for 1983 not available.

Source: Probation Statistics, England and Wales, 1983 and 1984.

contained (Home Office 1986: 95). These data also show that over 80 per cent of the report work and 90 per cent of the supervision stem from matrimonial proceedings.

There is, however, a dearth of evidence about how the service deals with this work. Since the mid-sixties, there has been a steady flow of research, much of it Home Office-led, into probation work with offenders. But, despite the more dramatic proportionate increase in civil work and the controversy surrounding some of the recent practice innovations, there has been very little actual research. The Home Office Research and Planning Unit Research Programme for 1985–6 shows that no projects on civil work were completed in 1984–5 (and none have been previously published) and only one project was being considered out of nine on probation topics. In 1979, probation areas themselves were only involved in three projects on civil work (Home Office 1979). Five years later, there were thirty-seven projects underway, reflecting the growth of interest in this area, but closer inspection shows that these were all demonstration projects or working parties rather than research (National Probation Research and Information Exchange 1984).

The major practice innovation has undeniably been the development of a conciliation-based approach to marital breakdown. Home Office inquiries in 1982 revealed that conciliation schemes were available in less than half the probation areas in England and Wales but only three years later similar inquiries by the Association of Chief Officers of Probation (ACOP 1985) showed that virtually all areas had some involvement with conciliation even if only in the way individual welfare officers prepared their reports. While only a few areas offered comprehensive coverage, with conciliation available throughout the legal process, this is still a substantial shift in a very short time.

But these inquiries have also been important in revealing the substantial confusion which surrounds the use of the term 'conciliation' in the probation service. James and Wilson (1986) have argued that the term is being used indiscriminately to refer to the *objective* of bringing peace to a dispute, to the *process* of trying to achieve settlement, and to a *method* of achieving agreement between disputing parties.

Divorce counselling, for example, either on an individual basis or through divorce experience courses, is sometimes referred to as conciliation in so far as it attempts to deal with the negative emotional by-products of divorce and reduce the feelings of anger, guilt, powerlessness, and frustration which so often contribute to post-divorce conflict. In trying to bring peace to the parties, conciliation is an objective. On the other hand, conciliation can also describe the process of preparing a welfare report in a way which includes advice or counselling over difficult issues such as access. James and Wilson (1984*a*) found that over 95 per cent of probation officers in their study claimed always or sometimes to take such an approach and that over 80 per cent favoured an increased involvement by the service in such activities. The same authors (James and Wilson 1984*b*) have also shown that some probation officers individually assist parties to negotiate agreements over access and resolve other problems in the course of preparing welfare reports, engaging in a form of 'shuttle mediation'. And, of course, the attempts to reach agreement on court premises described by Gwynn Davis may also be treated as a process of conciliation.

The term can, however, also be used to refer to a method of working with disputing parents intended to give them greater control of the resolution. This approach is based on certain principles about the primary and continuing responsibilities of parents in relation to decision-making and post-divorce parenting and uses theoretical perspectives, skills, and techniques which are comparatively new to the probation service. Whereas probation officers have traditionally worked individually, for example, this concept of conciliation encourages co-working in joint sessions with both spouses and, possibly, children and other interested parties. Of the three images of conciliation, this is probably the closest to the original vision of the Finer Committee. While there are debates about the rival merits of different versions of these methods, there is a general consensus that conciliation is concerned with dispute settlement and not with the general emotional issues involved in marriage breakdown (James and Wilson 1986). The view is well summarized by Kelly (1983: 37–8), who concludes that conciliation is about 'helping clients to resolve their disputes and reach an acceptable agreement . . . and within that context to allow the process to be psychologically beneficial as well'.

Much of the work involving conciliation as a method is done by probation officers carrying particular functional responsibilities for divorce and related work, sometimes as members of specialist civil work teams and often within the context of welfare inquiries for the courts. The enthusiasm which some probation officers have shown for these developments has not, however, gone unchallenged. Some critics (e.g. Davis 1985) have argued that there is a basic incompatibility between the use of such methods and the task of welfare investigation. There has also been a certain amount of judicial discouragement. In a judgment in *Re H (a Minor)* ([1986] 1 FLR 476), the liaison judge of the Family Division at Manchester, Mr Justice Ewbank, commented that 'conciliation and welfare reporting are quite different functions and should be carried out by different people in any particular case . . . a court welfare report should . . . involve a wide investigation'. Similar points were raised in *Scott* v. *Scott* (*The Times*, 2 April 1986) and have been endorsed by Sir John Arnold, President of the Family Division, in letters to both ACOP and NAPO. This has created further confusion in that some areas have responded to the criticism by ceasing to refer to the use of such methods in the context of preparing welfare reports as 'conciliation' (e.g. Shepherd and Howard 1985), being urged instead to adopt descriptions of practice which refer to 'family meetings', 'joint interviews', or 'settlement seeking discussions' (ACOP 1986).

The continued growth of civil work and the dissatisfaction of many staff with traditional styles of practice have led to a great range of innovations. At the same time, however, these should be seen as *ad hoc* and piecemeal local initiatives rather than a carefully managed and researched process of change. The result is considerable confusion about terminology, concepts, practice, structures, and management.

Practice Issues

With the exception of those few areas where there are developed in-court conciliation schemes of the type described by Gwynn Davis, the service's work is centred upon its statutory duty to investigate and report, at a court's request, on any matter arising in matrimonial proceedings which affects a child's welfare. In reaching its decision, the only test used by the court is its estimate of the best interests of the child. This test and the courts' view of the information needed to apply it are the framework within which the probation officer must operate.

The investigative approach

The 'traditional' approach requires the welfare officer to compile sufficient evidence to assess the relationship and prospects of a child with each parent. This was re-emphasized by the Court of Appeal in *Re W (a Minor) The Times*, 27 October 1982; [1982] JSWL 247; see also *Edwards* v. *Edwards* [1986] 1 FLR 187), which stressed the importance of observing the child in the home of each parent even if special arrangements were required to achieve this. Probation officers, then, would normally be expected to interview each parent on a number of occasions, with and without the children, at home and at the officer's base. Contact would be made with other agencies like schools, social services, or health services to request relevant information. If children are old enough to express a clear opinion, they would be seen on their own.

In practice, however, James and Wilson (1984*a*) found that only 41 per cent of officers always contacted social services and just over 20 per cent always contacted family doctors or health visitors. Nearly 25 per cent of officers did not routinely discuss feelings and attitudes towards the marriage breakdown with 9–12 year old children, rising to 70 per cent with 6–8 year olds, although these are the age groups most at risk of behavioural and emotional problems (e.g. Eekelaar 1982, James and Wilson 1984*b*, Wallerstein and Kelly 1980). Moreover, welfare reports are not widely requested: Eekelaar and Clive (1977) found they were available in about 8 per cent of uncontested and 53 per cent of contested cases. It has also been suggested that the intervention comes too late to be of much value. In half the cases where a report was called for James and Wilson (1984*b*) found that the request did not reach the welfare officer until six months after the filing of the petition. Although it could be argued that this has allowed time for the situation to stabilize and for the parties to sort out their own arrangements, there is a widely held view (e.g. James and Wilson 1986, NAPO 1984, Parkinson 1983b) that earlier intervention can be helpful in limiting conflict and preventing the polarization of attitudes. At present there is no substantial empirical support for either position and, certainly, no reliable basis for differentiating between cases in order to select appropriate responses.

Even within this approach there appears to be room for improvements in its efficiency at picking up cases where children might benefit from a welfare report and in developing a more uniform style of work. Factors such as access difficulties, larger family size, and the presence of 6–12 year old children all seem to be associated with disturbance to children in divorce. But, for example, welfare reports are more commonly ordered where custody changes between divorce and petition (Eekelaar and Clive 1977), although access difficulties, and consequent disturbances, seem more frequent where custody does not change (James and Wilson 1984*b*). Given the pressures to make financial savings by introducing conciliation (e.g. Gough 1982, Hall and Martin 1983) as a substitute for investigation, it ought not to be lightly assumed that the present mode of welfare reporting is as cost-effective as it could be.

Conciliation

The essential critique of this tradition within the probation service is, however, of a more fundamental nature. It rejects the role of the welfare officer as an assessor of families and looks to return control over the decision-making to the families themselves. Five elements are involved in this argument (Conference of Chief Probation Officers 1982, NAPO 1984):

1. No reports are requested in the vast majority of divorces. Families find themselves being investigated primarily because they are in dispute and only incidentally because there may be questions about parenting abilities. It is therefore illogical to try to assess these and identify the 'better' parent. If parenting abilities are questioned, by allegations of ill-treatment or sexual abuse, for instance, these should be brought to the attention of child protection services who properly have an investigative role in response to reports of this kind.

2. The investigative model undermines the authority and responsibility of parents by denying their capacity to identify and decide on their children's best interests.

3. Where there is no risk to the child, it is inappropriate, even arrogant to make value judgments about different styles of parenting. Adversarial and combative behaviour is encouraged by putting both parents under pressure to 'sell' themselves and discredit the other.

4. In the vast majority of cases, courts simply endorse the existing arrangements anyway.

5. If decisions have to be made as an outcome of assessments, they are legally the responsibility of the judge or magistrate and ought not to fall upon the welfare officer by default.

The specialist teams which have been in the vanguard of such developments have increasingly abandoned investigation and the preparation of traditional welfare reports for conciliation using methods derived from family therapy and task-centred social work (James and Wilson 1986). These often restrict welfare involvement to a small number of meetings, usually between two co-workers and the entire family, including the children, in an office setting.

There is a certain irony about these attempts to diminish the service's judicially valued activities in civil work at the same time as aspiring to increase the impact of its reports and recommendations in criminal justice. It does not, moreover, seem adequate to respond to the judges' disquiet (e.g. in *Re H (A Minor); Scott* v. *Scott*) about the new modes of practice merely by asserting the professional autonomy of welfare officers to determine their own methods of working. Certainly, it can reasonably be argued that the objectives of conciliation and welfare reporting are so different that the two should be kept entirely separate (e.g. Davis 1982*a*, Booth Committee 1985). If there is any attempt to combine them, the parties may be confused, the welfare officer's impartiality (real or perceived) may be prejudiced for any subsequent investigation, and the process delayed. Such a delay would systematically disadvantage non-custodial parents in disputes since courts prefer to endorse the status quo in order to minimize disruption for the child.[1]

On the other hand, as Robert Dingwall shows later, it is not clear that 'pure' conciliation is possible where there are third-party interests involved. No conscientious mediator, let alone an employee of a public agency with a moral and legal responsibility for a child's welfare, could be bound by any and every parental decision. The right of parents to make decisions concerning their children is contingent upon the consistency of those decisions with wider social perceptions of children's interests. But the boundary-setting which is implicit in this process is obscured by the way some welfare officers have turned conciliation into a therapeutic task. It may very well be that perspectives from family therapy can and should be used to understand the emotional and psychological impact of divorce and that the civil arm of the probation service should develop such approaches. However, the literature on mediation or conciliation stresses its short-term and pragmatic character. It is primarily concerned with dispute resolution, not with counselling. By failing to distinguish the two the 'conciliation' movement in the probation service is further confusing an already muddled picture.

The arguments against welfare reporting seem less conclusive than they might appear if we consider the general risks to a child in the context of divorce and the duty of the service to assist a court in applying the 'best interests' test. It seems undisputed that, if a child is alleged to be in physical or moral danger, an investigation should be conducted, although there is some disagreement about whether this should be triggered by the service or by the party making the allegation. Whoever conducts the investigation, though, its outcome will affect the future course of the divorce and the welfare officer's work. If nothing else, one parent may end up in prison or a child be taken into social services' care. But the evidence cited earlier suggests that many other children are placed at risk of behavioural and emotional damage by the experience of divorce itself and that parents may vary in their capacity to manage this. A child-focused assessment process by a suitably trained welfare officer could then be substantially more than simply making value judgments about parenting styles.

Undoubtedly, the selection of cases for welfare investigation could be improved. It needs to be more widely recognized, however, that a failure to agree does not necessarily indicate parental irresponsibility but the genuine difficulty of making decisions about complex and emotionally charged issues. And yet a decision is essential if the parties and their children are to be able to rebuild their lives on a firm foundation. The pronouncement of a court, on the best available information, is the socially accepted way of imposing closure on that dispute. If judges or magistrates are constrained from venturing outside the courtroom, they will continue to value the impartial professional assessment of a welfare officer, analysing the factors affecting the future prospects of a child, including the probable sources and likely impact of continued conflict. If there are deficiencies in the quality of these assessments, it seems defeatist simply to deny the need for them rather than looking actively for ways of improving practice. Certainly it is far from clear that the limits of advance have been reached in welfare investigation and reporting.

Management Issues

The enthusiasm to develop a more constructive approach to divorce-related work has raised a number of difficult issues for the practice of welfare officers. As Davis (1982*a*) has argued, the service is now faced with the task of managing the development of its civil work function with sufficient flexibility to absorb new techniques and sufficient confidence to set clear boundaries between different areas of work. As he might have added, it seems probable that it must do so within a context of static resources. In this, the most urgent task is to try to identify a set of agreed principles to underpin the practice of civil work and a shared definition of the role of the welfare officer. Some diversity is, of course, inevitable: the organizational solutions to the problems of service delivery in sparsely populated rural areas are likely to be different from those in culturally diverse inner cities. But these variations need to be seen as local adaptations of a uniform national approach, as means to a common end.

Genericism or specialism?

An immediate organizational issue is whether civil work should continue to remain part of the generic load of probation officers or should become an area of specialist practice. James and Wilson (1984*a*) found that about 15 per cent of officers had some degree of specialization in this area. Some of them were preparing over 70 reports a year, a figure which seems undesirably high. By contrast, a large majority of non-specialist officers were preparing fewer than 6 reports a year. It can reasonably be asked whether this will allow them to develop an appropriate level of competence and it certainly makes any degree of uniformity in practice almost impossible to achieve. Certainly, many of these officers felt under-trained for the tasks involved and there was evidence that it was being introduced much earlier in their career than used to be the case.

Such arguments favour a move towards specialization, a move which would also be consistent with recent approaches to the management and structure of the service (Home Office 1980). The service would need to give careful consideration to the place of such appointments in an officer's career development. But specialization would make the issues discussed above more accessible to debate and to proactive management rather than leaving them to *ad hoc* local initiatives. The relationship with the civil courts could then be subjected to more coherent analysis and development.

At present the National Association of Probation Officers (NAPO 1984) has identified two distinct approaches, both of which tacitly accept specialization. The first is a two-tier system, in which the provision of conciliation is kept separate from a court welfare service which continues to investigate and report. NAPO rejects this option, arguing that it is not possible to specify in advance which parents are suitable for conciliation and which for investigation, and that if conciliation is a process of helping parents to re-establish their ability to negotiate with each other, rather than simply a means of reaching an agreement, it has something to offer in all matrimonial disputes. Experience suggests, however, that some parents cannot be helped to negotiate and it is the recognition and acceptance of this in the course of conciliation that identifies cases as appropriate for investigation, rather than some predetermined criteria.

The other approach identified by NAPO is the completely integrated service, with conciliation central to all the work of the court welfare team. They also see this as problematic because of the need for a welfare officer to shift from conciliation to investigation if an agreement is not reached. In their view, the conciliator's neutrality is incompatible with making 'value judgments' and recommendations. The family's knowledge of this as a possible outcome may also prejudice the process of conciliation.

NAPO conclude that the role of the welfare officer needs to be fundamentally altered from that of informing the court's decisions to assisting families to rebuild their ability to negotiate. Reports should be prepared on the basis of meetings with the whole family, including children. If an agreement emerges in the course of such meetings, it will be reflected in a formal report. If there is no agreement, the report will simply describe the nature and areas of disagreement, but will make no assessments or recommendations. Such unresolved disputes do not indicate that conciliation has failed, merely that it is incomplete, although it must be wondered when it ever would be completed in some cases. Paradoxically, NAPO also hold that, after the court has adjudicated, continuing work may sometimes be appropriate, possibly under the powers of a Matrimonial Supervision Order, using time-limited and task-centred methods—that is, introducing those very elements of compulsion which the body of the document has rejected.

A more satisfactory approach, within the context of a specialist civil work team, would depend upon a clearer recognition of the difference between the three functions of divorce counselling, conciliation, and investigation/reporting. All families referred to the team might initially be considered for conciliation, defined as a time-limited process of dispute resolution. Those accepting this would be dealt with by appropriately trained team members. If, during the course of conciliation, it became apparent that emotional problems were blocking an agreement, one or both parents could be offered, possibly concurrently, divorce counselling by another team member. Where families declined conciliation or agreement could not be reached within its terms of reference, the case would be handled in an investigative manner by an officer trained for this task. In practice, of course, individual team members might be trained for more than one function but they would not be expected to exercise these different skills simultaneously in any one case.

Training

Boswell (1982: 186) noted that, 'to achieve credibility, an organisation should be able to point to the relevance and appropriateness of its training system'. But in spite of the growing importance of civil work, James (1985) found that officers did not feel well prepared for it. Only 58 per cent claimed to have had pre-service training specifically concerned with marital breakdown and its impact on children and only 50 per cent had received in-service training on these topics. Since these two groups overlapped, it seems that 25 per cent of officers currently involved in civil work have not had, or cannot recall, any training for the task. It must also be noted that there did not appear to be any substantial differences between the practices of those who had and had not received training. This suggests an urgent need to review the content of both basic and post-basic social work education available to the probation service and to identify officers who have missed out on this topic in their professional training and development. A concentration of work in specialist teams would make these issues much easier to tackle.

But the lack of evidence of effects from the training current practitioners have received suggests that its nature also needs careful analysis. Clearly it needs to take in not only divorce counselling and conciliation but it should also tackle investigation and report writing. These cannot be taken for granted as general probation skills, especially if an emphasis on children and their developmental needs is accepted as more appropriate for civil work reports.

Structures

Resources for civil work seem likely to remain limited in view of its modest place in the priorities of the Home Office. There is, then, a particular need to ensure that they are used both effectively and efficiently. Specialist teams may be part of the answer but they are not a substitute for explicit management attention to the issues of professional and organizational policy involved in the choice of methods and structures and to the identification of the costs incurred by each option. This need suggests that active consideration should be given to the formation of civil work subcommittees of Probation Committees[2] with a distinct budget for this area. These subcommittees should work through an Assistant Chief Probation Officer with specific overall responsibility for civil work practice.

The sort of structure described about would assist services to identify and manage the many issues currently arising from civil work rather than simply reacting to events. Reform, however, is increasingly urgent. Although the Finer Committee's (1974) recommendations for a Family Court have yet to be acted upon, there is growing pressure (e.g. BASW 1985, Hall and Martin 1983, Law Society 1985) for such a development in order to achieve a more consistent approach to family issues by the legal system. A separate family court welfare service is often presented as an intrinsic part of this change. If the probation service cannot demonstrate its ability to manage civil work, then it may lose the opportunity to do so.

The probation service can certainly, and probably rightly, argue that such a specialist agency would be too small to be viable and that they are better placed to meet the needs of the civil courts by virtue of their historical relationship, their professional skills, and their existing organizational structure. But the current confusion and diversity of practice and provision represent as much of a threat to the continued involvement of the service in civil work as does the increasing Home

Office emphasis on its contribution to the criminal justice system. It remains to be seen whether the service's management can find both the will and the way to meet these challenges.

Notes

Acknowledgement: The author gratefully acknowledges both the information and the helpful comments provided by Mrs Sheila Kenyon, Assistant Chief Probation Officer, Humberside. Responsibility for the views expressed remains the author's, however.

1. The procedural acceleration proposed by the Booth Committee could ease this constraint by making the status quo less of an obvious fixture because of its shorter duration.
2. Probation services are accountable nationally to the Home Office, but are administered locally by Probation Committees, which consist principally of magistrates. Because of the growing complexity of the service, the responsibility for some specialized functions is already devolved to subcommittees.

5. Divorce Mediation: An American Picture

JESSICA PEARSON AND NANCY THOENESS

Fifteen years ago, divorce and custody mediation in America was essentially an experimental approach advocated by only a few practitioners (Coogler 1978; Haynes 1981; Irving 1980; Kessler 1978; Lohman 1981). Today, it is an established area of practice pursued by a large number of individuals trained in mediation as well as in law, psychology, or social work.

Although a precise and current count of divorce mediation service providers is not available, a 1982 directory identified more than 300 groups and individuals in the public and private sectors (Pearson *et al.* 1982). Numerous states and jurisdictions make attendance at one or more mediation sessions mandatory in cases of contested child custody or visitation (Brown 1982; Comeaux 1983). While most court-based mediation services focus only on disputes dealing with child custody or visitation, a growing number are offering services for the mediation of all divorce issues including child support (Delaware Revised Court Rule 151) (Connecticut Special Act No. 84-74) and the division of property (Dispute Resolution 1980).

The reputed benefits of mediation are particularly compelling in child-custody disputes. Rather than have such matters investigated and evaluated by mental health professionals prior to judicial decision regarding custody, mediation proponents hold that parents should have primary responsibility for deciding on living arrangements for their children. Because mediation affords parents an opportunity to be heard and to explore all feasible alternatives, child-custody mediation is credited with being able to transform 'seemingly impossible . . . conflicts' (Bienenfeld 1983). In addition to enhancing parental communication and co-operation, another hypothesized benefit for mediation stressed by advocates is the superior adjustment for the children involved (Emery 1982; Coogler *et al.* 1979; Haynes 1978). Lastly, advocates stress that mediation reduces court congestion and costs and is more effective than adversarial interventions in improving compliance and reducing re-litigation.

Despite professional enthusiasm for mediation and its growing popularity and use, there have been only a few empirical studies of the efficiency of the divorce mediation process (Pearson 1982, McEwen and Maiman 1982; Pruitt and Kressel 1985). Moreover, the research conducted to date has generally suffered from methodological limitations (Kressel 1986).

The Research

This chapter summarizes the results of two major research projects dealing with the efficacy of mediating divorce disputes, particularly those involving contested child custody and visitation. One study, The Denver Custody Mediation Project (CMP), employed a quasi-experimental design in which comparable cases involving contested child custody were assigned to mediation and control group categories on a random basis, although ultimate participation in mediation was voluntary. The second study, The Divorce Mediation Research Project (DMRP), involved user surveys, observations, interviews, and an analysis of mediation tapes generated at public mediation programmes at the Los Angeles Conciliation Court, the Family Relations Division of the Connecticut Superior Court, and the Domestic Relations Division of the Hennepin County Family Court; surveys with divorcing parties who were contesting custody/visitation; and surveys of another group not contesting the issues in one state where court-based mediation was not available.

In both studies, mediation clients and their non-mediating counterparts were interviewed either face to face or by telephone at three time points.

The CMP and the DMRP offer a relatively reliable assessment of the effectiveness of mediation in achieving a broad range of goals. This chapter reviews our major findings to date. Specifically, we discuss the major research questions we have posed and the answers we have generated. Our review concludes with a discussion of questions that remain to be answered and most promising future research strategies.

The Use of Mediation Services by Divorcing Couples

With few exceptions, the divorce mediation programmes with the highest participation rates are compulsory services housed in courts. Voluntary mediation programmes, on the other hand, typically fail to attract a substantial number of participants. For example, half the disputants in the CMP rejected the offer of free mediation services to resolve contested child custody and visitation matters (Pearson and Thoeness 1982).

Not surprisingly, many courts are requiring that divorcing parties attempt to resolve their disagreements in mediation and permitting access to a judicial officer only after an attempt to mediate has been made. The concept of mandatory mediation of custody and visitation disputes enjoys strong public support. For example, among those who reached agreements in mediation in 1982 in Los Angeles, Minnesota, and Connecticut, the proportion favouring a mandatory attempt stood at 85–91 per cent. And even 62 to 68 per cent of those who failed to produce mediation agreement would 'definitely' or 'probably' favour a mandatory attempt.

A mandated attempt to mediate does not appear to affect the participatory nature of the process or the satisfaction with the outcome. Comparable proportions of users of mediation services in a mandatory programme in California (41 per cent) and voluntary ones in Connecticut (35 per cent) and Minneapolis (41 per cent) report reaching a final agreement in mediation. Comparable numbers also indicate that they definitely would recommend mediation to a friend (64 per cent in California; 43 per cent in Connecticut; 53 per cent in Minneapolis) and are very glad that they tried mediation (59 per cent in California; 42 per cent in Connecticut; 54 per cent in Minneapolis). Lastly, roughly comparable proportions of respondents in California (23 per cent), Connecticut (20 per cent), and Minnesota (12 per cent) agree with the statement, 'The mediator pressured me or my (ex) spouse into an agreement'. Methods of implementing divorce mediation services in the public sector including basis of legal authority, structure, and substantive provisions are chronicled in an article prepared by Comeaux (1983).

The mediation process

The mediation process varies in scope and duration in the public and private sectors. As a rule, cases are mediated more rapidly in the public sector, involve fewer sessions, and deal only with the issues of custody or visitation. For example, a 1981 survey of public and private sector services offering divorce mediation revealed that the average case in the private sector takes 8.7 hours and that half require 9 hours or more. In the public sector, the average case requires 6.3 hours and nearly half are handled in 4.0 hours or less (Pearson *et al.* 1983).

In addition to these distinctions between the public and private sector, we find differences in the scope and format of mediation at individual courts in the DMRP. In Minnesota, the process takes an average of 3.3 sessions and 4.3 hours. At the Los Angeles Conciliation Court, cases average 1.7 sessions and 3.0 hours. In Connecticut, the average number of mediation sessions and hours is 1.5 and 2.3 respectively.

Courts also differ with respect to the participation of children and attorneys. While 75 per cent of the Los Angeles respondents report that their lawyers were seen by the mediators, this is noted by only 16 per cent of the Minneapolis and 11 per cent of the Connecticut respondents. Children are most likely to have been seen by mediators in Minneapolis (66 per cent) and were seen in only 28 per cent of the Los Angeles and Connecticut cases, respectively. In addition, mediations in Connecticut are routinely conducted by teams comprised of a male and a female, while in California and Minnesota, sessions are most commonly conducted by single mediators of either sex. And in Connecticut and Minneapolis, mediation sessions are scheduled in advance using an appointment system, while in California families typically move directly to mediation from a preliminary court appearance.

Despite differences in format and duration, there are few differences in agreement rates for court mediation programmes. Approximately 40 per cent of disputants who use court-based mediation services in Los Angeles, Minneapolis, and Connecticut reach full agreements on custody and visitation and another 20–30 per cent report reaching partial or temporary agreements (Pearson and Thoeness 1984*a*).

Client, case, and mediator characteristics associated with successful mediations

Logically, successful mediation outcomes are a result of dispute and disputants' traits as well as mediator characteristics. To determine how well these factors are able to predict the actual outcome in mediation in the DMRP, we conducted a discriminant analysis. The analysis enabled us to predict settlements in 67 per cent of the cases that resulted in full agreements. Of the various factors used in the analysis, the one which aided most in outcome predictions was the mediator's ability to facilitate communication. This was followed by:

> providing clarification and insight;
> evaluation of chances using alternatives;
> magnitude of the dispute;

duration of the dispute;
relationship with an ex-spouse;
balance of power;
diffusion of anger;
acceptance of the divorce;
setting the stage.

In a second discriminant analysis, we used the factors to predict respondents' willingness to recommend mediation. We correctly predicted (93 per cent) willingness to recommend the process, but were less successful (75 per cent) in predicting unwillingness to recommend mediation. The following indicates the order in which the factors contributed to predicting respondents' willingness to recommend mediation:

facilitate communication;
provide clarification and insights;
diffuse anger;
magnitude of the dispute;
duration of the dispute;
relationship with an ex-spouse;
evaluations of changes of gaining custody;
balance of power;
acceptance of divorce;
setting the stage.

Thus to the extent that we are able to predict outcomes, we find that the two indices that appear to be best able to predict both settlement and willingness to recommend the process are users' perceptions of the mediator's ability to facilitate communication and provide them with a better understanding of their own feelings as well as those of their children and ex-spouse. This suggests that mediators' actions play a key role in determining the success of the process and underscores the need for mediator training and experience.

Our results are consistent with an analysis of audio tapes of ten successful and ten unsuccessful divorce mediations generated in the DMRP (Donohue *et al.* 1985), which found that more successful mediators use more intense *structuring* and *reframing* interventions in response to attacks than unsuccessful mediators. Finally our results reflect the importance of behaviours that mediators themselves value most highly. Asked how they approach the process, most mediators in the CMP stress making suggestions, giving opinions, and other active roles (Vanderkooi and Pearson 1983).

Types of mediated and adjudicated agreements

Theory alone would lead us to predict that mediation would be more accommodative and conducive to compromise. Not surprisingly, this appears to be the case. In the CMP, most couples who reach mediation agreements for custody disputes opt for joint legal custody, an arrangement rarely selected by those who are exposed only to the adversarial process. Among mediation couples who select sole custody, non-custodians receive more visitation than is commonly found in non-mediated agreements (Pearson and Thoeness 1984*a*). Joint custody is also the most common arrangement reported by couples who reach agreements in mediation programme in Los Angeles and Minneapolis, but not in Connecticut (Lyon *et al.* 1985). So, though it is not uniformly the case, there is usually more give and take in custody mediation than custody adjudication.

Because financial issues are not routinely mediated in public-sector divorce mediation programmes, it is impossible to compare reliably the financial effects of mediation and adjudication for adults and children.

Nevertheless, there is considerable public support for the mediation of financial issues. Approximately 50 per cent of respondents with custody or visitation disputes also report conflicts over child support and/or the division of marital property. When interviewed, approximately 50 per cent of respondents in California, Minneapolis, and Connecticut who used court mediation services 4–5 years ago as well as half of our sample of individuals currently mediating or litigating custody/visitation disputes said that they would 'definitely or probably' favour the mediation of financial issues. A number of courts are currently experimenting with the mediation of child support and property division issues (e.g. the Family Court of Delaware, the Superior Court of Connecticut). More systematic evaluation is needed before conclusions are made about the advisability of financial mediation.

User satisfaction

At all locations, mediation is associated with a high degree of user satisfaction, but satisfaction appears to taper off with the passage of time. For example, three months following the conclusion of mediation, between 85 and 91 per cent of the respondents at each court site who reached a custody/visitation agreement in mediation would recommend it to others. Among those who failed to reach an agreement, between 62 and 79 per cent would nevertheless recommend it to others.

At the third interview, administered approximately one year after the conclusion of the mediation experience, user satisfaction also remains strong. As before, both those who produced agreements and those who did not were likely to say they were glad they tried the process (90 per cent and 82 per cent, respectively) and would recommend it to others (76 per cent and 64 per cent respectively).

Among those who had used mediation 4–5 years earlier, however, reactions were less uniformly complimentary. Within this sample only about 65 per cent of those producing an agreement and 40 per cent of those who did not produce an agreement say they were satisfied with their mediation experience.

There are several possible reasons why mediation is rated more favourably by recent users. With the passage of time, users may be less impressed by the fact that they dealt rationally with an ex-spouse. The passage of time also allows more opportunity for non-compliance behaviours to develop and temper glowing reactions to the mediation process. Lastly, it is possible that mediation services provided in the courts have simply improved over time. In 1978, the year many respondents in our retrospective survey participated in mediation, court mediation programmes were new.

While the satisfaction rate may decline somewhat with time, there is little variation over time in the aspects of mediation that are most appreciated by users. For example, at all court sites, and at all interview phases, respondents tend to cite three factors when they praise mediation. First, 70 to 80 per cent believe that mediation helped them to focus on the needs of the children and that this orientation was beneficial. In the words of one Connecticut mother, 'it made me feel more considerate towards the kids and their feelings'.

A second benefit attributed to mediation by 70 to 80 per cent of the respondents at each of the sites, is the opportunity it provides to air grievances. These respondents agree with the statement, 'mediation gave me a chance to express my own point of view'.

A third feature of mediation endorsed by 70 to 80 per cent of the respondents is its ability to keep the discussion on track. In other words, the mediation sessions did not lapse into arguments, discussion of the problems of the marriage, or other non-child-related issues.

By contrast, court systems appear to be consistently rated as an unsatisfactory means of processing divorces or settling disputes. Thus, at every interview, regardless of whether or not mediation was attempted, between 50 and 60 per cent of those who formally contested custody or visitation voiced dissatisfaction with the court experience. In addition, 40 to 50 per cent of those exposed to a custody study, an investigative and evaluative process conducted by mental health professionals designed to identify the preferred custodial parent, expressed dissatisfaction with this process. Indeed, even those who divorced without contesting custody or visitation were critical of the courts. Despite their more limited contact with the judicial system, 40 per cent in this group reported themselves to be dissatisfied.

For the majority of the respondents, dissatisfaction with the courts stemmed more from the process than the performance of any particular actor. Indeed, most respondents (70 per cent) were satisfied with their attorneys. Rather, they objected to private issues being treated in a public forum. The impersonality of the experience, its criminal overtones, and the degree of control exercised by legal actors were shocking to many.

Sources of user dissatisfaction

Despite generally high levels of satisfaction, a substantial proportion of users do have criticisms of the mediation process. Like the aspects of mediation that are appreciated by users, these sources of dissatisfaction also remain consistent over time. For example, about half the respondents at each site agree 'somewhat' or 'strongly' with the statements: 'The sessions were tension-filled and unpleasant' and 'I felt angry during much of the session'. About 45 per cent of respondents at each location report feeling defensive about the session. There are several possible reasons for these reactions. For example, custody and visitation disputes may be so emotionally taxing that any method of dispute resolution will necessarily be unpleasant and evoke defensive reactions. This might account for the similar rates of dissatisfaction with court experiences and mediation. Alternatively, clients may feel that their point of view is either not understood or not respected by the mediator.

For other individuals, the sense of defensiveness may result from apprehensions about dealing with an untrustworthy but persuasive ex-spouse. As one Connecticut woman put it: 'he's smart . . . he can do anything . . . I was afraid they [the mediators] would believe him'. A Los Angeles woman noted that her husband 'did a better job of selling himself'. And a husband in Minneapolis believed that all his wife had to do 'was cry and she'd get her way'.

Still other respondents may well have felt tense, angry, and displeased as a result of faulty preconceptions about the mediation process. At each site, 20–30 per cent of the respondents agreed with the statement that 'mediation was confusing', and in-depth interviews with a few respondents often revealed profound misconceptions about the goals of mediation. For example, a number of respondents were under the impression that the process was designed to save the marriage and as a result they began the session feeling annoyed at unwelcome pressure to reconcile. Others who were interested in reconciling were upset by the fact that the mediators never urged their partner to give the marriage another chance. Still other respondents laboured under the false impression that the mediators would make the final custody decision or that mediation was merely another variety of counselling.

Finally, between 25 and 33 per cent of the respondents in each location felt that the mediation process was rushed and should be given more time. For some, the short duration of mediation created anger and feelings of assembly line treatment. In the words of one respondent: 'they should not take people and grind them through'. According to another: 'I was just another case. Case 62398-B, to be disposed of.'

Reactions of Men and Women

To assess whether men and women who participate in court-based divorce mediation evaluate their experiences differently, we analysed the responses of male and female interviewees separately and compared the results. The analysis revealed many significant differences. On the positive side, women were more likely to report that mediation helped them to: understand their ex-spouse's point of view; focus on the children; keep the discussion on track; bring issues and problems out into the open; identify lots of problems; understand their own feelings. At the same time, compared with their male counterparts, women were more likely to report that in mediation their ex-spouse pressured them into an agreement; they never really felt comfortable expressing their feelings; mediation was tense and unpleasant; they felt angry during much of the session(s); the mediator was very directive and essentially gave them the terms of the agreement. The items that male respondents were more apt to note about the mediation experience were: waiting too long to get into mediation; spending too much time in mediation on the past; feeling comfortable and relaxed and feeling mediation was rushed. Thus, although women appreciate many positive aspects of mediation, they are clearly more apt to report unfavourable reactions including feeling pressured by an ex-spouse.

To distinguish women who felt pressured by an ex-spouse in mediation from their unpressured counterparts, we conducted a discriminant analysis using a variety of attitudinal and background variables as possible predictors. There were no differences that could be attributed to several measures of the balance of power during the marriage including: level of violence, who won arguments during the marriage, or the ability to present one's side of an argument. Indeed, the best predictor of a sensation of pressure was the report of communication problems during the marriage. This was measured by respondents' reports that 'thoughts became jumbled and confused during discussions with an ex-spouse'.

Many women reported having such problems. This did not vary with income levels during the marriage. Indeed, the only women who did not report having this problem were women with graduate school educations and/or women over the age of 45.

Despite the prevalence of communication problems and their sensation of being pressured during the mediation sessions, women are not statistically different from men in their post-mediation ratings of the experience. They report comparable levels of satisfaction with the division of property, the child support arrangement, their willingness to recommend mediation, and their belief that mediation should be mandatory intervention. Indeed, compared with men, they are most apt to express the view that mediation should be offered to resolve financial disputes.

This suggests that while the intervention is perceived by many women to involve elements of coercion and pressure by an ex-spouse, many aspects of their overall assessments are favourable, and not unlike those reported by males.

Compliance and Re-litigation

There is mixed evidence regarding the compliance patterns associated with mediated and adjudicated agreements. A long-term follow-up interview in the CMP revealed better compliance among those who mediated. While 33 per cent of the adversarial group reported that serious disagreements had arisen over the settlement, this was noted by only 6 per cent of successful mediation clients (Pearson and Thoeness 1982). These patterns persist after controlling for pre-existing factors, most notably the initial co-operation level between spouses.

In a similar vein, an analysis of compliance with child support and visitation orders in the 1981 sample of the DMRP reveals patterns that favour the mediation group. Based upon reports from those who are supposed to receive support, it appears that about a third of those who mediated or agreed custody reported irregular or absent child support payments, while this was the case in over half of those who contested custody. A comparison of accounts by those who are supposed to be exercising visitation rights reveals that none of those who resolved their custody dispute in mediation report visitation to be infrequent while this is reported to be the case by 30 per cent of non-custodians in every other dispute category.

An analysis of compliance patterns reported by DMRP samples who mediated and adjudicated in 1978, however, reveals few differences. Approximately 60 per cent of all mediating and adjudicating respondents report satisfaction with custody arrangements today. The highest proportion of respondents reporting very regular visitation and child support payment patterns are those who adjudicated custody 4–5 years ago and were never even exposed to mediation. And comparable proportions of respondents in each mediation and adjudication category report frequent disagreements over visitation (8–13 per cent).

There is also some debate about the capacity of mediation to reduce re-litigation. For example, in the CMP, there is evidence of lower recidivism among mediation clients. At a two-year follow-up, only 13 per cent of successful mediation clients had filed court modifications as opposed to 35 per cent of their adversarial counterparts (Pearson and Thoeness 1984*b*).

We also observe statistically lower levels of re-litigation by those who produce final arrangements in mediation versus all others in the 1981 sample of the DMRP. Thus, between the first and final interview, 21 per cent of those who resolved the custody dispute in mediation had been back to court to file contempt citations, to take out temporary restraining orders, or to change custody, visitation or child support. Among those who reached no agreement in mediation, 31 per cent had returned to court. Among the adversarial group, 36 per cent had returned, and 13 per cent had been back at least twice. Only 6 per cent of those settling in mediation had returned to court that often.

Our survey of individuals who disputed custody/visitation in 1978, however, reveals that families who mediate and those who use the adversarial process are equally apt to return to court to modify. Based on self-reports, a quarter of those who reached agreements, a quarter of those who did not reach agreements in mediation, and about a quarter of the adversarial group had returned to court on custody/visitation matters within the last 4–5 years.

Given the contradictory findings in our two research projects, it may be safest to conclude that while mediation may not always be more effective than court adjudication in preventing recidivism, it certainly does not produce a rash of re-litigation activity. Mediated agreements are no more or less stable than those originating in lawyer negotiation or court orders.

User evaluation of spousal co-operation patterns

Does custody and visitation mediation enhance couple communication and co-operation? Three months following their mediation and/or litigation experiences, we asked DMRP respondents whether their exposure to the court system and mediation had made a difference in the way they interacted with their former spouses. The response was as follows: 15 per cent credited the court system with improving their relationship with an ex-spouse; about 40 per cent indicated that court had a detrimental effect on the relationship; and the remainder said it had no impact on their relationship.

Asked the same question 12–15 months after the initial interview, DMRP respondents were slightly more positive about their court experience. About a fourth now said the court system had improved their relationship with their ex-spouse while only 25 per cent, not 40 per cent, claimed it had hurt the relationship.

Unfortunately, respondents were only asked to assess the impact of mediation three months following the initial contact. As a result, it is impossible to tell whether mediation might also have been viewed more positively over time. The patterns elicited at the three-month interview however, suggest that respondents view mediation as a less damaging intervention than court. Thus, three months after mediation, regardless of the outcome, less than 15 per cent feel that mediation hurt the relationship. However, only those who settled in mediation are likely to credit the process with improving spousal co-operation. Thirty per cent of those who settled in mediation say the process improved the relationship, while only 7 per cent of those who 'unsuccessfully' mediated perceive that the process benefited the relationship.

Additional evidence that mediation is a less damaging intervention than court emerges from responses to questions regarding the degree to which individuals are able to co-operate with their ex-spouses. Between the three-month and twelve-month follow-up interviews there was a small increase in the number of mediation group respondents reporting that some co-operation was possible. This pattern holds both for those who produced agreements in mediation, and those who did not. In the adversarial group, however, there was some decline in the proportion expressing co-operation between the second and third interview.

The final measure of spousal co-operation that we consider is the incidence of problems with visitation following the mediation or litigation of custody issues. The evidence suggests no particular benefits to those who mediate. Before any adversarial or non-adversarial intervention, 45 to 50 per cent of all respondents who were contesting custody/visitation reported that three or more visitation issues were sometimes or often a problem. These issues included concerns about the children's safety/well-being; the amount of time spent with an ex-spouse's family; lack of discipline/over-indulgence; late return following visitation; a lack of activities during the visit; or one parent criticizing the other in the presence of the children. Among respondents in the non-contesting category, only about half that figure (25 per cent) reported three or more problems. By the final interview, the number of respondents reporting three or more problems had declined to 30–40 per cent of all mediation and adversarial group respondents and remained at about 25 per cent in the non-contested group.

Overall, it appears that while mediation fails to transform hostile couples into co-operative ones and eliminate future conflict, it is perceived to be a less damaging intervention than court.

Effects on children

To assess parental perceptions of child adjustment, we focused on a single child per family within the age range of six to eleven years. Two child adjustment instruments were utilized. One consisted of nineteen statements, original items as well as several developed by other researchers (Olsen *et al.* 1979), about the child's divorce, custody and visitation experiences. Parents responded to each statement using a five-point scale. The nineteen statements were subsequently factor analysed. The four indices that emerged appear to measure: the custodial parent's relationship with the child, the child's acceptance of the divorce, the child's satisfaction with the custody and visitation arrangement, and the parent's perception of the child's maturity following the divorce.

Our second instrument of child adjustment was a 119-item checklist of child behaviours developed by Achenbach and Edelbrock (1980) which can be used to create a variety of subscales measuring specific behaviours as well as to yield an overall measure of the child's well-being. Given the size of our sample and the number of dispute resolution categories we wished to compare, we restricted our analysis to those subscales and items which were common to all age groups and both sexes. This resulted in modified subscales for depression, aggression, delinquency, social withdrawal, and somatic complaints.

We employed multiple regression to identify the factors that might best help to explain the variance in the global Achenbach score; the subscale scores of aggression, depression, social withdrawal, delinquency, and somatic complaints; and the indices created.through factor analysis that appear to measure quality of the custodian–child relationships, acceptance of the divorce, satisfaction with the custody arrangement, and maturity as a result of the divorce. Our list of possible predictors of child adjustment included a variety of items that have been mentioned in the literature. These independent variables fall into five major categories. These are: (1) the general background of the family; (2) dispute/divorce specific variables; (3) characteristics of the child; (4) variables related to custody and visitation; and (5) characteristics of the parental relationship.

Using the backward model of regression, variables are entered simultaneously and removed step-by-step until the optimum combination remains to explain the variance in the dependent variable. This technique allows us to explain a modest amount of variance (8–20 per cent) in each of the child adjustment measures.

Looking across all ten regressions, we find five variables that appear in more than half of these regressions. These variables are in descending order of frequency: the parent's degree of interest in reconciling at the initial interview; the level of physical violence in the home during the marriage; custodian's financial stress as reported at first interview; the parent's level of co-operation at the first interview; the parent's level of co-operation at the final interview. The pattern is for better adjustment in those families where parents are co-operative. Thus, despite the mixed messages that may have been sent, we find better adjustment in homes where reconciliation was considered at the time of the initial interview. Adjustment is also greater in families with no history of violence and where custodians did not experience high levels of financial stress at the initial interview.

Another nine variables appeared in half the regressions: the custodian's attachment to the ex-spouse at the initial interview; the non-custodian berating the custodian to the children during the visitation; the age of the parents; the age of the child; the child's sex; the number of changes in the child's life (changes in schools, residences, and so on); the regularity of visitation at the final interview; non-contested group status; and adversarial group status. Among these variables, we find child adjustment to the ex-spouse; regular visitation at the final interview; no berating of the custodial parent to children during visitation; younger parents and children; fewer changes reported in the child's life; no dispute over custody; and non-adversarial group membership. In addition, we find better adjustment for girls than boys.

These analyses suggest that variables dealing with family dynamics, child characterics, and the parent–child relationship and, to a far lesser extent, those related to the dispute resolution category are relevant in understanding children's adjustment.

Savings in time and money

Mediation procedures tend to translate into time savings for disputing parties although savings vary with programme format and outcome. In the Denver Custody Mediation Project, mediation translated into time savings only if it was successful since those who were unsuccessful in mediation also had to pursue a custody investigation.

The greatest savings in attorney fees were realized by those who were diverted to mediation early in the dispute and succeeded in resolving the dispute. For example, individuals who successfully mediated before receiving a final divorce decree paid an average of $1,650 in legal fees— about $680 less than the average $2,330 paid by pre-decree members of the control group.

Reports from the 1978 and 1981 samples of the DMRP also suggest that mediation may produce modest financial savings for users. For cases involving a custody dispute in 1978, whether prior to and following the promulgation of a divorce decree, only about 20 per cent of the respondents who successfully mediated in a final agreement reported attorney fees in excess of $3,000. For the adversarial group, the percentage was approximately 45 per cent. About 30 per cent of those who did not produce a final agreement in mediation incurred attorney fees over $3,000. Among those contesting custody, both prior to and following the divorce decree in 1981, about 35 per cent of those who were unsuccessful in mediation and 35 per cent of the adversarial group had legal fees in excess of $3,000. By contrast, only 20 per cent of those who successfully mediated final custody/visitation arrangements paid this much.

Public cost savings are more difficult to calculate for mediation programmes. Because they lack large volume and perhaps attract cases that would not otherwise be adjudicated, some researchers conclude that mediation programmes are more expensive than per case costs in courts. For example, an evaluation of a court-connected family counselling service that offers custody mediation to divorcing couples in Clackamas County, Oregon, concludes that the service cannot be justified on economic grounds. The average cost of providing services to divorcing couples at the Family Counselling Service comes to $307 to $338 per case; trial costs for comparable cases range from $96 to $247. Moreover, since the counselling service only handles child-related disputes, a sizeable proportion of couples must use the court to resolve money and property disputes and are consequently involved in both a court trial and mediation (Cohen 1981).

The director of the Domestic Relations Division of Hennepin County (Minneapolis), on the other hand, finds evidence of savings while noting that any conclusions require reliance on numerous estimates. In 1982, estimated per case costs for those needing only mediation treatment was $238. Per case costs for those requiring a custody evaluation was $1,530. Cases requiring both treatments cost the county $1,645, although only 16 per cent of 1982 cases fell into this category. According to the Director, the use of mediation in 1982 rather than the automatic assignment of contested cases for an evaluation saved the county approximately $139,000 (Cauble *et al.* 1985).

Lastly, mandatory mediation programmes appear to be decidedly cost effective. For example, in 1978, the Los Angeles Conciliation Court, the largest jurisdiction offering public-sector mediation services, handled 747 cases with an estimated net saving to the County of Los Angeles of $175,004. The procedure was found to be so satisfactory and cost effective that it was made mandatory in 1981 with the enactment of S.B. 961. It is paid for by an earmarked increase of $15 for the divorce filing fee, $5 for the marriage licence fee, and an assessment of a $15 fee for any motion to modify or enforce a custody and visitation order (McIsaac 1981).

Conclusions

Our research indicates that mediation provides a valuable complement to the existing domestic relations court process. For example, in our research, one criticism voiced by parents is that the court system is overly formal and complex. Divorcing parties perceive it to be a cold, indifferent, and confusing setting in which to deal with a former spouse and their children. More to the point, the court setting is frequently perceived to undermine whatever degree of co-operation may exist between the spouses.

Mediation, on the other hand, is widely recognized by these parents to be a more personal and private approach and it is appreciated for these qualities. Compared with assessments of court processes, mediation receives high ratings of user satisfaction and these differential evaluations are largely maintained over a period of four to five years.

To some extent, mediation also appears to foster a sense of commitment to abide by the agreement produced in mediation, to encourage continued co-operation, to reduce re-litigation in the short run, and to produce a sense of equity and fairness even among those who fail to 'win' custody. Unlike court processes, mediation allows for emotional ventilation and outcomes that embody compromise. It is also regarded as less damaging to relationships with ex-spouses than court intervention. These properties of the process are reflected in' the evaluations offered by users immediately following mediation and one year later.

However, the expectations for mediation should not be overstated. The process seems to be associated with few or no consistent improvements in long-term compliance, spousal co-operation, and re-litigation. An analysis of child adjustment to divorce finds that mediation appears to have few measurable effects and private- and public-sector cost savings appear to be detectable only in compulsory programmes in large jurisdictions, where litigants are diverted to the process in the early stages of dispute.

In many respects, these findings are consistent with previous research comparing mediation and adjudication in a variety of substantive settings (Merry and Rocheleau 1985; McEwen and Maiman 1982; Block and Kreger 1982; Pearson 1982). While all studies seem to find evidence of strong user satisfaction with the mediation process, the data on more basic behaviour changes such as compliance, re-litigation, and relationship between ex-disputants are more ambiguous with some studies finding evidence of improvements and others finding no differences. There are several reasons why mediation may have only a modest ability to enhance child adjustment to divorce, alter basic relationship patterns, or promote co-operation between disputants.

First, mediation in court settings is a brief intervention. For example, in Minnesota where the process took the greatest amount of time, the average number of mediation sessions reported by respondents in our sample was 3.3 and the average number of hours was 4.3. More commonly, in California and Connecticut, cases were processed in an average of 1.6 sessions and 2–3 hours. There are clearly limits to the types of basic or long-lasting changes that would be expected to ensue from any limited, short-term intervention.

Second, divorce mediation differs dramatically from mediation between non-strangers in other civil settings. It involves parties with lengthy, intimate, and problem-ridden histories and deeply established behavioural patterns. Mediation cannot and does not address the underlying emotional problems of families. While the intervention might help families as they struggle to adjust to a divorce, and to develop custody and visitation plans, the process cannot generate a final resolution to the multitude of problems faced by some of these families.

In addition, couples who mediate typically face the prospect of years of frequent, complex, and emotion-laden interactions surrounding issues such as child support, visitation, and child care. Such interactions are likely to afford many opportunities for conflict and non-compliance. For example, if one ex-spouse is perceived to be hostile or non-compliant, it may be possible for the other to violate the terms of the agreement without a sense of failing to live up to an agreement entered into voluntarily. By comparison, most mediations between non-strangers with continuing relationships, such as landlords and tenants, employers and employees, and neighbours, are simpler; the emotional and financial stakes are usually lower and the opportunities for continued contact and interaction are typically more limited.

With respect to the absence of findings dealing with child adjustment to divorce, it is relevant to note that there may be too much heterogeneity in conflict and functioning in both intact and divorcing families to allow any prediction of adjustment on the basis of labels regarding parents' adjudication, mediation, or non-contesting status. Indeed, data published from the New York Longitudinal Study revealed that parental divorce or separation was not related to the child's level of adjustment as a young adult when the effects due to conflict were taken into account (Chess *et al.* 1983). Several investigators have found that children from relatively conflict-free single-parent homes are better adjusted in general than are children from conflict-ridden two-parent families (Emery *et al.* 1983; Hetherington *et al.* 1979).

Finally, there may also be too much variation in the adversarial experience to make comparisons between children of adversarial versus mediating couples meaningful. For example, research shows that while some divorce attorneys are 'litigators' who push their clients to a full court battle, many are conciliatory and seek to minimize hostility (Kressel *et al.* 1979; Mnookin 1975).

Nevertheless, over the span of twelve to fifteen months we observe some notable differences between those who mediate and those who adjudicate and find that in some attitude and behavioural categories these differences hold up over a 4–5 year period of time. Moreover, as in our previous research comparing these who mediate and those who adjudicate child custody (Pearson and Thoeness 1984*b*), the differences continue to hold after statistically controlling for the initial level of co-operation reported by the respondents. Thus, the differences that do exist between successful mediation clients and other respondents are not merely the result of the fact that co-operative individuals are likely both to succeed in mediation and later to co-operate and comply. Rather, these patterns indicate that even brief mediation interventions with a troubled population have modest but positive effects that hold up over time.

Remaining Research Questions

Our research raises several policy issues that warrant additional research and attention. One such issue deals with the pros and cons of mediating the financial aspects of divorce. As we have noted, most court programmes restrict mediation to the child-related issues of custody and visitation although the problem of non-payment of child support is at epidemic proportions. Our research confirms that at least 50 per cent of individuals with custody/visitation disputes also have disagreements about financial issues and that the same proportion of divorcing litigants favour the mediation of these matters. While some mediators contend that the mediation of financial issues will result in more generous financial settlements and that this will enhance the financial status of women and children following divorce, others maintain that mediation is often harmful to women, since husbands frequently possess greater financial acumen. Empirical research is clearly needed to assess and compare the quality of mediated and adjudicated financial settlements and resolve the largely hortatory debate surrounding this issue.

A second policy consideration deals with the setting, duration, and format of mediation sessions. Without a doubt, the greatest volume of divorce mediation activity occurs in public, court-based programmes, some of which are compulsory, that are typically available to litigants at no charge and supported by ear-marked filing and/or marriage licence fees. Qualifications for court mediators vary from jurisdiction to jurisdiction with some assigning mediation duties to probation officers, custody evaluators, special masters, and referees. The number of hours expended on each case also varies by jurisdiction with cases usually terminated with or without a resolution well before the upper limit of permissible hours is reached and well in advance of the time typically devoted to a case in the private sector.

Naturally, these patterns raise legitimate questions about the compatibility of programme efficiency and programme outcome. For example, many feel that mandatory mediation contradicts the ideology of the movement and requires disputants to submit to resolution procedures that lack adequate procedural and constitutional protections. Still others maintain that programmes that achieve large case volumes must devote less time to each case and that this undermines the qualitative programme objectives of favourable and durable outcomes, user satisfaction, and perceptions of equity. Needless to say, it will take additional experimentation and evaluation to identify the ideal format for implementing mediation programmes so that they are effective in attracting litigants and achieving a broad array of qualitative goals.

A third issue is public and professional education about the mediation process. Such education may promote client usage of mediation and eliminate erroneous client expectations of lengthy counselling or evaluations and enhance satisfaction. Goal clarification may also enhance client co-operation and eliminate the resistance shown by those that view it as complementary to legal interventions and not a source of competition. A future area of needed experimentation and evaluation will attempt to discern the most effective methods of public and professional education.

Finally, additional research is needed to document the differential impact of various types of mediators. Mediation is currently a non-regulated profession. With the exception of a two-year post-graduate programme just begun at Catholic University of America, mediation courses typically run for about a week. Although some mediation training programmes require that trainees hold an advanced degree in law and/or a behavioural science and possess a certain amount of working experience with families, other training programmes are open to people of all ages and all backgrounds. Indeed, divorce mediators may be lawyers, mental health professionals, clergy, and laypersons.

In the public sector, there are few statutory and administrative provisions dealing with the qualifications of divorce mediators who work in courts. While these provisions usually call for a master's degree in family counselling, social work, or a related field and a substantial amount of working experience, this is not always the case. Some courts utilize clergy, marriage counsellors, mental health professionals, or trained volunteers to perform mediation services. Others hire employees exclusively to do mediation. Still others retain employees who perform other agency duties such as probation supervision, custody investigation, and domestic relations counselling. In the private sector there are no regulations governing the training or education of mediators.

There is only sparse research on the qualities and training of effective mediators working in any substantive setting. In the light of this fact there has been a reluctance to impose requirements or even to endorse guidelines in mediation training and certification. It is to be hoped that future research will identify the type of professional orientation, personality characteristics, and training associated with effective mediation interventions dealing with divorce disputes.

Acknowledgements

The authors would like to thank the staff and directors of the mediation programmes included in this research. Recognition is also due to the following site researchers: Margaret Little, Eleanor Lyon, Maria Ring, Martha Cleveland, and A. Elizabeth Cauble. The CMP was funded by the Piton Foundation, Denver, Colorado. The DMRP was funded by the Children's Bureau of the Administration for Children, Youth, and Families, US Department of Health and Human Services (Grant No. 90-CW-634). The grant was awarded to the Association of Family Conciliation Courts. Earlier versions of this manuscript have been published or are scheduled for publication in the following journals and books: 'Mediation in Custody Disputes', *Behavioural Sciences and the Law*, 4, No. 2, pp. 203–16 (1986); 'Divorce Mediation: An Overview of Research Results', in *Columbia Journal of Law and Social Problems* (forthcoming); and *Divorce Mediation: Theory and Practice*, edited by Jay Folberg and Ann Milne, The Guilford Press (forthcoming).

PART II

Mediation on Court Premises

6. The Halls of Justice and Justice in the Halls

GWYNN DAVIS

This chapter is concerned with *court procedure* and its inclusion in this collection reflects the fact that the terms 'conciliation' and 'mediation' are applied to preliminary appointments on court premises, as well as to a whole range of extra-legal services. These appointments were first introduced in Bristol County Court in 1977 (Parmiter 1981). Initially limited to decree proceedings, the system was extended in 1979 to cover contested custody and access applications. Most county court registrars have since followed suit and, from January 1983, a similar scheme was introduced in the Principal Divorce Registry. The latter now involves some 1,000 appointments per annum (Parkinson 1986*b*: 98).

There has of late been growing enthusiasm for this procedural experiment, partly in the belief that the values underpinning 'conciliation' may be applied to the legal process itself, but also in the hope that these preliminary appointments will promote legal settlement and thus save money. Most recently, the recommendation that there be an 'initial hearing' in most categories of divorce cases formed the cornerstone of the Booth Committee's report on matrimonial procedure.[1]

It will be my contention in this chapter that the arguments as to which form of 'conciliation' has most to offer (or, more pragmatically, which is most deserving of government support) reflect a lack of clarity concerning both the objectives of these various forms of intervention and the actual processes involved. The empirical base for the thesis which I shall try to develop is provided by the 'Conciliation in Divorce' research project carried out in the Department of Social Administration, University of Bristol, from October 1981 to June 1984.[2] This included a detailed study of court records (Davis and Bader 1983*b*); observation of preliminary appointments in Bristol County Court (Davis and Bader 1983*a*); and an extensive programme of interviews carried out among parties to contested divorce proceedings (Davis and Bader 1985).

An Autobiographical Note

My own interest in 'conciliation' as an integral part of legal procedure arose from observation of judicial appointments with divorcing parents. These 'Children's Appointments' are the means by which courts carry out their duty under s. 41 of the Matrimonial Causes Act 1973 to establish whether the proposed arrangements for the children are 'satisfactory, or the best that can be devised in the circumstances' (Davis *et al.* 1983). As far as any prospect of 'conciliation' was concerned, the omens were distinctly unpromising. First, this procedure is intended as a welfare check, not a means of resolving custody or access issues. Second, only the custodial parent need attend. Third, the judges taking these appointments are under great pressure of time, with as many as thirty cases being listed for one morning. (The average duration of the appointments which we observed was four-and-a-half minutes.)

Nevertheless, we came across several cases in which, although no formal application had been made to the court, the couple were still locked in dispute. In some of these, both parents attended the appointment and, on a few occasions, the judge attempted to mediate between them. These judges demonstrated an impressive capacity to come to grips with parents' disagreements and anxieties. Having listened, they might give advice, invite parents to return to them if they continued to experience difficulty, or attempt to resolve the dispute there and then.

Most parents attending the s. 41 appointments are unrepresented and it seemed to us that immediate access to a sympathetic judge, skilled in developing rapport, was of considerable benefit to some of them. Whether we were correct to characterize the judge's intervention as a form of 'mediation' is, of course, a separate question: the few judges who took on this role tended to handle parents quite firmly and there was no doubt that they were utilizing the authority vested in their judicial role.

Other contributions to my interest in procedural reform came from my two attempts to monitor the work of the independent Bristol Courts Family Conciliation Service (Davis 1980, 1982*a*, and 1982*b*). Most of the Bristol solicitors whom I interviewed about this new scheme appeared reasonably well disposed towards it, but also tended to regard it as a fairly marginal activity which would be of value only to a minority of the divorcing population. Even allowing for solicitors' tendency to regard the formal mechanism of the court as at the heart of divorcing couples' experience, it seemed very strange that all reforming energies were being directed at these independent schemes, while the legal process itself was regarded as immutable. Even stranger was the notion that these extra-legal services were to be judged in terms of their impact on court process and legal costs, as was reflected, for example, in the approach of the Inter-departmental Committee on Conciliation.[3] It was possible to conceive of these voluntary schemes as providing a convenient smokescreen, diverting attention from the shortcomings of legal process (Davis and Westcott 1984).

Subsequently, the interviews which we conducted with divorcing couples in the course of the 'Special Procedure' research revealed widespread dissatisfaction with solicitors' handling of these cases.[4] The 'Special Procedure' survey comprised legally uncontested cases, but we discovered that many couples had, in fact, been in dispute over custody or access. They were often disappointed at their solicitor's failure to engage in a dialogue with 'the other side', suggesting the need for a more constructive approach to negotiation on the part of at least some partisans. It seemed reasonable to suppose that the introduction of a forum for negotiation on court premises might help to achieve this.

Just as all was becoming clear, a more sceptical voice was raised. It was suggested, in particular, that court appointments could never have a genuinely mediatory character; that a mediator should not be someone who relied for his influence on a position of formal authority; that he should remain at the edge of events, an unobtrusive rather than a dominating figure and one, moreover, who could communicate easily with the parties, employing language and ideas which they could understand. Mediation on court premises, it was argued, would not succeed in focusing attention on the parties' view of the problem and on what they wanted to get out of the meeting (Roberts 1983).

In support of this argument, it is apparent that the various professional actors who are likely to be present at a court appointment will all be accustomed to exercising a good deal more authority than is consistent with the above definition of the mediator's role. Solicitors are used to negotiating in their own style, often without consulting their clients directly. Welfare officers are used to making a formal recommendation to the court. Registrars are used to adjudicating. Even if they wished to do so, these powerful figures could hardly become 'unobtrusive', whilst the parties themselves might find it equally difficult to revise *their* expec-tations of courts and the legal process.

These were powerful arguments, although I did not regard them as decisive. For example, they still did not meet the point that independent services cater only for a small minority of the divorcing population. Might it not be easier to change people's perceptions of court personnel than to 'sell' the virtues of informal mediation? What of those who could not contemplate negotiating without the support of legal advisers? Also, was there not a risk that by virtue of our applying the same language ('conciliation') to both extra-legal services and an aspect of court procedure, we were inviting a false and almost totally misleading comparison, and one which might lead to our jettisoning these appointments because they failed to live up to a quite impossible standard? Any procedural experiment (whatever title it happens to be given) ought to be compared with other mechanisms for *settling legal issues*, such as negotiation between solicitors, negotiation following the preparation of a welfare report, 'door of the court' negotiation on the morning of the trial, and negotiation conducted on adjournment. Preliminary appointments might prove to be a useful adjunct, if not an alternative, to these other mechanisms. Out-of-court services, on the other hand, might be regarded as an entirely separate matter, a contribution to divorcing couples' attempts to resolve these matters between themselves.

This was the point which my thinking had reached when my colleague Kay Bader and I embarked on our survey of the parties' response to 'conciliation appointments' conducted at Bristol and Newport County Courts.

The 'Conciliation in Divorce' Consumer Survey

Any attempt to measure the outcome of these appointments is far from straightforward, even if one restricts the definition of 'success' to the achievement of legal settlement of contested applications. This is because many cases involve a number of related issues; secondly, there may be several preliminary appointments in the one case; and thirdly, in many cases in which it would appear from the record that settlement was reached at the appointment, the actual negotiation took place beforehand, with one or other solicitor turning up on the day merely to inform the registrar of the outcome.

Bearing these reservations in mind, the settlement-rate achieved at Bristol County Court, *either prior to or in the course of a first or subsequent conciliation appointment*, was in the region of 70 per cent for access disputes (n = 47 cases); 45 per cent for custody issues (n = 36 cases); and 56 per cent for disputes relating to the award of divorce decrees (n = 9 cases). Of course, even where *no* agreement was reached, this did not mean that the case would necessarily proceed to trial: in one way or another, most cases are 'settled' in the end.

But the main drawback of a measurement of outcome expressed in terms of 'settlement' is that this does not enable us to answer the most important questions—such as whether the parties have successfully resolved their differences, whether they have arrived at a workable compromise, or whether they have constructed a basis for future negotiation. In terms of these more subjective assessments, there is reason to be rather more sceptical about the worth of the procedure. For example, even in cases in which an 'agreement' was reached at or prior to the appointment (n = 107 individuals), 48 of those interviewed (45 per cent) told us that the hearing had served no purpose in their case. We also asked our Bristol group how they had felt when they left the court following their (final) preliminary appointment: 35 per cent had been 'relieved' or 'pleased', but 55 per cent had been 'upset', 'angry', or 'disappointed'.

These responses reflect what is perhaps the dominant theme to emerge from our interviews, namely that, judged from the standpoint of the courts, the preliminary appointments make a significant contribution to the efficient processing of disputes; but judged from the standpoint of the parties, the procedure may appear coercive, or somewhat removed from their real concerns. In order to understand why this should be, we need to look more closely at the conduct of these appointments. (A more detailed account is available in Davis and Bader 1985.)

Conduct of the Appointments

In the Bristol court, much of the 'work' involved in these appointments takes place in the court waiting area. Two private interviewing rooms are generally available, but much of the 'nitty-gritty' of negotiation takes place out in the open, including, sometimes, that involving the welfare officers. Appointments are listed for every half hour, but there is no question of the court sticking to this timetable. The registrar and welfare officer cannot tell beforehand which cases will be adjourned immediately and which will take all morning. Many of our informants were highly critical of the overcrowding and lack of privacy which they experienced.

I was sitting there for a good half hour on my own. [Husband] there with his solicitors . . . me sitting there all on my own with nobody. It was awful. He [solicitor] turned up eventually. He was actually in the building somewhere with another case. But I was there for a good half hour on my own, thinking, which way to look, what to do with my hands, you know, that sort of feeling. I felt quite lost and alone watching all of these other transactions going on and I thought, 'How can human beings come to this?'.

The strength of people's reaction to this period in the waiting area no doubt reflects the way they felt about the whole business of getting a divorce. This may have been the only time they had to go to court and whilst some were able to cope with it reasonably well, it was common to find that the time spent in this very public arena crystallized all their negative feelings.

Each appointment may involve several 'stages'; for example (*a*) waiting period, including discussion between the parties and solicitors and conversations between solicitors; (*b*) welfare officer interviewing the parties; (*c*) registrar's chambers. The process can be compressed, so that effectively only one (or perhaps two) of these stages is gone through.

Given the anxiety which many people experienced when having to confront their spouse in the waiting area, how were they to negotiate together? The answer, quite simply, is that in most cases they did not do so. In 56 per cent of the preliminary appointments in Bristol (excluding five in which only one party was present) we were told that the parents had not discussed the issue together at any stage. Some had been anxious to avoid this, with the result that solicitors were driven to act as intermediaries. But it was more common for us to be told that solicitors had not wanted the parties to negotiate directly with one another.

His solicitor was one side and my solicitor was the other and we were about twelve feet apart. And they just kept swapping over. He'd go back and say, 'What about 7 o'clock?' and I'd say, no, and he'd go back and say, 'What about half past seven?' It got a bit pathetic. It got ridiculous. I almost stood up and said, 'Look, can we stop this game?' because it just seemed so childish to me. I could talk to him, he was only twelve feet away from me. He [solicitor] told me I couldn't. I said to him, 'Surely we could sit by a table'—oh no, we must do it like this—and they [solicitors] kept going off in a corner, having a little discussion and coming back and I just found it very stupid. It cost me £160, which absolutely flabbergasted me. I couldn't see any necessity for it at all. I went up to [husband's] solicitor afterwards and gave him a piece of my mind. That happened all the way through really. I don't think anyone encouraged you to communicate—you were told not to communicate. Everything had to go through your solicitors.

Some of the parents who remarked on their solicitors' practice of keeping them apart acknowledged that it was their own inability to resolve matters amicably in the first place that had got them in this position. Nevertheless, they were taken aback at the almost complete loss of authority and loss of control which they experienced once having embarked upon their litigation. It is one of the key messages of this research that this form of court-based 'mediation' does not succeed in rectifying this.

But it is also very important to acknowledge that not everyone wants or feels able to resolve these disputes through negotiation. That is why we have courts. For those who have tried and failed to reach an agreement, there may be a kind of tyranny in the expectation that, even when they have got as far as a court-room, they should once more attempt to exercise a responsibility which they have come to regard as beyond them. They may well prefer, by that stage, to be relieved of all the burden of decision-making. This feeling may be exacerbated, in the course of negotiations on court premises, by the lack of time and a general expectation that some kind of agreement will be reached despite all the recent history. This was one woman's account:

If you have to rely on solicitors and the welfare they put pressure on you to come to an opinion and that's difficult. I don't agree with it [mediation]. It's an effort to put your opinion across. Ideally it should have gone to the solicitors and been left at that. I don't see that a lot of good comes out of the mediation—you are left with tremendous guilt if you haven't done enough yourself. It is so informal as to provide no guide-lines at all and it is rather hard to expect two people who do not talk, or cannot talk because their relationship has broken down so completely, to start talking again. You accept that there has to be a mediation appointment because that's the way it's done here, but my immediate thoughts [at having to go back a third time] were 'Oh gosh, not again'. Nothing is achieved by them by my mind. You see a welfare officer who, in my opinion, has read a book and has read your notes and that's the end of it. You're under pressure of time and a tremendous pressure to reach a decision—which you do, and it's only *after* that you wonder if it was the right decision. And because you're given the impression that it's *your* decision you have to live with your guilt. That's another aspect of it. You already have enough guilt without having more to add to it. I suppose, really, you need a scapegoat. If you have solicitors, you can always turn round and blame them. . . . To have come face to face with your ex-husband and know that people expect you to come to an opinion together on it is asking too much when the very reason that you're there is because you have broken down. It's a contradiction.

The woman quoted above had experienced three preliminary appointments, it being a feature of this procedure in the Bristol and Newport courts that more than one appointment may be held, on the same issue, in the one case. In fact, of those who told us that they had attended a preliminary appointment in Bristol, 38 per cent had done so more than once while 11 per cent had experienced at least three appointments concerned with the one issue. It was even more common in Newport for there to be several appointments in the one case. These repeated adjournments came in for severe criticism:

As we went in [registrar] just said, 'Is there any progress between Mr W and Mrs

W sorting this out—custody, before we go to court?' Then he said, 'We'll adjourn it for today'. We were only in there 5 minutes—'adjourn it for today and come back in, say, a month'. Went back in a month's time . . . he said exactly the same thing . . . it was just getting me down. We weren't getting anywhere! I said to my solicitor, 'Is it going to be over with today, or anything sorted out?' 'No', he said, 'there'll be nothing finalized today, it's only [registrar's chambers] again', he said, 'it's got to go to the proper court to be decided by the judge, you know'. So I said, 'Why are we going?' He said, 'I don't know. It doesn't make sense to me why we're going again.' You know, even my solicitor was baffled why we went to [registrar's chambers] three times. He said, 'We've got to go, we've been summoned to go' and that's it, we've got to appear there. But then on the third time [registrar] said that he'd make a definite date for a hearing.

In the absence of anything more constructive, 'conciliation' on court premises becomes synonymous with delay. It is generally accepted that the Special Procedure has taken us into the realm of 'administrative divorce'—in other words, courts exercise only minimal supervision where both parties say that they want a decree. That in itself was a radical departure when first introduced, but what we now appear to be observing is an attempt to apply a cloak of consensus even to contested legal applications, so that courts seek to respond in administrative rather than judicial terms. No doubt this reflects the perceived difficulty of adjudicating family disputes (Ormerod 1973), but cost considerations also loom large, as does a miasmic faith in 'conciliation' as the *only* appropriate or necessary response to child-related issues (Shepherd, Howard, and Tonkinson 1984).

The Solicitor's Role

Most people, in anticipating the appointment, had wanted their solicitor to be there—and were glad, after the event, that he or she had been present. It is not surprising, given the present tendency in Bristol for solicitors to negotiate *on behalf of* their clients, that parents found it difficult to conceive that they could have managed on their own. This indeed was the view taken by the Lord Chancellor's Legal Aid Advisory Committee. They argued that if formal court orders were to be made at an initial hearing, '. . . then it will be necessary to allow, and where appropriate for legal aid to finance, legal representation for the parties. The wish to encourage agreement between parties should not override the need for parties to have dispassionate legal advice as to the advisability of such settlements.'[5]

One could hardly object to this as a general principle, but we gathered from our interviews that whilst some solicitors did indeed protect their clients against the very powerful settlement-seeking momentum which could be generated at these appointments, others were perceived as fifth-columnists, undermining their client's resolve from within. In many instances it appeared that solicitors were at least as keen to 'get a result' as were the welfare officer and registrar:

The discussion was really between the solicitors and the welfare officer. The pressure was terrific to get the matter sorted out and out of the way. It came from the solicitors and the welfare. They wanted a decision.

I didn't feel that he [solicitor] was forceful enough; I felt that he was backing down a bit. And at the end, my opinion was that all they [solicitor and welfare officer] wanted was it sorted out and out of the way—they wanted an ending to it all.

By far the strongest criticism of solicitors, at both Bristol and Newport, was that they had not given their client sufficient backing. An ironic response to the Advisory Committee's recommendation might therefore be to the effect that, these days, the threat of coercion by one's own legal adviser is almost as serious as that of coercion by 'the other side'. This arises from a quite fundamental shift in the legal profession's approach to matrimonial litigation over the past ten years or so. Whilst some would argue that solicitors and barristers have always been keen to 'settle', the greatly increased volume of divorce cases, coupled with pressure from the judiciary and the change in thinking wrought by the conciliation movement, has brought us to a point where, for some solicitors, the achievement of 'settlement' appears to be their sole *raison d'être*. This has two equally serious consequences. The first is that 'justice' in matrimonial disputes becomes simply a matter of adhering to professional bargaining norms. The second is that the preliminary stages of the legal process can become even more excluding than the admittedly highly intimidating experience of the traditional form of trial. This is because litigants may have literally *no* opportunity to convey their point of view to the court. Both these aspects are conveyed in the following account:

My solicitor was telling me that [husband] had certain rights and the judge would probably agree to this, that, and the other, and I was saying, 'How can they? They don't know me, they don't know my children, they don't know him.' And I said to him, 'Well, I'm not going to let you stand up' . . . and he said to me, I couldn't address the registrar, he'd have to do it. I said to him, 'No, I don't see that. If we're discussing my children, I feel I have every right to say how I feel.' I don't think you should be told—because he's a solicitor and because he can use longer words and make it sound more complicated than it really is—I don't care if he's a registrar or what he is, I think you should be able to speak to him in plain language. I thought that was wrong, that he [solicitor] could tell me that I had to go through him. I can relay words to you but you might not relay them the same way. You could use the same words and not in the same context that I want them used and they could sound completely different. Solicitors to me have got blinkers on and they just look one way. I think in divorce, custody, and children, you can't do that. It's too personal, too emotional. You've got to look at each case individually. I just think it's too standardized really.

As one might have gathered from the above account, women were more likely than men to experience a lack of support from their solicitor at the appointment. In many instances the whole atmosphere of the court was perceived to be stunningly patriarchal. In the words of another of our informants: 'It frightened me to death, to be quite honest with you, you know, with all the men sat around and just me sat there. It was just all men. I felt small.'

The Welfare Officer at the Appointment

Of the two non-aligned, potential mediating figures who are present at the Bristol appointments—the welfare officer and the registrar—it is the welfare officer who is regarded as the principal negotiator. For the most part, he or she will work directly with the parties (rather than their solicitors), the discussions taking place either in the waiting area or in one of two interviewing rooms.

The impression conveyed by the majority of our informants was that in both the Bristol and Newport courts the welfare officers were as keen to achieve a 'result' as were the solicitors and registrar. This was reflected, for example, in the fact that welfare officers appeared loath to contemplate any change in the current arrangements for care and control. There was a general reluctance to acknowledge that the designated 'loser' might also have a case. These dissatisfied customers tended to be either custodial mothers having to grant access to the husband, or non-custodial fathers, frustrated in their desire to assume care and control. These are the classic 'losers' in the present system; their case is seen by everyone to be weak and 'in-court mediation' might almost have been designed to secure their reluctant compliance.

The kind of negotiation which takes place in these circumstances, as Roberts (1983) has pointed out, retains precious little element of 'party-control', being more a means of lubricating *third-party* decisions arrived at by court personnel. Nevertheless, there were circumstances in which the blunt, no-nonsense approach of some welfare officers came as a welcome relief, *particularly where parents had given up any hope of being able to resolve the issue themselves.* The 'negotiation', if we can call it that, was highly pragmatic, but given the stage these parents had reached, they felt this to be necessary: indeed, it was what they had been hoping to get from the court. Roberts (1983; 1986) has been highly critical of those processes, partly on the basis that they are wrongly characterized as a form of 'mediation', and partly because they represent an absorption of extra-legal processes, it being feared that this will enable regulation to become both more pervasive and more covert.

It is obviously necessary to acknowledge the coercive nature of 'in-court mediation', but it may nevertheless provide us with an imperfect model for a more accessible, less professionally dominated framework for decision-making. I suspect that this would be positively welcomed by some litigants: many people feel they need more *control* than can be provided by an extra-legal mediation service, but either cannot get access to judicial determination, or are put off by the professional mysteries surrounding it.

It is very important from the point of view of the thesis which I want to develop in this chapter that it is understood that many of our informants would positively have welcomed the opportunity of a face to face meeting with their former spouse, on the understanding that they were going to *have* to come to some decision because this was a *court.* One account of a successful negotiation of this type appeared in Davis and Bader (1985). Another is given below, to convey some idea of the flavour, if not the substance, of the negotiation.

The welfare officer comes out and chats to both solicitors and next thing I know she says, 'Your husband and you—I'd like to speak to you in the office.' So we got in the office and then my husband started—screaming, shouting, forgetting that it's just a partition wall against where we are and where the children are with his wife [as she is now]. I said, 'I'm very sorry, I'm not saying anything else, I want my solicitor in here'. She said, 'you can't'. I said, 'I beg your pardon'. She said, 'You cannot have your solicitor in here.' I said, 'Well I'm sorry, I'm not saying anything else because I'm not going through a slanging match, I've just spent 13 years going through a slanging match and there's no way I'm going to go through it again.' And I've got to give her credit—after I said this, she did wipe the floor with him a bit—she said to him, 'For crying out loud, stop screaming and shouting. Act like a man and sort this out. I'm sitting here and I'm trying to do a job, I'm trying to stop everything being dragged through the courts.' She was only a young girl, and I don't know how long she'd done the job, but I mean, she did do a good job. She said, 'Mr D, if you're going to talk like this, we're not going to get anywhere . . . if you can't calm down, remember your children are next door and they're going to hear.' Anyway, she did calm him down and quite out of the blue he said, 'she never wants the children', and I thought, What's going on here? I'd been having the kids every fortnight—every weekend for however long we'd been separated—I said, 'hold on a minute, I have the children' . . . 'Oh, you're always putting the children off'. Then this young girl looked up and said, 'The children, talking to me, decided they do want to see you every week.' She said, 'My suggestion to you, if both of you will agree, is that you have the three children from 9 o'clock in the morning till 8 o'clock at night on a Saturday', which, you know, without my thinking, Oh God, here he goes again, he's going to have a right go at this, he agreed to it! And I sat there and I thought well, why in hell couldn't he sit and talk to *me* and say this. . . . It's all sorted out from there and it's gone on great.

In cases like this it would appear that the parents participated actively in, even if they did not control, the decision-making process. But other accounts of these proceedings do not convey the same impression. The problem was not so much that the process was coercive—after all, it is in the nature of courts to be coercive and we need only worry about that if the extent of the coercion is denied (as, for example, through the appointments being labelled a form of 'mediation'). It was rather that the appointments were too settlement-orientated. Such a criticism may appear almost paradoxical given the 'mediation' or 'conciliation' label which is applied to them, but I use the term 'settlement' here to refer to an exclusively professional preoccupation with the need to terminate contested applications without resort to trial. The accent is not on the service being offered to the parties: such a description would be wholly misleading. The objective, on the contrary, *is to restrict access to a service*, the service in question being that of judicial determination. It is inevitable that a procedure which is concocted as a form of rationing, rather than a means of expressing valued principles of justice, will serve the interest of courts and professional personnel, rather than of litigants. 'Settlements' arrived at in these circumstances may make not the slightest contribution to a resolution of the problem as this is experienced by the parties.

The Registrar's Chambers

The dominance of these professional 'values' is reflected in the way in which the proceedings are conducted, with legal advisers acting as the mouthpiece for their clients. This is most apparent at the final stage of the appointment, when the parties and their solicitors are ushered in to see the registrar. These were some parents' reactions to this stage of the proceedings:

I was shocked. I thought I was going into a place where I would be allowed to have a say in the matter. I expected, not actually to go in a dock, but to stand up and be allowed to say your piece. But it didn't happen like that. I didn't feel you could [speak up]. You didn't breathe, let along regards talking.

You don't feel as though you're allowed to speak. I suppose if you're the type of person who didn't mind speaking up, you could. You weren't stopped, but you had the overall impression you weren't allowed to.

I was left wondering what happened. I didn't say a word. Neither did my husband. Neither did the solicitors even. The registrar just made a few comments and that was it. I didn't really know what was going on. I was still wondering when I came out of that place. I thought—what's the point? What have I gone through? Why did I bother to come down here? I didn't know what was what. I was only in there seven or eight minutes. And afterwards, when I thought about it, I thought, I wonder why I paid all that money.

This is what 'settlement-seeking' by professional third parties can be like. At its worst it is a thoroughly unsatisfactory hybrid: a kind of 'mediation' without party control, or 'adjudication' without the opportunity to give evidence. The preliminary appointment system builds on a very long-established tradition of negotiation by legal advisers on court premises. It takes an exceptionally customer-orientated registrar, or an exceptionally determined customer, for these traditional patterns of professional court-room behaviour to be overcome.

The final extract in this section reveals much of what is wrong with the procedure, but it also points to elements which are valuable and which might be developed. As it happens, the appointment was concerned with the divorce decree.

It's a mess. Courts are such drama, even when you go before the registrar. There's such awe. Everybody bends and scrapes and you don't quite know why you're doing this because you don't really know how great his position is, but you get the feeling that they are all scared to death of him so you'd best not open your mouth. So the first time I went I was amazed at all this and I said: Can I say something? And [solicitor] was flabbergasted—I thought he was going to write me a note saying 'shut up'. So I explained that I didn't really want to divorce. I didn't know enough about my husband's financial background and how my finances would settle and how it would affect me and my children—if I knew that, it would go a long way to helping me make up my mind what I wanted on the ethical side. I thought divorce was failure and I really don't think I've failed so why should I have to—I'll have to anyway in the end because everyone has to in 5 years—but at that time I felt angry that I was having failure forced upon me. When I spoke out [registrar] listened and he was very kind and I wished I'd spoken out before. I hadn't done anything wrong but the way the solicitors were putting it, I was afraid he'd get the wrong impression.

Other Research

Pearson and Thoeness (1984a), who investigated the 'mediation experience' in the three courts of Los Angeles, Connecticut, and Minnesota, report that 'at all locations, mediation was associated with a high degree of user satisfaction'. Even amongst those who failed to reach agreements, 'a clear majority . . . would encourage others to try'.

These results appear to have been arrived at on the basis of quantification of responses to the researchers' direct questions—reflecting a style of interviewing which tends to produce 'findings' which confirm (or more occasionally, refute) the researchers' prior conceptions. The limitations of this approach are reflected in Pearson and Thoeness's own figures. For example, 70–80 per cent of their informants appreciated (on being asked, presumably) the benefit of an opportunity to share grievances. But 30–40 per cent complained of not being heard or understood. One-third of those who reported reaching an agreement also informed the researchers that 'little or no progress' had been made in their case. The latter finding is described as 'intriguing' and as revealing that 'mediation is a complex process'. The researchers make the laconic observation that 'an agreement is not synonymous with a solution', but do not go on to draw any conclusions about the true nature of 'mediation' on court premises. Instead, Pearson and Thoeness make a number of references to the parties' *confusion* about the process. We are told that some people were under the erroneous impression that the procedure was intended to save their marriage; that the mediator would make a *decision*; or that mediation was a form of counselling. The researchers refer to these ideas, without equivocation, as 'misconceptions'. They advocate 'client education about the mediation process . . .' in order to 'eliminate erroneous client expectations of lengthy counselling or evaluations'. Acknowledging that some people 'had no idea why they were mediating', Pearson and Thoeness suggest that '[g]oal clarification may . . . enhance client co-operation and eliminate the resistance shown by those who believe that they are being asked to reconcile or that they are being judged'.

It would appear from this that litigants are the problem: confused, behind the times, or just plain thick, they need to be knocked into shape in order to appreciate the benefits of this new procedure.

Discussion

Researching the same field over a period of years can be an uncomfortable experience, as new insights (whether one's own or other people's) undermine old positions. As it now appears, some of my best articles have been based on misconceptions, although there are fortunately one or two arguments which still stand up. For example, I was muddled, in 1983, when I claimed that procedural reform *and the development of in-court mediation* were of overriding importance, and when I suggested that it was essential that *the values and strategies appropriate to mediation* should be accommodated as part of the legal process. My own research, and Simon Roberts's strictures, have convinced me that decision-making on court premises can never have a genuinely mediatory character, if by that is meant a form of negotiation which continues to reflect *the disputants'* view of the quarrel, rather than that of professional third parties. It has been suggested (Parkinson 1986a: 81) that '[t]he perceived dichotomy between in-court and out-of-court conciliation becomes an anachronism if mediation is recognized as a particular method of working which different families may need at different stages in the transition through separation, divorce, remarriage and, in some cases, re-divorce'.

There was a time when I might have said the same, but I now regard such statements as far removed from the realities of negotiation on court premises. However, I still believe (as I wrote in 1983) that the *first* priority should be to remedy those defects which prevent access to the legal system or make it an unsatisfactory mechanism in so many cases. Extra-legal services are struggling to attract customers; solicitors and courts, on the other hand, are overwhelmed by the 'demand' on their service. It has been suggested (Roberts 1983) that some of these litigants would do better to take their quarrels to a conciliation service; that they have fallen victim to the legal profession's self-promotion to such an extent that they consider it 'dangerous' to act without professional legal advice and regulation. But if divorcing people—who are perhaps being bullied or manipulated by their spouse—consider they need legal advice, and perhaps judicial determination, then we should respect their judgment—not attempt to fob them off with 'mediation'.

The rationing motif dominates our civil justice system. It is evident, once again, in the Booth Committee's proposals for reform of matrimonial procedure (paras. 3.1 to 3.16). The net effect may well be to further restrict access to judicial determination, rather than, as I would like to see, making judges and registrars *more* accessible—not as mediators, but as adjudicators.

This is an aspiration quite at odds with that which Dingwall (1986) has identified as being at the heart of the mediation movement, namely, a withering away of state power as people take more responsibility upon themselves. The latter is reflected in Roberts's argument (1983) that mediatory intervention should be kept separate from the places and personnel of the law, that it should be seen as 'other' than adjudication, something to be tried first. I have no quarrel with that, but it is important to recognize that Roberts is not considering the whole picture: he is confining himself to 'non-law' and arguing that these processes should be allowed to retain their clearly non-legal identity. He has not set himself to consider the cost, the delay, the stultifying ritual—indeed, the plain inaccessibility—of judicial determination. He has identified the non-mediatory character of 'in-court mediation', but he has not addressed the problems of courts. He warns that in-court mediation, so-called, may result in 'disputants . . . having decisions moulded for them without the procedural safeguards attending formal adjudication' (1986) but it is also necessary to consider the plight of those divorcing couples who, although experiencing major disagreements about aspects of their divorce, feel bound to soldier on without help (Davis *et al.* 1982). Others may apply to the court, only to find that their dispute is not fully aired, or that it is 'settled' without providing any real solution. What use, in these circumstances, are the 'procedural safeguards attending formal adjudica-tion'? These avail only those who reach the summit: we ought also to be concerned for the majority, miserably wandering the lower slopes.

The evidence which I have outlined suggests, unfortunately, that the preliminary hearing is best understood as a further element in the court's rationing, deflecting strategy. It is clear from accounts which we were given of these couples' experience from the point of separation onwards that, at the time when all the really important decisions were being taken, one party (if not both) might feel totally unprotected. This, I suspect, indicates something quite fundamental about the role of the courts in family disputes. They are perceived, by all those professionally involved, to be a highly expensive blunt instrument which cannot hope to grapple with the complexity and the rival versions of 'truth' characterizing custody or access disputes.

So what is the court's response? The answer is simple, if unpalatable: it is to avoid tackling these issues at all unless forced to do so. To this end, the *cost* and the *delay* associated with the legal process act as rationing devices. This is central to my understanding of the reasons underlying the introduction of 'mediation' on court premises, and also, the form which that mediation is likely to take. These appointments do not necessarily reflect any desire on the part of courts to become more accessible to divorcing couples at a time when outside intervention is most needed, or to engage in a deeper examination of complex family matters; on the contrary, the hope may well be that in some rather ill-defined way, the proportion of disputes which 'survive' to the stage where they have to be adjudicated may be yet further reduced. The same judgment may be applied to the Booth Committee's concept of the 'initial hearing'. Whilst this innovation could have its positive side, the main object is to enable courts to exercise greater control over proceedings in the interests of administrative efficiency and 'savings'.

Critics of informalism (and specifically of 'conciliation' as a response to family disputes) have suggested that, for some couples, these services will come to replace genuine dispute resolution. In the words of Richard Abel (1982*a*), they represent 'a neutralization of conflict that presents itself as a new and better mode of expressing conflict'. Bottomley (1984) also emphasizes the role of 'due process' in protecting the rights of adults and children affected by divorce. But what needs to be recognized and understood is that 'due process' is itself in flight from due process. In other words, 'diversion' is endemic within the legal system itself. Everyone contributes: solicitors, barristers, court welfare officers, and registrars. The Bristol and Newport preliminary appointments, I would suggest, can appropriately be viewed in this light.

This still leaves us with what I regard as the key question, namely, how to provide readily accessible judicial authority in the context of a court procedure which is sufficiently informal to enable the parties to state their views. A very useful starting point is Silbey's (1981) defence of the lower courts, its relevance in this context having been identified by Dingwall and Eekelaar (1984), who used it in order to mount a defence of magistrates' justice.

Silbey refers to the distance between the litigant's conception of his trouble and the judge's ability, *within the law*, to deal with it. This is not helped by the tendency to develop increasingly formal rules and procedures, reflecting the tension between 'legal formal rationality' (or due process) on the one hand and 'substantive justice' on the other. According to Silbey, 'the desire to "do justice", but have it done in a regular, procedurally correct way, according to the known, general, clear, consistent rules of law, characterizes the dilemma of western legal systems'. An ethic of responsive justice is inconsistent with adversarial due process. She suggests that the disposition of cases in the lower courts often involves a dialogue between *all* the interested parties (professionals and litigants) concerning the nature of the problem and what might constitute a reasonable solution:

> It appears that they go beyond narrowly assigned powers, beyond procedures and restraints which define their role . . . in fashioning individualized solutions to cases of grievance, trouble, or differences of interests and values. But it is not a chaotic enterprise. People come to court because the courts respond to their trouble and respond by providing compulsory, often final, resolutions.

This is an attractive image, and one that may be thought especially appealing in the context of *matrimonial* disputes. However, one should be wary of assuming that this is the kind of service which the lower courts actually provide. It is not only the due process rights of the parties which may be compromised: as Silbey herself acknowledges, the lower courts tend to emphasize *rapid case processing* and *volume control*—in other words, a form of rationing which operates not by restricting access, but by limiting the service that is offered and imposing rapid termination.[6] This, it could be argued, is precisely what the preliminary appointment system in the County Court offers us at the moment. I see no reason why rapid processing should encourage 'individualized solutions'; it is more likely to promote stereotyping.

The accounts which we were given certainly cast doubt on any suggestion that Magistrates' Courts, simply by virtue of their being 'lower courts', are more responsive to the parties than single professional adjudicators. In general there appeared to have been even less opportunity to contribute directly to the proceedings that was offered in the County Court. The registrars whom we observed in Bristol and Newport were keen to secure a legal settlement, but on the occasions when they were able to wrench themselves away from this preoccupation, they were not insensitive. In the words of two of our informants: 'He gave her what she wanted, but he also gave me what I wanted. He was as fair as he could be.' 'He was very observant and quite intelligent—full of commonsense, which I find is quite unusual in the legal profession.'

'In-court mediation', so called, can readily be criticized because of its non-mediatory character, but it also provides us with some useful clues as to how third-party decision-making might be rendered more accessible and meaningful to the disputants. One should not imagine that all trials conform to an ideal type, with the judge or registrar making a pronouncement at the end. Some adjudicators display considerable flexibility in the course of 'trying' a custody or access dispute. Take the following account of a *defined access hearing*. Despite what was in this instance an avowedly *adjudicatory* framework, it appears that the registrar did all he could to encourage the parties to work out their own solutions.

The last one [registrar] was quite nice and quite fair, he had just as much to say to me as to [husband]. He did actually suggest that we were very close to agreeing and maybe we ought to just try and sit down somewhere and have a cup of coffee and talk about it. And [husband] said, 'Absolutely not' and I said, 'Well, I wouldn't mind' and so it was actually arranged there and then. I think he was quite fair not to make a decision when he could have done—that's what it was for. He was just there to make a decision. And I thought that was quite good of him really, he seemed human.

I have not read any other accounts of this 'non-adjudicatory' judicial style, although anthropologists have described forms of dispute-resolution which combine adjudication with 'settlement by consensus' (Epstein 1971; Gulliver 1979: 27). One very interesting model, albeit occurring in the field of child protection rather than divorce, is that of the French *juge des enfants*. This is Michael King's (1984: 148) account of some of the features of a typical hearing under the French system of judicial control of child care:

Hearings before the judge, it must be emphasized, are not lengthy formal affairs —they can be over in ten minutes and usually last no longer than an hour—yet nor are they the mechanical rubber stamping of social workers' decisions. They take the form of informal discussions between judges, social worker, and parents with the judge controlling the sequence of such discussions. The child will be brought to the court and the judge will in the case of older children talk to the child, either seeking his or her views on possible solutions to the problem or to explain what has been decided.

The attraction of this procedure for King is that it provides a measure of protection against arbitrary social work judgments. The single judge, in his view, is *more* effective in achieving this than the combination of legal representation and complex procedural rules which is to be found in English courts. But there are two other important features of the French procedure, each of which has a bearing on the present discussion. The first is that it is a vehicle for judicial decision-making, rather than the pursuit of 'settlement'. And the second is that parents contribute actively to the process.

King himself warns of the 'greener grass' syndrome, and one must be particularly careful given that the system described is not only operating in a different country but relates to a different area of judicial responsibility. There may nevertheless be lessons to be learnt, particularly with regard to the court's attitude towards involving the parties in its decision-making. According to King, family rights in France do not depend on procedural protection and legal representation to the degree which one finds in English courts. They rely instead on 'an ideological approach to child protection that sees the family, including the extended family, as central to the child's future welfare'.

The element which King has identified, and which I think is often missing from the English system, in relation both to trials and 'in-court mediation', is an acknowledgement that it is the *parties* (that is to say, parents and their children) who will have to sort out these matters in the end. They are the ultimate decision-makers. They ought therefore to be involved as much as possible in the *court's* decision-making processes, whatever label is attached to these.

Unfortunately, it appears that little thought is currently being devoted to reform of the core of the family law system, by which I mean judicial determination of contested applications. Suggestions for procedural reform are dominated by the rationing motif. One even finds extra-legal conciliation services being co-opted by courts as a further element in their 'diversion' strategy. A recent illustration of this is the Practice Direction (1986) which instructs judges and registrars to consider referring contested cases to local conciliation services, where these exist, in preference to ordering an enquiry and report by a welfare officer.

One might well ask: what does this do to the image (and the practice) of non-coercive, independent mediation schemes? Even more important, at least in relation to the themes developed in this chapter, are the implications of this kind of development for divorcing couples' access to adjudication. The *Guardian*'s report of the new practice direction (1 October 1986) was entitled: 'How to end a marriage without tears'. I would have thought, on the contrary, that it might cause considerable additional distress to find yet another barrier placed in the way of judicial determination. This is precisely the kind of development which critics of conciliation in family disputes have warned against. The aggrandizing tendency of the conciliation 'movement', coupled with the rationing, deflecting strategies employed by courts, could lead to adjudication becoming so much a last resort that it is stigmatized as the refuge of the obsessive and the intransigent. Richard Abel (1982: 306) warns that:

. . . informalism helps to legitimize the legal system by distracting attention from the problems of formal institutions. These, it is argued, are not defective; they are simply being asked to do too much and to do the wrong kind of things. The solution, therefore, is not to reform the core of the legal system . . . but rather to create alternative institutions at the periphery.

I agree with Abel. The legal process should not be allowed to atrophy whilst we concentrate all our energies on developing extra-legal alternatives.

Notes

1. Report of the Matrimonial Causes Procedure Committee (Booth Committee), Lord Chancellor's Department, 1985.
2. This research was sponsored by the Nuffield Foundation.
3. Report of the Inter-departmental Committee on Conciliation, Lord Chancellor's Department, 1983.
4. This study was conducted in the Department of Social Administration, University of Bristol, from 1979 to 1981. The research was directed by Mervyn Murch and sponsored by the Joseph Rowntree Memorial Trust.
5. Lord Chancellor's Legal Aid Advisory Committee's submission to the Matrimonial Causes Procedure Committee (Booth Committee).
6. I am grateful to Profession Roy Parker, Department of Social Administration, University of Bristol, for his elaboration of this idea: Parker (1975).

7. *Kaji Chotei:* Mediation in the Japanese Family Court

SATOSHI MINAMIKATA

One of the central issues in debates about divorce mediation relates to the protection of the parties' legal rights. Questions have been raised about the degree of freedom individuals are allowed in deciding whether or not to participate in mediation and the extent to which the process actually gives them an opportunity to reach an agreement without explicit or implicit coercion. This chapter discusses the experience of court-based family mediation services in Japan, *Kaji Chotei,* and the lessons this well-established system may have for comparable developments in other countries.

As in most jurisdictions, approximately 90 per cent of all divorces in Japan are obtained by consent, although these may involve some private mediation. The remaining cases go through a more formal procedure, including *Rikon Chotei,* a mandatory attempt at mediation. This system has its origins before the Second World War. It has clearly benefited a large number of individuals and offered an effective means of resolving family disputes. Nevertheless, an increasing amount of criticism is now being voiced about its principles, practices, and quality of service. To provide a context for discussing these issues, however, the chapter begins by outlining the Japanese court system and divorce procedure.

Getting a Divorce in Japan

The Civil Code of 1898, which introduced a Western legal concept of divorce to Japan, provided ten grounds for dissolving a marriage. With the exception of clauses relating to 'missing parties' (essentially people presumed dead) and to the dissolution of a particular type of adoption all of these were based on the offence doctrine. In practice, however, Japanese courts never enforced this rigidly and it was substantially eroded by a series of precedents before being swept away in the post-war Civil Code of 1947. This remains the current law and is essentially a no-fault provision. A divorce may be granted solely upon the irretrievable breakdown of a marriage, with some qualifications where a court considers that the applicant was responsible for the breakdown. The Code (ss. 763, 770) provides two ways of obtaining a divorce: 'divorce by consent' and 'divorce in court'.

Divorce by consent

Although divorce by consent is uncommon among modern divorce systems, it has a long history in Japanese society. There has never been a dominant religious doctrine emphasizing the importance of marital unity and marriage was traditionally regarded as a private, secular arrangement between two *Ihe* or families. Divorce could disgrace the honour of a family and there was a preference for discreet consensual dissolutions. In modern times, an alternative ideology has become important, namely the view that if a marriage can be contracted by the mutual consent of parties, they should also be able to end it by agreement alone. Moreover, divorce by consent is cheaper, quicker, and simpler than the cumbersome procedures of divorce in court. It remains, then, the preferred means of ending a marriage, except where parties are particularly concerned to secure their legal interests.

There are two procedures for obtaining a divorce by consent. One involves the filing of a notification form with the family registry section of the relevant local authority. The other involves a visit to the family registry office and an oral declaration of divorce in front of two witnesses. If the parties agree about the divorce and related issues, including the distribution of property and arrangements for custody, there is no judicial intervention. But if one of the parties subsequently breaches the agreement, the other can ask a court to order its performance.

While some couples dissolve their marriage without outside help, people often seek assistance in reaching agreements. This process is not well understood and any account must be somewhat impressionistic. However, it seems that assistance can be drawn from two sources: the parties' 'primary groups' give informal and individualistic support while 'secondary groups' are more formal and institutional.

Primary groups include friends, relatives, 'matchmakers', and influential persons in the community or organizations to which the parties belong. Help may be sought from such sources because of the parties' trust in a particular individual, because the prospective mediator has a position of authority, or because the person shares common interests with the parties. The amount of freedom retained by the parties varies. Sometimes they can maintain their decision-making power throughout the process. But mediators have been known to put undue pressure on the parties to accept a decision based on the mediator's own value system. In other cases, parties seem to abandon any attempt to decide for themselves and leave their problems entirely in the hands of the mediator.

How effective are these primary group members as mediators? The answer seems to be that they are in decline as a result of long-term changes in Japanese society. Greater social and geographical mobility mean that people may not have anyone appropriate to involve who is reasonably accessible. Traditional community structures have become weaker and the role of influential authoritarian individual leaders has diminished over the last thirty years or so (Fukutake 1982: 134–5). More recently, a growing tendency to separate work and family life has reduced the influence of workplace superiors over their subordinates (Fukutake: 1982: 147–9). Thus there are fewer people in a position to mediate than there would have been a generation ago. Those that remain are increasingly reluctant to become involved. Even the matchmakers who still arrange a significant proportion of marriages tend to shy away from the traditional extension of their role in helping to maintain those marriages by mediating in disputes.

The secondary groups include professionals such as lawyers and local welfare commissioners. In theory, the role of a lawyer is different from that of a mediator because the lawyer is, strictly, the representative of one party in negotiating the settlement of the matrimonial dispute. But, just as Richard Ingleby describes for England, Japanese lawyers often end up performing mediation functions (Forum 1983: 55). On the basis of information obtained from interviewing the client and communicating with the other party, a lawyer may suggest to the client a 'fair and reasonable' plan for resolving the dispute within legal principles. To the extent that the client often attempts to reach an agreement based on such a plan, it may be said that the lawyer performs functions similar to those of a mediator.

These secondary relationships based on the simple business principle of retainer and client seem to be filling the space left by the decline of traditional relationships noted above. There seems no reason to expect that this trend will not continue, especially as the professionals seek to improve access to their services. The Japanese Bar Association, for example, established an inexpensive advice service mainly for legal aspects of divorce in 1984.

Whether an agreement to divorce by consent is reached by the parties' own efforts or with the assistance of informal mediators, it is not unusual for one of the parties, normally the wife, to be in a weaker bargaining position and less able to protect her own interests. In 1981, for example, divorce disputes taken to the family court resulted in 19 per cent of husbands winning custody of their children, as against 74 per cent of wives. Divorces by consent in the same year resulted in 24 per cent of husbands and 69 per cent of wives gaining custody. Women going to the Family Court obtained 'special payment for divorce', a type of maintenance award, in 55 per cent of cases, compared with 47 per cent in divorces by consent. (Economic Planning Agency 1983: 150–1) These differences are not large but they do suggest that divorce by consent produces outcomes less favourable to women (Kobayashi 1984: 124).

Divorce in court

When a couple fail to agree about a divorce or related matters, either or both may apply to have the case dealt with in court. Japan established a family court system in 1948 with predominant jurisdiction over family disputes and juvenile delinquency, although district courts, of the same status, retain some jurisdiction in property matters. Both courts come under the appellate jurisdiction of the High Court and, finally, the Supreme Court.

Family courts offer two legal procedures for resolving disputes. *Kaji Chotei* is a process intended to encourage reconciliation or agreement between the parties. *Kaji Shimban* deals with the cases affecting a wider public interest, such as the change of a family name, which is regarded as a fundamental alteration in a person's social identity. In this procedure, the judge makes an order. Divorce cases reaching the court system may go through three stages of proceedings: mediation (*Rikon Chotei*) and 'court order' (*Rikon Shimban*), both in the family court, and litigation (*Rikon Hanketsu*), which is obtained in the district court.

The process of *Rikon Chotei* begins when an application is made for a divorce through the court. Even if this is filed with a district court, litigation cannot proceed there directly. The case must first be transferred to the family court in 'the system of compulsory *Chotei* prior to litigation'. Once an application is received, a *Chotei* committee is formed. This is made up of at least two lay people, one man and one woman, known as *Chotei* commissioners, and a family court judge. *Chotei* commissioners may, but do not necessarily, have a background in social work, counselling, or law. They tend to be chosen from among middle-class housewives, lawyers, company executives, and retired legal professionals. The committee conducts the mediation in a private room on the court premises. The public are not admitted and both parties are required to attend. If they wish, they may be accompanied by lawyers, relatives, or new partners. The purpose of the meeting is to promote the settlement of the dispute by conciliation, or reconciliation, on the basis of information provided by the parties, although the *Chotei* committee also has the discretion to ask for a report from an 'investigation officer' whose role is similar to that of an English divorce court welfare officer. At any stage, the committee may make its own proposals for a settlement which its members would consider reasonable, but, in theory, the parties are free to decide whether or not to accept this. If an agreement is reached, it is incorporated in a '*Chotei* document', whose binding force is equivalent to a court decree. It may be enforced by a 'performance recommendation' or a 'performance order' in the family court.

If an agreement is not reached through *Rikon Chotei*, the judge involved has the power to issue a divorce order (*Shimban Rikon*). For example, mediation may prove unsuccessful if one of the spouses resists an agreement in order to save face, although not necessarily being opposed to the divorce in principle. The judge must consult the lay commissioners and the divorce order must be within the scope of the parties' original application. If either party objects to the order, it ceases to be valid. In fact this power is rarely used: there were only thirty-one cases in 1982. More commonly, the case will go to the district court for divorce by decree (*Hanketsu Rikon*), where it will be examined by a procedure which introduces adversarial elements. A dissatisfied party has the right to appeal further to superior courts.

Legal Protection of the Parties in *Chotei*

One of the major concerns for a couple throughout the entire *Chotei* process is the protection of their interests, in the broadest sense of that term. This would, at a minimum, seem to require recognition of the right to self-determination, implying respect for the parties' free will and their ability to control the progress of the case and the supply of information, and the right to receive fair treatment from the court. It is generally believed that such criteria are met by the current system. Fukaya (1983: 245), for instance, describes *Chotei* as 'one of the legal procedures provided by the family court through which parties are expected to reach agreements *voluntarily* in order to resolve their marital disputes with the assistance of a *Chotei* committee' (emphasis added). But a closer examination reveals three serious problems with this procedure. These derive from its basic assumptions, from the nature of the existing law, and from the way in which it is operated.

The basic assumptions of *Chotei*

In theory, *Chotei* should accord with the Japanese Constitution, which guarantees the fundamental rights of individuals. This is elaborated by the Civil Code of 1947 in its provisions relating to family life. Thus, *Chotei* ought to operate in a way which respects the equality of the sexes, their rights to family life, and a body of 'democratic' legal principles. In reality, however, some of its underlying ideas seem to be inconsistent with this aspiration.

These ideas may be clarified by an examination of the historical background to *Chotei*. Its origins go back to the nineteen twenties (Tanaka 1976: 493–5). An Ad Hoc Deliberative Council on the Legal System was established in 1919 to review those parts of the 1898 Civil Code dealing with family matters. This was a period of considerable social unrest in Japan (Isono 1985: 203–4). Since the turn of the century, there had been an escalation of industrial conflict and disputes between tenant farmers and landlords, reflecting the strains of the rapid modernization of Japanese society (Kawashima 1976: 269). The Imperial regime interpreted these phenomena as evidence of the obsolescence of traditional methods of settling disagreements between citizens, which represented a threat to the stability of the established social order. These anxieties were compounded by their observations of the Russian Revolution and their fear that its example might make the short sea crossing to Japan.

This social disorder was explained in terms of changing attitudes among the lower classes, particularly their growing awareness of individual rights not only as citizens but also as family members (Haley 1982: 130–1). Although the Civil Code of 1898 had been drafted under the influence of Western legal ideas of individualism, Imperial family policy never recognized this. State education, for example, emphasized that families were not groups of independent individuals who had freely chosen to form a relationship with a particular exchange of legal rights and obligations (Isono and Isono 1958: 29–30). The family was said to be based on 'inviolable' principles of authority and piety, the duties owed to the head of the household and through him to the state. If part of the programme for containing or eliminating social unrest was the restraint on individuals from conceiving themselves as independent agents with legal rights, then it was particularly undesirable that family conflicts should be dealt with in the formal setting of a court.

The Ad Hoc Council responded to this élite analysis of Japanese society by proposing the establishment of a family tribunal (*Kaji Shimbansho*) which would delegalize family disputes and lead to peaceful settlements. It was proposed that this tribunal would use *Chotei* as its method of proceeding.

The implementation of these ideas was, however, delayed until 1939. It needs to be analysed in the context of the development of an increasingly totalitarian and militaristic society in Japan during the nineteen thirties. Following the Manchurian Incident of 1931 and the Japanese invasion of China, the government was faced with an increase in disputes among soldiers' families over rights to war pensions or other special allowances. As Robert Dingwall and John Eekelaar observe for England, attention to domestic social policy became an important factor in maintaining morale in the armed forces (Naito 1974: 90). However, in Japan, the financial and political pressures of the war caused the government to abandon the project for a family tribunal, although the idea of *Chotei* was retained. The Conciliation of Personal Affairs Act 1939 provided for family disputes to be dealt with through *Chotei* on the basis of 'ethical principles' and 'paternalistic compassion' indigenous to 'traditional Japanese culture'. These matters would not be treated through the legal language of individual rights and obligations in an ordinary court. *Chotei* was established as part of the ideology of an authoritarian state rather than any spirit of liberalism.

When the Japanese Constitution was revised after the defeat and surrender of the Imperial regime in 1945, family problems were, in theory, supposed to be managed in a new spirit of American-style democracy. But *Chotei* was absorbed into the new system of family courts without any attempt to rethink its fundamental assumptions. The traditional paternalism was simply restated in a new language of welfare. This example is from a family court judge writing in the nineteen fifties.

[Before 1945, *Chotei*] emphasized that family disputes should be resolved on the basis of ethical principles and paternalistic compassion. Despite the old-fashioned terminology employed, such an understanding reflected correctly the fundamental principles which should be followed in handling family problems: family conflicts should be dealt with against a flexible standard rather than by a rigid one, and, moreover, they should be handled through conciliatory procedures rather than an adversarial one. (Hiraga 1974: 157.)

Even today *Chotei* commissioners praise the procedure as an 'effective measure to encourage the parties to reach an ambiguous settlement (instead of a clear-cut resolution)' (Forum 1983: 49). The family court was established under the dominance of a welfare principle without any serious discussion of the extent to which this could compromise the rights of individuals. As a result its authoritarian heritage from the pre-war period has remained essentially unquestioned.

The legal framework of *Chotei*

This lack of attention to parties' rights pervades the legal provisions for the *Chotei* process. It affects both the treatment of the ideal of self-determination and the provision of equitable procedures.

Chotei is usually said to have two objectives: the first is to harmonize the emotional and social relationship between the disputing parties with a view to reconciliation and the second is to mediate their legal dispute. Conflicts can, however, arise between these goals. In order to achieve a successful outcome in the first respect, the committee needs to encourage the parties to present as much information about themselves as possible. This allows both the committee members and the parties to develop their insight into the reasons for the failure of the marriage. But this information could include evidence of misconduct, such as adultery or violence, which may discredit the culprit. There is, though, no restriction on such information being used against the parties in consideration of the legal dispute. Indeed, *Chotei* committees do not even seem to acknowledge that there could be a possibility of the inappropriate use of information offered or obtained from the parties for one, welfare, purpose to affect the legal outcome.

The compulsion to participate erodes the parties' control over the provision of information and its use. Although the relevant legislation is rather vague about who has the legal control of the *Chotei* process, the committee manual encourages members to treat it as under their direction (General Secretariat 1976: 6). Thus the parties have little scope to control the flow of information by resisting the committee's inquiries. The law appears to leave the committee with a virtually unfettered discretion to collect and use information as it sees fit. Although the law requires that one committee member must be a judge, in order to ensure that the procedure is conducted in a fair and equitable manner, the Civil Code refrains from establishing a standard, to which the parties could appeal, in the name of respect for family privacy. It is not that the parties are acting under the shadow of the law but that the law's deliberate lack of clarity prevents it from casting any shade at all. In the absence of any legal framework, there is no effective guarantee of protection for the parties against *ad hoc* oppressive treatment in the *Chotei* system.

The practice of *Chotei*

These worries are not merely theoretical but are grounded on the actual practice of *Chotei*. Publicly, it is characterized as a procedure through which couples resolve their own disputes without coercion, aided by commissioners who are fair, impartial, and understanding (General Secretariat 1976: 1; Numabe 1977: 26). At the same time, committee members are expected to maintain a firm and resolute attitude towards an unco-operative party in the interest of conducting the meetings smoothly (Numabe 1977: 10). They are also supposed to 'persuade' the parties to reach agreement in accordance with the general principles of family law (General Secretariat 1976: 16–17). There would seem to be a fine line between the coercive imposition of a committee's values about family life and persuasion to follow an undefined standard by a firm and resolute commissioner.

The tone is well captured by this commissioner's account of his expectations about the approach to be taken with parties who resist disclosure of information about themselves.

> . . . the parties to *Chotei* tend to be reluctant to speak out about matters which they would much rather conceal. They are particularly determined to conceal certain types of information. Commissioners are, therefore, expected, to some extent, to develop the art of extracting relevant information from the parties. (Forum 1983: 54).

Such an attitude seems to be at odds with the ideal of party control in the mediation process. It is reflected in the frequent complaint from younger couples about the way that commissioners tend to fasten onto a particular aspect of a case and to ignore the real wishes of the parties. Some are reported to hector couples merely on the basis of their own moral beliefs (Osaka Women Lawyers 1983: 38). This is accentuated by the generation gap between parties and commissioners. The latter must be recruited from people aged between forty and seventy years, whose experience of life and personal values reflect a very different era in Japanese social development.

Restraints on procedural abuse are also weakened by the shortage of family court judges and their lack of interest in the work. Although a number of judges have consistently devoted themselves to the improvement of the family court, others have been discouraged by the low status which the system appears to attach to this work. Typically, judges are only assigned to the family courts for three or four years in the course of their career, without any consideration of their interest or their understanding of the issues they will have to handle. The development of expertise in family law seems to make only a marginal contribution to a judge's prospects of advancement (Mikazuki 1976: 457 n. 9). As a result, there are few incentives to encourage or reward those who take a close interest in the cases presented to them. The low regard for the work is reflected in, and reinforced by, the staffing levels which mean that judges are frequently absent from *Chotei* hearings. In busy urban courts, one judge may be responsible for several cases simultaneously, slipping from room to room to monitor their progress (Forum 1979: 256). Although the judge can ask the lay commissioners for reports and advise them on the management of a case, his lack of physical presence means that no great reliance can be placed on his ability, even if motivated, to ensure due process treatment of the parties. Certainly, there is no routine system for evaluating the quality and results of the process although it processes a very large number of disputes. There were approximately 90,000 cases in 1984, of which 53 per cent related to divorce. Data on the consumers' views of the experience are notably lacking. This is consistent with the paternalist attitudes of the court but seems an inappropriate basis for public policy debates.

The available material on the history, principles, and practice of *Chotei* does not encourage the view that parties' rights are treated with much sensitivity. The number of unsuccessful attempts at mediation has been increasing (Asahi-Shimbunsha 1985: 201; Family Bureau 1986; Ministry of Health 1984). In 1970, 41.6 per cent of matrimonial disputes (mainly divorces) were settled through *Chotei*, declining to 38.9 per cent by 1984. Over the same period, the proportion of *Chotei* cases where parties failed to settle increased from 11.1 per cent to 16.4 per cent. The number of petitions for divorce originating in the district court has also increased more rapidly than petitions to the family court: a 250 per cent rise between 1966 and 1983, as against 180 per cent in the same period for the latter court. It appears that the consumers may be trying to vote with their feet against mediation by diverting their petitions into a more legalized setting.

It is, of course, true that the Japanese experience of divorce mediation reflects a very particular set of historical circumstances in a society which has undergone rapid and occasionally convulsive social changes in the last half century. However, it is a well-established working model of court-based mediation in a culture which does not traditionally favour adversarial means of resolving disputes. As such the value of its study should not be underestimated. It should, for example, sensitize us to the complex politics of mediation. In the West it has often been identified with self-consciously progressive social movements. In Japan, *Chotei* is a deeply conservative institution, which diverts disputes away from the public forums of the society into private arenas where people's troubles can be isolated and personalized, concealing the imposition of particular ideals of family life. Democratic legality is crucial to the protection of weaker parties, normally women. This account of *Chotei* also reminds us of what could happen when mediation work becomes the routine practice of an overloaded or under-resourced legal system. The ambiguities which enable well-meaning and committed mediators to give of their best may also confer a disturbing potential for abuse and oppression.

PART III

Mediation out of Court

8. Mediation, Conflict, and Social Inequality: Family Dispute Processing among the Bakwena

ANNE GRIFFITHS

The movement in support of alternative means of dispute resolution—mediation or conciliation—in divorce, forms one part of a wider international interest in the concept of informal justice. Debates in this field have drawn extensively on research carried out in Third World settings where the institutionalized systems of dispute resolution do not show the formality characteristic of Western practice. Like Satoshi Minamikata's discussion of *Chotei* in Japan, this contribution examines a working model of an informal approach to the resolution of family disputes, in this case among the Bakwena of Botswana, to consider what questions it may pose for similar developments in European societies.

'Informal justice' is an ill-defined term because it has normally only been used in a loose fashion to contrast with formal legal systems. As an ideal, however, it seems to involve at least five elements.

(*a*) There are no specialists involved in the representation of the parties to a dispute.
(*b*) The parties control the processing and outcome of the dispute.
(*c*) The parties are not subject to coercion or sanctions.
(*d*) The system expresses communitarian values.
(*e*) The system leads to social integration rather than division.

Informality of process (whatever that is) is said to encourage the parties to produce agreements of their own choosing which are likely to be more enduring. Any third-party mediator acts only as a channel for communication, somebody who facilitates rather than imposes a settlement. The person is presented as a benign, non-authoritarian figure. It is an image of voluntarism, equality, and private ordering.

By contrast, formal justice is seen as alienating and associated with blame, fault-finding, and all the potential for conflict, defeat, and humiliation contained in an adversarial process. A feminist rhetoric has linked such formal approaches with the concept of 'maleness' and associated informality with an ideal of female non-aggression and directness of address. The advantages of informal mechanisms for coping with family disputes are said to be that they are 'inexpensive, discretionary, personalized, voluntary, consensus-oriented and thera-peutic, and that, unlike the formal methods, they empower the participants' (O'Donovan 1985: 195). In the area of family law, especially with the growing abandonment of fault-based divorce, such a settlement-oriented approach has seemed preferable to perpetuating or escalating conflict through formal processes.

It is always dangerous simply to transplant models of informal justice without reference to their original social, historical, and cultural context. But an examination of family dispute processing among the Bakwena can be instructive for two reasons. Firstly, even within its own cultural terms, the system confronts problems which make it necessary to examine the ideal specifications of party control and the role of third parties with some caution. Secondly, although it is difficult to understand disputes in an alien culture, the anthropologist's distance from everyday involvements may make it possible to adopt a more detached perspective on events. Thus, it becomes possible to focus on issues underlying the system and the way they may, or may not, also arise in settings closer to home where familiarity or sectional interest may conspire to obscure their relevance.

This chapter presents an in-depth analysis of a single case study, a method defined by Mitchell (1983). The dispute chosen is representative of those arising from contests over the distribution of property at the end of a marriage. It is used to provide a framework for the analysis of three particular issues: the concept of 'justice' in an informal setting; the value of a dichotomy between 'formal' and 'informal' justice; and the relationship between the gender order in a community and its concepts of 'justice', 'equality', and 'fairness'.

The Bakwena

The Bakwena are one of the eight major Tswana tribes in Botswana, a landlocked state in Southern Africa. They inhabit the Western part of the country, in Kweneng district, which had a population of just over 20,000 in 1981. Their economy is based on subsistence agriculture, cattle raising, hunting and gathering, and migrant labour. Research on family dispute processing was carried out in the Bakwena's central village. Molepolole, between January and September 1982 and from June to August 1984.

Family disputes are initially dealt with in a customary system, for reasons both of tradition and ease of access. People only use the formal system and the courts if, for a variety of reasons, the customary system fails them. This happened in more than half the cases studied (Griffiths 1984). As in the case examined here, disputes may return from the statutory to the customary system at a later stage.

The Bakwena have a hierarchical system of social organization. This begins with the *kgotla*, a group of huts and a central meeting place where important administrative, political, ritual, and ceremonial events take place. The *kgotla* is presided over by an individual male known as the 'headman'. Several *kgotlas* are grouped to form a sub-ward and these, in turn are grouped into wards. At the apex of the system is the Chief's *kgotla*, which is the final arbiter in questions of dispute.

When there is a disagreement between husband and wife, the first step is normally for the couple and their relatives to meet at the home of one of the families to discuss the matter. If these negotiations are unsuccessful, the dispute may be taken to the *kgotla* (usually the man's) where the headman will attempt to mediate. Should this prove unsuccessful, the matter can be referred to the sub-ward and the ward until it finally reaches the Chief's *kgotla*. This process may take several years. It is only the Chief's *kgotla* that has power to fine or attach property: at other levels tribal officers may only mediate or make recommendations to the parties.

When a dispute is brought to the *kgotla*, the procedure begins with the complainant stating his or her position. A third party, normally the headman, then asks any questions he considers necessary and invites the other party to question anything that has been said. After this, the other members of the community present in the *kgotla* at the time are invited to question the complainant. Although women may be present, they rarely participate in this stage. The other party will then be asked to put their view of the dispute and questioned in a similar manner.

At the end of this process, the couple will be asked what they want to do about the dispute and members of the *kgotla* will make suggestions which may be formulated into recommendations by the headman. The parties are free to accept or reject the advice given but it is hoped that these lengthy discussions will have enabled them to reach a basis for settlement. The customary system places great emphasis on reconciliation. Couples are almost invariably urged to go and 'live in peace and harmony'.

Where they fail to do so, as in the case discussed here, and are sufficiently tenacious, the dispute will eventually end in the Chief's *kgotla* for the breakdown of the relationship to be socially confirmed and the consequences discussed. The Chief's *kgotla* is not a pure example of the ideal type of informal justice. It is recognized by the formal legal system of Botswana and dispenses statutory criminal justice in minor offences, subject to review by the District Commissioner and the District Magistrate. Some of the language of the formal system has been borrowed: it is often referred to as the Chief's Court; those who deal with the disputes are referred to as 'Presiding Officers' who give 'judgments' and make 'orders' and the person raising a family matter is the 'complainant'. In family disputes, there is power to impose a settlement. On the other hand, there is no involvement of legal specialists. The Presiding Office is the Chief Regent, the Deputy Chief, or the Senior Chief's Representative (SCR), all of whom are appointed by virtue of their relationship to the Royal Family. Parties are not represented by lawyers. Procedure within the *kgotla* takes the same forms as elsewhere in the system and the third parties hearing the dispute operate within the same cultural values at all levels. The behaviour of the SCR in this case is, then, typical of the system, although he happens to have greater formal powers in reserve than do subordinate dispute resolvers.

The Facts of the Dispute

The dispute analysed here involves a couple, Mr and Mrs Busang, from Molepolole. They had married under Botswanan statutory law in 1960 and had eight children. When their relationship ran into difficulties, their problems were initially taken to the customary system, reaching the Chief's *kgotla* in 1979. These attempts at resolution were unsuccessful and the statutory marriage was dissolved by a divorce petition in the High Court in 1982, on the ground of irretrievable breakdown caused by Mrs Busang's behaviour. Mr Busang was awarded custody of the six minor children but the distribution of property was referred back to the Chief's *kgotla* at Mrs Busang's request.

   Under the customary system, property is divided according to the source from which it derived and the conduct of the parties. Thus, this dispute revolves around both the definition of marital property and its origins, and the behaviour of each spouse. Proceedings begin with Mrs Busang outlining her claim and its justification.

I am complaining about the property which I acquired jointly with Mr Busang. I say this because it is he who divorced me. I have asked him to let me have some of the things which we acquired jointly and these are the items of property which we jointly acquired, a home, a vehicle, bank savings amounting to 1,500 pula (about £1000), 10 head of cattle, 10 goats, and a ploughfield.

She went on to list chairs, saucepans, hoes, and so on. She also claimed 135 pula, 'which is the proceeds of jerseys I was knitting'. Mrs Busang was then questioned by the third party hearing the dispute, Mr Sebele, the Senior Chief's Representative (SCR). He asked specific questions relating to property—for example, when Mrs Busang referred to 1,500 pula in the bank, she was asked, 'Is this money in the bank at the moment?' When Mr Sebele had finished she was questioned by Mr Busang. His questions were aimed at discrediting her version of the property involved by disputing her account of its source and thus her credibility in general. For example he questioned her about the money.

Are you aiming at this figure of 1,500 because some time back I told you that there is a certain amount of money paid by the government for each child in the family? Are you certain that you never got this information from anyone but me? Do you think this is so that anyone can rely on? It is certain that this is just what you have made up.

Similarly he attacked her claim for ten cattle by suggesting that this was based on the non-existent reproductive capacities of an ox (a castrated bull).

After Mr Busang had finished, she was questioned by the *kgotla* members. They shifted the discussion from the issue of property to that of conduct. The first question was put by the Chief Regent (CR), participating as an ordinary *kgotla* member (but, as will be seen, a rather powerful one).

CR. I've got one question to ask. Here it is. When you started making your statement you said you wanted this property because your husband had divorced you. My question is did he just divorce you without any cause? [i.e. the concept of irretrievable breakdown is not being recognized].
MRS B. He just divorced me.
CR. Since you say he divorced you without any cause, have you heard of a case of that nature where a husband divorced his wife without any reason?
MRS B. No, I've never heard of such a case.

This exchange is crucial because it establishes Mrs Busang as being at fault in the eyes of the *kgotla* and sets the tone for Mr Busang's statement. This has nothing to do with arguments related to specific items of property, but concentrates on his wife's conduct. It begins:

In connection with the case I do not see anything that entitles this woman to the property that she is claiming. She is not entitled to anything according to traditional custom. I'm saying this because she is the person who caused all the troubles in our married life since we married on 12th November 1960.

He goes on to specify the faults in her conduct. This is a brief catalogue:

(*a*) that she practised witchcraft;
(*b*) that she was a 'harlot' and after one of her affairs had to have an abortion;
(*c*) that she contributed nothing to the home;

(*d*) that she assaulted him;

(*e*) that she deserted him and the children;

(*f*) that she refused to co-operate in efforts made at reconciliation and, when divorce was inevitable, with the arrangements for the divorce.

In contrast he stressed how reasonably he had behaved: that he forgave her the affairs and abortion; that he tried to cure her of witchcraft; that he offered to make arrangements over the property.

Before I conclude let me clarify a certain point regarding certain things I discussed with her before the case was decided at the High Court. I told her she did not have enough grounds to claim a share of the property because the matter will be referred to the *kgotla* to be settled in accordance with our tradition and custom and you are going to lose the case. Then I suggested that she should let me know what items of property she wanted and I would give them to her. I wanted her to list what she wanted so that I could tell the *kgotla* the division we had agreed to. I even gave her the option that if she wanted to take all the property I would let her have everything. Then we listed out the items and I came to Molepolole with the list so that we could both sign an agreement which included the custody of the children. Then she refused to sign and there and then I knew that someone had advised her not to sign. Then on this wrong advice she made a different list with her lawyers which included things which did not exist.

He seems here to be trying both to present himself as reasonable and to use the High Court to endorse his behaviour and her fault. This is also marked at the end of the catalogue of misdemeanours when he states:

I presented all the evidence to the High Court to Justice Hannah. She did not contradict all this. She was represented by certain lawyers who I paid for. I had only paid the legal costs—she consulted lawyers all on her own, all I did was pay for the lawyer. This indicates that she was aware of everything that I presented to court and she accepted it *in toto*. It now astounds me that she, being aware of the fact that she had been instrumental to the breakdown of the marriage in collusion with her parents as previously stated, claims any property.

Mr Busang was then questioned by his wife who attempted to clear her character. He was not questioned by Mr Sebele. The members of the *kgotla* then put their questions, which were an attempt to see if he was willing to concede anything to his wife. For example one *kgotla* member asked, 'Is it right that a woman should forfeit everything because of a mistake she made in her past? Haven't you got any sympathy with your wife?'—to which he replied, 'No'. All his replies indicated that he was not prepared to alter his position on the division of property.

The members of the *kgotla* were then asked to give their advice. Some members felt that Mrs Busang should get something although this might be difficult to justify. 'We have been listening to this case all day and it is difficult for us to base our decision on customary procedure—all we can do is to ask Mr Busang to be sympathetic and give her something.' Others felt that she had been at fault and should, therefore, receive nothing.

I don't have much to say but I'll say what the other speakers have already said. I don't see any reason why the woman should be given a share of the property. Our Tswana expression is that she has committed suicide and someone who does so you don't cry for. When her husband wanted to sympathetically consider her position and give her property she turned that offer down. The husband had a kindness to ask her to make a list of all the items she wanted so that he could give them to her and she refused and insisted on having a case against the husband in connection with this property. She did not see the implications in the offer made by the husband, that he was willing to give some property voluntarily but did not want to argue about it. It is on those grounds that I see no reason why this woman should be entitled to any of the assets. I contend that they belong to all the children she has deserted together with the husband. If she had been submissive to her husband and co-operated with him when he made her an offer there would not have been all this trouble. She is instrumental to the division so I contend that she should get nothing.

The Senior Chief's Representative adopted this latter view. Mrs Busang had no entitlement, merely whatever she might receive from her husband's goodwill.

When the *kgotla* considered Tswana custom it found that Gofetamang his wife was not entitled to any property due to the fact that she was instrumental to the divorce, and further that when the marriage was dissolved at the High Court, the children were given to the father. This property should be used for their maintenance. It is true and at the same time in accordance with customary law. I agree with the *kgotla* members that Gofetamang is not entitled to anything. It is reputed that she has all her clothing. Nevertheless this court pleads with Mr Busang to be sympathetic. It is not a court order, it is a request. He should take into account the duration of their marriage and how many children they have had together. He must try and consider her position sympathetically, it is not an order but a humble request.

Informal Justice

How far does this picture conform to the image of informal justice promoting party control and agreement? It is true that both parties to the dispute were asked to express their own views on the situation and respond to each other as well as to the community at large, represented by the *kgotla* members. However, as Abel has noted, 'adversaries in pre-capatalist societies are often unequal in which case the outcomes of informal processes inevitably reflect and reproduce those inequalities' (Abel 1982*a*).

Mrs Busang was less well educated than her husband. She was less articulate and did not share his knowledge of the formal system of justice. Her earning capacity and political influence were not comparable with his. Mrs Busang had never been in formal sector employment and had only begun to generate income for herself outwith traditional sources when she started knitting jerseys at home. Her family was not particularly influential in the village. Mr Busang was a civil servant. He had been a District Commissioner, a highly regarded occupation in Tsabong, and was at the time of the case an Under-Secretary of Works and Communications. Not only was he close to ministerial rank but he belonged to a family that is considered very influential in Molepolole. Clearly the parties were not equally matched in terms of education, earning capacity, and social status.

Mrs Busang did not seem to 'control' the dispute or its outcome at any point. She was consistently subjected to questions and interruptions by the Senior Chief's Representative, while Mr Busang was allowed to state his position virtually uninterrupted, at length, and with no subsequent questions by the SCR. Mr Sebele played an active role throughout the dispute, controlling the boundaries of discussion between the parties. The dispute opened with Mrs Busang setting out the property that she was claiming. The SCR played an inquisitorial role here, geared to specificity and accuracy of statements regarding property. To give an example, he said to Mrs Busang: 'You said there were 10 goats, we would like a full explanation as to how you arrived at the number 10.'

He pursues an aggressive policy towards her statements concerning property:

SCR. Since you have no knowledge of the savings account for the 1,500 pula and no proof that there is any money in the bank, are you withdrawing that claim because there is no evidence of it?

MRS B. Yes.

SCR. A while ago you claimed 10 animals that were reproduced by an ox, from the evidence this is not true because an ox cannot reproduce. Are you withdrawing this claim too?

MRS B. Yes.

SCR. Since you initially claimed 10 goats and there is no convincing evidence that 10 exist are you withdrawing your claim and asking for 6 only?

MRS B. Yes.

SCR. Now there is the question of a claim for 135 pula. The court feels incapable of allowing this claim.

This was the money Mrs Busang claimed from the proceeds of knitting jerseys. She does not agree that the claim should be dropped. He tries two different approaches to get her to abandon it. He begins by maintaining that the claim is not an appropriate one under the customary system and then strikes back by saying that she can only claim what is actually there and she must prove its existence. When she continues to protest he asks her, 'At the High Court, who won the case?', immediately closing the discussion of property and shifting the emphasis to conduct and the underlying assumption of fault on her part.

Immediately after this interchange he throws the questioning open to the *kgotla*. One member picks up the question of conduct and asks, 'Now that they are here, what is the cause of their division?' Unlike the Chief Regent, however, he is told by Mr Sebele,

The time for that question has gone. This case was tried at the High Court and that was where all such questions were asked. All the questions must be based on distribution of property.

Once again he has shifted the area of discussion. This time from the general question of conduct back to the specifics of property although a moment earlier he had altered the focus of the discussion in the opposite direction. When Mr Busang gives his statement it is centred on the case that he presented to the High Court. Mr Sebele has just said that the divorce is not to be discussed and yet Mr Busang is allowed to present the history at length. Mr Sebele only intervenes when Mr Busang starts expressing what he claims are the wishes of the children, that their mother should not receive any property.

When Mrs Busang seeks to question Mr Busang, Mr Sebele intervenes several times. For example, Mrs Busang addresses several questions to Mr Busang aimed at dealing with conduct. 'You stated that at a certain time I deliberately had an abortion. When you noticed this what action did you take? In connection with the statement about bewitching what action did you take? If it's true that I contributed nothing towards the maintenance of the home how is it that I was knitting jerseys for which you have the money?' At this point Mr Sebele intervenes to tell her that she must deal with the reasons put forward for the dissolution of the marriage in the High Court. She is informed that her questions about jerseys are irrelevant.

When she carries on questioning in the same way, for example, by asking—'Was I wrong to desert and go to our people and tell them about our trouble?'—Mr Sebele again intervenes saying that such questions are irrelevant and that she must base her questions on distribution of property.

> Your husband has divorced you and has given his grounds as to why you should forfeit everything in connection with the marriage so you must concentrate on this if you think you should get a share of the assets.

This, however, is what she is doing. Her questions are addressed to the general question of conduct on which her husband rejects her claim to the property. They are not—the ramblings of an incoherent woman. For example, the question—'Since you say I'm a harlot, what action did you take?'—is highly relevant because, in the customary system, if Mr Busang considered her to be unfaithful he should have arranged meetings with her family or the *kgotla* to discuss the matter at the time, rather than raising it long after the event. Yet the intervention of Mr Sebele shifted the focus of debate and she finally ceased to ask any further questions because she became confused.

These few observations on the part played by the Senior Chief's Representative illustrate that in this case the third party was an authoritative figure who directly controlled the proceedings and made (contradictory) decisions about what the focus of the discussion between the parties should be.

If control was exercised by any party in this case it was surely Mr Sebele. As Abel has stressed, 'third parties in pre-capitalist institutions occupy the role of intermediary because they already possess legitimate authority' (Abel 1982a: 4). The SCR is a man of considerable wealth and political power whose position and authority are recognized by the formal system of justice.

Structured Inequality

Thus far, the analysis has concentrated on the position of individual participants in the dispute. Left in those terms it might be dismissed as a unique case, a freak occurrence from which one cannot make generalizations. The outcome is, however, also explicable at a deeper level, in the construction of the gender order among the Bakwena.

Comaroff and Roberts (1981: 18) have warned against the dangers of presenting rules as an internally consistent code, rather than a more loosely constructed repertoire. They maintain that any conduct or relationship is 'potentially susceptible for competing normative constructions' and find that 'Tswana dispute processes simply cannot be reduced to or explained by formalistic models or derivative legal logic'. However, they do admit 'that the normative repertoire plays a significant part in the arguments and discussions that occur in the dispute process' (19).

Schapera has described the dominant role of the husband in Tswana societies.

The husband, once he sets up his own household, is for all practical purposes his own master. The woman on the other hand, passes from the legal control of her parents into that of her husband, who now becomes her guardian and as such responsible for her actions. He is the official head of the household, while she is regarded as his *mothlanka* (servant). She must be in all respects subservient to his will and must live wherever he chooses to build his home. (Schapera 1955: 150–1.)

In using the language of master and servant Professor Schapera is invoking a repertoire of subservience and power. Although he was writing of the 1930s, prevailing norms in the customary system have altered little.

Mr Busang's speech was designed to refer to a normative repertoire relating to conduct, establishing what a bad wife Mrs Busang had been in terms of community values, rather than concentrating on specific issues of property. Good wives are supposed to work for their husbands. Good wives are not harlots and do not subject their husbands to public humiliation—by gossiping as his wife did with his subordinates in Tsabong or by insisting on raising a case in the *kgotla* against his wishes. The most damaging allegation that he makes, on which a large part of his statement concentrates, is that she was involved in witchcraft.

The subject of conduct was raised by a senior member of the *kgotla* after Mrs Busang had given her speech about property. The exchange that took place informed the rest of the debate. It was picked up and manipulated by the SCR and the *kgotla* members who put the onus on her to establish that she had adhered to the role of a good wife and mother. Mrs Busang had an uphill struggle because she had to appeal to a set of norms which place women in a subservient position. The man is the dominant partner and if he makes an assertion the onus is on the woman to disprove it.

When Mrs Busang failed to respond to the very first exchange regarding conduct between the Chief Regent, as *kgotla* member and herself she was seen to accept that she was at fault, because she could not say that her husband did not divorce her without cause. Her position, however, was not quite as clear cut as it might seem. When Mr Busang filed for divorce Mrs Busang was advised that a contested divorce was a costly process. She accepted that their marital relationship had come to an end and was told that Mr Busang had offered to make a settlement regarding property. None of the matters alleged in the divorce were put to proof. However, Mr Busang repeatedly referred to the High Court as endorsing his claim that his wife was at fault and this was accepted by the *kgotla*. This emphasizes the importance of the role that the formal legal system may play in disputes of this kind and the problems that may be created by using it as a reference point. It may be used to legitimize something that is taking place in another context where substantive concepts, here of conduct and its relevance, may be quite different.

The influence of the formal legal system is also apparent in the way that the third party, Mr Sebele, handles the dispute. It was noted earlier that he controlled the dispute by shifting the discussion from property to conduct in an apparently contradictory manner. It might be argued that in so doing he was simply responding to Mr Busang as the more powerful party. This would probably be an over-simplification. Another interpretation might be that his behaviour reflects a blurring of cultural norms and the problems of dealing with the distribution of property on the basis of a European-style community property principle where fault is irrelevant, alongside distribution within the customary system which is based on fault. Mr Sebele's handling of the dispute continually shifts from a European to a Tswana mode of enquiry. When he silences the *kgotla* member who asks about the cause of divorce and declares that the matter has already been dealt with in the High Court and all questions must relate to the distribution of property, he is acting like a European judge, treating the matter as one that has already been adjudicated upon. When he allows Mr Busang to restate the case he raised at the High Court he is acting in a Tswana mode which considers the conduct relevant for Mr Busang to establish that, according to the customary system of the Bakwena, she has no claim to property. He may be seen as trying to provide a synthesis from the two systems. As Gulliver (1979: 22–4) notes, in a parallel discussion of 'negotiation' and 'adjudication', formal and informal legal processes are not mutually exclusive but are influenced by each other and by the same wider social values.

Conclusions

To what extent does this case support or reject the image of informal justice systems as a free bargaining of equals mediated by a benign third party? One view may be that this is simply an individual case and that the outcome is more a reflection of Mrs Busang's inability to negotiate than of any inequality. Another might be that Mrs Busang was 'less skilful' in manipulating the dispute because she could not refute Mr Busang's allegations regarding her conduct and that, in terms of the prevailing ideology, she was indeed at fault as a bad wife and mother and that the outcome in the eyes of the community was therefore perfectly acceptable. But it would be naive to assume that the distribution of negotiating skills is totally unstructured by gender or to assume that community-approved outcomes are consistent with the 'equality' of parties. One cynical male observer commented after the case, 'divorce is based on fault and the woman is always found to be at fault'.

Nor was the third party totally powerless and non-directive in determining the outcome. Although none of the parties were legally represented or trained, the third party hearing the dispute did have the power to impose a solution. Here an objection might be that this case does not provide a true model of informal justice and that this model is closer to a court. There is force in this but it must be noted that this model is not unique to the Chief's *kgotla*. It provides the base for all disputes within the customary system. This is important because one should not simply ascribe Mr Sebele's behaviour to the possession of such formal powers. Even when distinguished between a 'mediator' and an 'adjudicator' on the basis that the former does not possess such powers, Gulliver (1979: 213–14) accepts that a mediator

is not and cannot be, neutral and merely a catalyst. He not only affects the interaction but, at least in part, seeks and encourages an outcome that is tolerable to him in terms of his own ideas and interests. He may even come into conflict with one or both of the parties.

Third parties hearing disputes at every level within the system can be seen to behave in the same way as Mr Sebele, although they do not possess the same formal powers. This indicates one of the conundrums of using Third World examples as instances of informal justice. It is simply impossible to ascertain, on the basis of contemporary studies, the extent to which we are examining traditional or 'mixed' dispute-processing methods. But, as the problem of structural gender inequalities indicates, it is probably romantic to assign all injustices to the influence of the formal system.

It may also be argued that dispute processing among the Bakwena is so far removed from informal justice in Britain that it can only be viewed within its own particular social context. Yet in its own cultural terms this case highlights some of the problems of dispute processing that make one aware of the need carefully to scrutinize concepts of party control and the role of third parties. Such problems are not necessarily unique to one culture. In connection with conciliation in Britain, Bottomley (1985: 179) has warned:

Private ordering can only be detrimental to women; economic, social and psychological vulnerability all militate against the image of the equal bargaining situation which is presumed to be present in mediation for it to be a truly mutual agreement. Ignoring power relationships within the private domain can only reproduce them.

It also shows the problems that women may face when presented with an approach that is said to be in the best interests of the child. The Robinson Committee (1983: 6) sets out its approach to conciliation on the basis that 'it seems to us that if there is a justification for creating special machinery for matrimonial causes it must surely be primarily for the sake of the children'. One of the factors that weighed heavily against Mrs Busang in the *kgotla* was that she was not a good mother. Her husband was given custody of the children. As one *kgotla* member stated:

When considering cases of this nature usually we base our consideration on the position of children whether they are minor or grown up. But in a case where a woman left the husband and left the children with the husband as the case now, she is just like somebody who is dead. I do not think her claim for property is justifiable.

His sentiments were echoed by other *kgotla* members. This is partly a reflection of the Tswana concept of property, which involves a 'collective' notion of property geared to ownership by the family rather than by an individual. Those who own property are seen as being the custodians of it on behalf of their children.

While this difference must be recognized, Mrs Busang's case illustrates that where notions of the family and the interests of children prevail an individual may suffer. In this country, Bottomley (1985: 171) has also warned:

informal patterns of judgment made in the interests of children may hide the value content of their judgments. On both counts the needs of women are likely to be subverted in a concern to maintain parenting. Those who are not mothers, or who are mothers whose children are grown up, will not find their position given any priority.

Finally, to turn a vice into a virtue, the objections to the 'purity' of this instance of informal justice may well be the most significant feature of this in considering Britain. Mrs Busang's case raises interesting questions about 'bargaining in the shadow of the law' and the *relation between* formal and informal justice. It alerts one to the problems of two systems operating side by side; to the possibility that processes and procedures in one may be influential on the other without a full understanding of how those processes and procedures operate.

While these problems may be culturally specific, they point to dangers which may be encountered with conciliation in Britain which will always take place against the backdrop of the legal system. There may be a conciliation process labelled as 'informal' and a court process labelled as 'formal', but they are not separate systems for dealing with marital breakdown. Can one be sure that the norms and values of one will not become blurred with those of the other? In this case, which is typical of Tswana family dispute processing, we have seen the influence of the formal legal system at work on the *kgotla*. But the influence is not all in one direction. Other material illustrates the reverse. It is misleading to view the customary and statutory systems as two independent entities. They are rather part of one process of justice. They are mutually effective and, while labels of 'formal' or 'informal' justice may be applied, these are of little relevance.

Mrs Busang became defined as a troublesome individual who refused to fall within the norm of negotiated agreement without court intervention. May there not be a danger in this country that with the advent of conciliation, those individuals involved in marital breakdown who seek to redress their grievances in the courts may also be regarded as deviants rather than as acting on an entitlement to engage in conflict?

9.   Three Models of Family Mediation

SIMON ROBERTS

There seems to be widespread agreement that the objective of family mediation should be to initiate, nourish, and sustain those fundamental bilateral processes through which parties to domestic conflict may themselves reach joint decisions about the issues which divide them. Beyond that, the picture in Britain today appears to be one of bewildering diversity. The most cursory inspection of the growing literature on 'conciliation' reveals a wide range of assumptions about what constitutes this form of intervention, an impression which is reinforced by such limited research evidence as is available on agency practice.

In this paper, an attempt will be made to identify three basic models of family mediation. These are not derived from observation of any particular agency and it is not argued that practice anywhere conforms directly to one or other of these ideal types. Nor would many contemporary family mediators necessarily be willing to accept one of the labels proposed here as a description of their practice. But it is suggested that the aspirations of most mediators and the realities of their work fall generally within the boundaries marked out here. These models are framed in abstract terms as a means of identifying critical variations in practice and establishing criteria by which their rival approaches may be more rigorously evaluated. The paper begins by defining each model.

Minimal intervention. This type of mediation has the objective of reviving and sustaining a flow of conversation between the parties in much the same fashion as it would have continued but for the conflict. It is based on two assumptions: that the parties are competent to negotiate and implement arrangements for the future; and that it is their meanings, understandings, and objectives that should inform the exchange between them. I have suggested elsewhere that this model identifies four specific tasks for the mediator: '(1) establishing and maintaining contact between parties; (2) providing a forum, in the physical sense, where they can meet face-to-face; (3) constituting, within that forum, a neutral presence supportive of the projects of negotiation; and (4) stimulating a two-way flow of information' (Roberts 1986: 37).

Directive intervention. The second form of intervention involves active steps on the part of the mediator to provide additional information and to influence the content of the decisions to be reached by the parties. The parties are assumed to require the help of a skilled professional to deal with matters at issue between them (such as the future management of children or the rearrangement of existing financial provision). In this type of mediation, the intervener's view of the quarrel becomes central, and energy is devoted to modifying or affirming the parties' perceptions to fit with it. The aim is to achieve and implement decisions which are objectively optimal given the circumstances of the case. This form of mediation thus involves three principal tasks: obtaining and assessing information about the disputants and their quarrel; identifying and evaluating the options available to them; and persuading the parties to adopt the courses of action which the mediator considers, in the light of his or her professional experience, to be most suited to their particular circumstances. The directive mediator thus openly combines 'advice' and help with joint decision-making and is presented as an authoritative specialist who knows better than the parties how the issues confronting them ought to be resolved.

Therapeutic intervention. In this third type of intervention, joint decision-making on specific issues is postponed in favour of an examination of the relationships that have broken down within the family. The mediator begins from an assessment of the parties' approach to each other and uses, openly or covertly, professional therapeutic techniques to reveal and correct pathological elements in this relationship. It is assumed that the particular dispute presented for mediation is a symptom of some underlying and unexamined family malfunction. The problem can only be resolved when these deeper problems have been recognized and the parties' relationship transformed. At a practice level it implies three tasks for the mediator: an examination and assessment of the relationships involved; ensuing corrective intervention to redress the malfunction, or at least to bring the parties to terms with it; a process of joint decision-making in the light of the transformations wrought with the help of therapeutic techniques. This form of intervention inevitably involves the combination of advisory and therapeutic help with assistance in joint decision-making. It aims openly at a break with the original conversation in which the parties were engaged; a new situation is evoked or imposed.

The Models Compared

All forms of mediation—and this, after all, is the objective—change the ways in which disputants view and handle their quarrels. In this process, mediators exercise power, generally in private and under conditions which escape the conventional forms of surveillance to which adjudication is subject. Consequently all mediation carries the risk of unregulated coercion and manipulation.

This risk is reduced where an openly minimal form of intervention is employed. The more the parties remain responsible for the shape of the exchanges between them, and for the content of any decisions that may ultimately be reached, the less likely are they to feel coerced or to suffer the consequences of covert manipulation. There is a more positive advantage in the minimal form: the parties are likely to have a stronger commitment to an outcome they themselves have constructed. Such an outcome will require less in terms of external 'policing'. Similarly, the more weight the parties themselves can be encouraged to carry in the context of mediation, the greater is the possibility that they will later be able to 'manage' any necessary renegotiation of their arrangements by themselves.

The disadvantages of a minimal form are equally clear, and have been widely discussed. These are that the parties will together make arrangements which are to the disadvantage of others, notably their children; or that the stronger of two parties will be able to exercise a coercive domination over the weaker.

The obvious advantage of a directive form of intervention is that the parties will enjoy the benefit of skilled, specialist help in constructing a decision. Options can be identified and evaluated, advice given, and an appropriate outcome proposed. Further, the very presence of a dominant, authoritative professional may provide the necessary stimulus to settlement. These possibilities are all absent in the context of a minimal form of intervention. The potential hazards of activist mediation are just as clear. We are no longer contemplating a bilateral conversation between the parties; as we move away from minimal intervention the mediator's view of the quarrel and his/her preferred solutions are progressively substituted for those of the actors principally involved. At the same time the possibility of unregulated coercion increases.

In favour of a therapeutic form of intervention, it can be argued that in many cases it will be necessary to undertake an examination of relationships within the former family group, and of the circumstances surrounding breakdown, before the parties will be able to cope with their changed circumstances sufficiently to participate in joint decision-making. Against this important advantage it may be argued that necessary counselling and therapeutic help must be kept distinct from joint decision-making if the danger of covert manipulation is to be avoided.

The Context of Family Mediation

The burden of what has been said here is that a number of disparate activities pass for 'mediation' in the family context today. It is important that those practising, and those experiencing, mediation should know exactly what is going on, and be aware of the implications, hazards, and advantages of different kinds of intervention. These points are obvious, but they need to be taken very seriously at this moment when mediation's relationship to adjudication (the ultimate form of coercive intervention) and to the whole complex of diagnostic, advisory, and therapeutic practices lies in the balance.

Take, first, adjudication. In Britain today, and for a number of years now, the encouragement of joint decision-making by the parties themselves has become entangled in the very different project of renovating and refurbishing adjudication. Specifically, mediation has become associated with the long-awaited birth of the family court. As far back as 1974, the Finer Report (1974: 183, 185) at once proposed the establishment of a 'family court', advocated the encouragement of conciliation (which has generally been taken to have meant mediation, although this was never directly spelled out), and required that this conciliation should be 'conducted through the court'. So we find proposed, there, refurbished adjudication together with new official surveillance of extra-judicial attempts at resolution.

Exactly the same mix reappears in the Booth Report of 1985. Formalized conciliation is advocated; but again encapsulated in the court process. Conciliation, says Booth, 'should form a recognised part of legal procedure' (para. 4.53). This juxtaposition of joint decision-making by the parties and court process is taken for granted as an unqualified good to be aimed at. While these proposals have yet to be implemented, experiments along the same lines are taking place in many courts in Britain today. We also hear of similar moves in North America towards 'integrating alternative dispute resolution processes into the public justice system'. The idea of the Multi-door Courthouse, conceived and advocated by Professor Sander, encourages the courts to appropriate the supervision of diagnostic and alternative dispute resolution functions (Sander 1976; 1985).

This direction of developments should be regarded with profound misgivings. The very nature of mediation decision-making, in which the essence is an outcome constructed by the parties in accordance with their own meanings and objectives, is incompatible with being incorporated in, and made auxiliary to, adjudication.

One difficulty with in-court, or court-related, schemes of mediation lies in the inescapable, and indeed desirable, authority which the courts and court personnel widely enjoy. Courts are places where authoritative seniors tell us what to do, and are explicitly coercive in doing so. We are all aware of the apparatus which is held in readiness if we disobey judges. This circumstance makes court-related mediation extraordinarily problematic. I do not believe that free, uncoerced negotiation is possible in the vicinity of the court or under the supervision of court personnel. The evidence so far available on how parties feel about court-directed mediation in Britain suggests that they experience it as coercive. Meanings are at the very least going to get muddled in the minds of disputants if processes over which they supposedly retain control are conflated with those which are essentially about externally imposed decisions. The beauty of adjudication, if you can call it that, is that we know unambiguously what we are experiencing.

There is a second, equally serious, cost in relating mediation and adjudication too closely. That is harm to the court process itself. Judges are authoritative superiors in whom power to decide is vested and few would want that position changed, however they may feel about the performance of particular incumbents. But that authority may well be damaged if judges get too closely identified with mediation and the general management and oversight of negotiation. The relation of the mediator to the disputant is quite different to that of the judge, and I am not persuaded that a shifting back and forward between those two postures is feasible.

Family mediation also seems to be at risk from another quarter—the whole field of advisory, diagnostic, counselling, and therapeutic forms of intervention. In themselves these are desirable kinds of help, but they are not appropriately combined with decision-making on specific issues, which I see as being the core object of mediatory intervention.

In Britain today mediation is increasingly informed by theory derived from family therapy, notably family systems theory. It is widely argued that the process of mediation must be preceded by an investigation, examination, and assessment of the feelings and family circumstances of the disputants, leading to a process through which the conflict can be 're-framed' with the help of the mediator, and the views of the parties transformed. Such a process seems to me fraught with serious hazards and potentially extremely harmful, when practised in close association with attempts at joint decision-making. Assessment processes involve a power on the part of the mediator very different from that of the judge: covert in the sense that it may not be experienced by the parties; unregulated in the sense that institutional safeguards are absent.

Overall, mediation should remain removed from adjudication and therapeutic intervention in terms of time, place, and the specialist personnel involved. It should ideally develop as a discrete, autonomous form of third-party help, towards the minimalist, rather than the activist, end of the spectrum. Why this insistence on a minimal form? As I have argued elsewhere (Roberts 1986), the most valuable help which a mediator can give in family disputes—particularly those where children provide a continuing link between the parties—is in creating and sustaining a productive dialogue between them. Bilateral negotiation, where it is possible, represents the surest route to an outcome acceptable to both parties—they are most likely to live with what they themselves have constructed. Subsequently, too, a continuing conversation must remain, after the transition and reorganization associated with break-down, the means through which business relating to surviving aspects of the relationship—here children—can best continue to be transacted.

If the objective of mediation is seen to be to revive the flow of conversation which would have taken place but for the family conflict that led it to be discontinued, and if both external coercion and covert manipulation are to be avoided, a limited, clearly defined role for the mediator suggests itself. This should be broadly confined to securing communication and promoting the exchange of information between the parties that is essential to joint decision-making. In achieving this, four basic tasks have been identified above: (1) establishing and maintaining contact between the parties; (2) providing a forum, in the physical sense, where they can meet face to face; (3) constituting, within that forum, a neutral presence supportive of the project of negotiation; and (4) stimulating a two-way flow of information.

A truly minimal form of mediation would be complete at this point but arguably the kind of mediator I have in mind might go further in three directions: (1) providing some ground rules in accordance with which the exchange is to take place; (2) helping the parties to articulate the issues which divide them; and (3) identifying the various options that seem to be available.

10. Empowerment or Enforcement? Some Questions about Power and Control in Divorce Mediation

ROBERT DINGWALL

Adversarial forms of dispute resolution are deeply embedded in Anglo-American law. Since the late nineteen sixties, however, they have been the target of an increasing barrage of criticism. Family law has stood in the front line of this attack, over its handling of divorce cases. Critics have argued that the adversarial process is simultaneously inefficient and ineffective. It imposes unnecessary costs on the parties and the legal system, fails to promote compliance with support obligations, and stimulates continuing disputes over custody and access. If only people could reach their own agreements rather than have solutions forced upon them by court decisions, money would be saved, arrangements for support payments, custody, and access would be more reliable, and settlements would evolve with the changing circumstances of the parties. Mediation, or conciliation, provides a forum in which such agreements can be made. More recently, however, this movement has itself been criticized (e.g. Abel 1982*b*). Its partial institutionalization is seen as a response to the success of traditionally disadvantaged litigants in gaining access to the public arena of the courts and using its formal procedures against previously dominant groups. Informal justice may be a way of moving these disputes back into private settings where weaker parties can be pressed into settling for less than they could gain from litigation.

The question of control is central to these debates. Does mediation really offer a party-controlled settlement process or is it merely substituting the insidious influence of the mediator for the open decision of the judge? This chapter begins by examining the mediators' own discussion of these issues. But the question is fundamentally an empirical one. The core of the chapter, then, is a detailed analysis of mediator behaviour in a voluntary-sector, British conciliation agency. It will be argued that the answer is less simple than the question might imply and that this gives rise to considerable problems for organizational design and public policy.

Party Control: The Mediators' View

One of the principal claims of divorce mediators is that they act merely as facilitators, using their professional skills to contain the emotional charge of the conflict and focus the disputants on the task of agreement, while leaving the determination of the actual outcome to the parties. As Roberts (1983: 540 original emphasis) puts it, mediation represents 'a move *away* from third-party decision making toward a solution which the parties themselves have constructed: the power to decide is taken from outsiders and is shifted back to the parties themselves'. This process is frequently described in terms of *empowerment*. In one influential American text, for example, Haynes (1981: xi) asserts that,

The nature of the legal system removes a great deal of power from the couple. Thus, one of the most important events in their lives, the dissolution of the marriage, takes place in large part outside of their control. This book proposes an alternative way of dissolving the marriage: divorce mediation. I seek to establish that people can be empowered to negotiate their own divorce settlement outside of the legal system and in a nonadversarial way.

In its pure form, however, party control would entail the possibility of grossly unequal and insensitive settlements being imposed by the strongest disputant.

While Haynes contemplates this prospect with equanimity in indus-trial conflicts, he clearly has a well-defined sense of what he considers to be morally acceptable behaviour in family disputes. As he insists, 'the mediator does not simply facilitate a divorce: s/he does it within a value context' (Haynes 1981: 131–2). Neutrality in a situation of social, economic, or psychological inequality between the parties may allow one spouse to exploit the other. 'Real' negotiations, according to Haynes (1981: 62–3), are only possible if the mediator can deliberately enhance the power of the weaker party, usually the wife. Similarly if other parties, especially children, seem likely to be victimized by an agreement, the mediator has a duty to speak out and 'act forcibly' (Haynes 1981: 129–32). As Parkinson (1986b: 161) comments, from Britain,

Many conciliators are reluctant to accept that their responsibility is exclusively towards the two parties to the dispute, as though children were no more than sacks of corn to be haggled over or divided in half . . . at some point there has to be a dividing line between supporting parental autonomy and, to take an extreme but possible situation, colluding with child abuse.

It would seem, then, that divorce mediation can incorporate some elements of *enforcement*, where settlements are required to meet moral criteria external to the standards of the disputants.[1] If this is the case, then it would raise the possibility that mediation does not increase party control of disputes but merely imposes a different set of norms about their conduct and outcome. One way of investigating this is to examine the process of social interaction between mediators and clients.

Mediation as an Encounter

Mediation sessions are encounters, defined by Goffman (1972: 17–18) as gatherings with a 'single visual and cognitive focus of attention; a mutual and preferential openness to verbal communication; a heightened mutual relevance of acts; an eye-to-eye ecological huddle that maximizes each participant's opportunity to perceive the other participants' monitoring of him.' The participants organize their interaction in such gatherings by reference to a frame, an array of presuppositions which establish which topics, motives, actions, and affects are to be treated as legitimate. Two categories of encounters can be distinguished: those which are institutionalized, in the sense that they are replayed with some regularity by members of a recognized group of people, and those which are one-off, where one or more participants may be unfamiliar with the framing. Each of these categories can be further divided according to the type of regulatory practices which are adopted to secure compliance with the frame: *mundane conversations*, where participants keep each other in order by a variety of informal and consensually based techniques; *orchestrated encounters*, like seminars, where order is maintained by the actions of one party who is recognized by the others as an arbiter; and *pre-allocated encounters*, like court hearings, where order is based on an elaborate and formal body of rules about who may speak when and on what topics and from what location (Dingwall 1980). Any party who is considered to have failed correctly to orient to the encounter framing, or to come to order when required, risks being judged socially incompetent or mind-less (Goffman 1983).

From this, it can be argued that, if the nature of mediation encounters tends towards empowerment, their organization should tend to look like that of a mundane conversation. Given that the need for mediation arises out of some breakdown in the relationship between the parties, some intervention by the mediator may be anticipated but this should take the form of guaranteeing that the conventions of mundane conversation will be honoured. If, on the other hand, mediation sessions look more like orchestrated encounters, where the organization is closely controlled by the mediator, we may conclude that a particular version of the process and outcome is being enforced.

The Data

The data presented here are taken from fieldwork in an independent divorce mediation service run by a charitable trust in an English provincial city. At the time of the study, the agency employed five women: three mediators on a sessional basis, together with a full-time co-ordinator, who performed some mediation as well as administrative, public-relations, and fund-raising work, and a full-time secretary/recep-tionist. All the mediators were qualified social workers. The agency dealt with about 300 cases per year. Most of these were referred by lawyers at an early stage in the divorce process but there was also some self-referral. Clients were invited to donate funds to the agency according to their means, but the main sources of revenue were central and local government programmes for aid to voluntary social services. Forty-five interviews were recorded from fifteen cases. In addition, ten days' observation was completed, covering office duties and intake and yielding about 28,000 words of fieldnotes.

This study was intended as a pilot for a larger project to examine the impact of different organizational settings and theories of practice on the process of mediation. That objective was frustrated by funding and access difficulties. These data, then, are not collected in a way which would justify claims that they were necessarily representative of British practice or even of practice in this particular agency. Nevertheless, they are of importance as evidence of what *can* happen and, as Mitchell (1983) observes, single case studies have a validity of their own in the development of a theoretical understanding of social institutions and processes through their exploration of the possible logical connections between a series of observations.

Framing-up Interviews

Mediation encounters differ from institutionalized settings, like the medical consultations discussed by Strong (1979), in that, at least for the divorcing couple, they more typically have a one-off character. Seeing a mediator is not like seeing a doctor, something which we do from an early age with some frequency and with ample opportunity to observe various idealizations in books, film, or television. The first task for the agency personnel, then, was to construct an appropriate frame for mediator--client encounters. After a brief discussion of this process, the remainder of the paper will examine some of the possibilities made available to the participants by this framing.

The mediation service was officially a 'drop-in' agency, although about half of its clients were referred by their lawyers. Self-referral can, however, present difficulties for the staff. Too close an involvement with a spouse who initiates contact with them unilaterally is seen to have a possibility of compromising their ability to involve the other party.[2] Their attempts to overcome this provide some of the most explicit descriptions of the encounter framing. Data extract 1 is my hand note of a mediator speaking on the telephone to a woman whose husband had previously visited the office to ask them to take on the case.

Extract 1

Well there are two questions really—one is whether you should see me or someone else—I just asked him to take a message to you, but you might want to start with someone new, but I didn't talk to him for very long. The second question is whether we can actually fit it in this week . . . He came in as an enquiry, and I explained to him that we only work with both partners, and that our task is to clarify issues rather than to make assumptions . . . We can only help if we can actually start afresh with you and you actually want that contact . . . I didn't ask him a lot of questions . . . But he has now agreed to go with you to the Marriage Guidance, that's fine . . . the great thing is for there to be some sort of dialogue and discussion . . . It may just serve to show each of you that you had some needs that the other wasn't meeting and some part of you that the other didn't recognize. It doesn't mean to say the marriage isn't workable . . . when he said that your son was taking his 'O' levels, I said that you must take the children's needs into account, even if it was a sudden decision (. . .) I could see him on his own if I was going to see you on your own. Sometimes when people have deep doubts and confusions, it's difficult to bring them out in front of their partners. It sounded so complicated, I asked him to come in and see what we could offer (. . .)

The frame described here sets out the character that will be ascribed to the parties as self-directed but not selfish individuals, motivated by a desire to reach a settlement which is fair to each of them and to their children through a process of talk drawing on their capacity for reasoned discussion. In this process, the mediator will be neutral as between the parties. To the extent that her ability to display such neutrality has been compromised by her previous contact with the husband she will stand down. But she is not neutral with respect to the frame. First of all, she sets herself up as the distributor of the opportunity to talk. It will depend upon whether a mediator is available and whether the parties are prepared to accept the service's policies about the conditions on which sessions will be held. Secondly, she makes it clear that she will determine the consistency of conduct and frame, 'I said that you *must* take the children's needs into account' [emphasis added]. The mediator will control the organization of interaction and judge compliance with the moral character ascribed by the frame, features which are characteristic of orchestrated encounters.

In this agency, framing-up was reinforced by an institutionalized preference for meeting each party separately for about one hour a few days before a joint session. These separate interviews are, however, more than just occasions for telling one version of the story: they also provide an opportunity for mediators to perform additional work on the framing of the joint encounter. We can bring out the effects of this by tracing the development of a specific case, handled by another mediator.

Frame Work

This case involved a working-class couple, Mr and Mrs Pinnock, who had been married for more than thirty years. They lived with two adult sons in a local authority house, whose tenancy was in the husband's name. One son was working but Mr Pinnock and the other son were both unemployed and receiving social security benefits. Mrs Pinnock's professed motives for petitioning were the lack of emotional support from her husband and his arguments with their sons about contributions to the rent. He claimed that he had always been a good provider and that he was only pressing the sons for rent because the calculation of his social security benefit assumed a contribution from them. If his wife really wanted a divorce she could have one as long as he kept the matrimonial home in order to stay near his friends.

The prospects for a settlement might seem quite good once Mrs Pinnock understood that her husband would not contest the petition unless she wanted the house. She believed that the local authority would rehouse the two sons and herself, even if it meant leaving the neighbourhood. But the mediator told me after the joint session that she thought the wife was seriously misinformed about the availability of alternative local authority accommodation and the likelihood of this being offered for her sons.

The amount of frame work in the mediator's session with the wife is fairly small, probably because the impetus for mediation has come from her solicitor and she is assumed to be well informed. Nevertheless, the mediator does take at least one opportunity to reiterate the framing principles we have already documented (extract 2).[3] Mrs Pinnock asserts *her* compliance with the moral assumptions of the frame (lines 1–2). She has a capacity to talk which she is willing to use in order to settle the dispute, a statement which she recycles into a progressively stronger form (lines 4–10) as the mediator witholds any display of affiliation (lines 3, 6, 8). It is not just her word, there is also the evidence of her son. It is not just that her husband is not willing to talk, he 'flares up'. Thus, *his* capacity to act within the frame is proposed as problematic. But the mediator has not yet met him. The neutral responses are consistent with her official stance of not making judgments until both sides have been heard, a message which is reinforced as she formulates her role as an orchestrator at lines 11–15. In contrast with the mediator's behaviour, Mrs Pinnock enthusiastically affiliates herself to this statement of the frame. Here is an opportunity to display rather than assert her compliance.

EXTRACT 2

```
1    W    Well if he wants to talk I mean I'm willing to talk
2    W    because you can't talk at home because ⌈as, as
3    M                                           ⌊mm
4    W    the eldest boy said if only you'd sit down and talk
5    W    dad
6    M      Mm
7    W        we might get somewhere
8    M                              Mm
9    W                                  but you see ee would never,
10   W    ee won't do th⌈at, ee just flares
11   M                  ⌊Well sometimes if you come to a neutral
12   M    place
13   W        Yes
14   M           with somebody else there ⌈it makes it that mu⌈ch easier
15   W                                     ⌊thas right          ⌊ Yes
16   W          Oh well I yes it do  don't it, yes⌈
17   M                                            ⌊Hmm⌈
18   W                                                ⌊Well thank you ever so
```

Frame work is more explicit in the opening and closing sequences of the husband's interview (extract 3). In this opening sequence the mediator seems to be uncertain about how far Mr Pinnock understands the nature of the mediation process. He is bursting to get his problem on the floor (lines 11–15) but the mediator tries to hold him back while she formulates the framing (lines 21–47). She takes him through this quite slowly with frequent micro-pauses opening opportunities for him to come in and clarify any problems. In some detail, we can note the establishment of a joint focus on this topic (lines 22–5), the assertion of the conciliator's neutrality (lines 31–45), and the statements of acceptable conduct in the

EXTRACT 3

```
 1    M    Did you realize your wife had been to see me already today
 2    H    No my love no
 3    M                No she came this morning
 4    H    I don't know nothing
 5    M    Right but you, you were told about us by your solicitor were you
 6    H    I was told that er you would be writing to me
 7    M                                              Yes
 8    H                                                 that er
 9    H    y'know
10    M        Yes
11    H            It's a pity really because erm (0.4) well I'll tell
12    H    what I'm havin' trouble (   ) now (0.6) (   ) now officially my
13    H    social security (0.2) my two eldest boy well my eldest boy my
14    H    youngest they're to give me so much for the rent you know what
15    H    I mean
16    M          Ye:s
17    H             (Well)
18    M                    Social security said that did the⌈y
19    H                                                     ⌊Well that's what
20    H    they said (        )
                          ⌈
21    M                    So before we get too fa:r Mr Pinnock can I
22    M    just make sure that we both understand you know why you've come
23    M    that we both understand you know why you've come ⌈here and the
24    H                                                     ⌊Yeh
25    M    way in which we can help I don't know if your solicitor explained
26    M    very much about it did he
27    H    Not a lot n⌈o
28    M               ⌊Noho well (.) we exist (.) to see if we can help
29    M    cou ⌈ples
30    H        ⌊Yeh
31    M            you and your wife (.) to resolve any (.) difficulties
32    M    between you
33    H            Mmm
34    M                really at a point when your marriage is probably or
35    M    possibly ending (.) so (0.2) today I'm hoping to discuss
36    M    with you how you see things and what you see as the main
37    M    difficulties
38    H            Yeh
39    M                um to see if there is some way in which I can help
40    M    you and your wife resolve them (.) and sort them out in a more
41    M    friendly way but I don't have to report to anyone I don't have to
42    M    ⌈to r⌉eport to your solicitor an I won't be repeating to  your wife
43    H    ⌊N o ⌋
44    M    anything unless you ⌈(.)⌉ are happy about it so we are talking just
45    H                        ⌊No ⌋
46    M    the two of us togeth⌈er
47    H                        ⌊Yeh I know what you mean my love yeh
48    M    Right sorry I just wanted to get ⌈that clear
49    H                                     ⌊s'all right I know what you mean
50    M    but as I say it's gonna be a waste of time because I'll tell you
51    M    why because (0.2) now (0.4) they'll owe me twelve (   ) my rent now
52    M    because I've got the two boys livin at home.
```

joint interview (lines 40–1). This last comes out more conspicuously in the closing sequence (extract 4). The prospects for the joint session are made to hinge on Mr Pinnock's behaviour. He depicts his wife as intransigent and attacks her motivation. She is not a self-directed actor but is being

EXTRACT 4

```
 1   M   Well if you feel like that then I feel we can do something
 2   M   because if you don't you want to sort of be nice but sort things
 3   M   out
 4   H       Yeh
 5   M           fairly then I think there's a very good chance we can
 6   H   I don't think so my love
 7   M                       Wehhell
 8   H                           She got the boys behind er
 9       an tha's
10   M           Ye⌈:s
11   H            ⌊they wants me out (0.5)
12   M   Well let's see
13   H               that's straight up ⌈I mean I'm not I said I'm not
14   M                                  ⌊Mm
15   H   beatin about the bush
16   M                       Mm (.) well you're saying OK to the divorce
17   M   aren't you
18   H       Yeh
19   M           but you'd like to keep the home
20   H                                   I'd like to keep the
21   H   home yeh
22   M   Mm and she's saying I want a divorce and I'd also like the home so
23   M   the thing you're really not agreeing about is the house ⌈isn't it
24   H                                                           ⌊that's
25   H   right my dear yeh
26   M   OK well we'll discuss that on Tuesday
```

pressed by their sons (lines 6–15). But the mediator focuses upon his aspiration to be 'nice' and to be 'fair' (lines 2 and 5), although she leaves open the crucial question of what will actually count as behaviour recognizable in these terms. As in the earlier interviews, she witholds her support from one party's attack on the other (lines 10, 12, 14, and 16). She begins to close the session by emphasizing the limited nature of the disagreement, although this might seem to be a zero-sum game. Nevertheless, her formulation of the dispute attracts Mr Pinnock's endorsement (lines 20–1, 24–5).

The Pinnocks came back for a joint session the following week. The meeting began with the mediator summarizing the contents of the separate interviews and re-emphasizing the joint commitment to solving the outstanding problems. She stated her understanding that the parties had agreed on the principle of the divorce, which they both accepted, and then introduced the dispute over the tenancy of the house. She acknowledged its symbolic importance to both of them and focused them on the practical implications of the divorce for their living arrangements. If they could not live together, someone would have to move out. Mrs Pinnock asserted a moral right to the house based on her care of it while Mr Pinnock put forward a legal claim based on his payment of the rent. The mediator suggested that he might not be able to rely on this in court but the introduction of the topic of the rent diverted the discussion into the dispute between Mr Pinnock and the sons over their financial contributions, which Mrs Pinnock uses to question his capacity as a father (extract 5). The mediator tries to head this off (lines 15–17) and Mrs Pinnock then springs an offer to abandon her claim to the house (lines 19–20). What is the response to this? The first point to make is that neither the mediator nor the husband rush to respond. There is a perceptible pause at line 21 before the mediator takes the next turn. Her utterance (line 22), however, appears to undercut the status of the offer. Mrs Pinnock's statement at lines 19–20 opens the possibility of the mediator's next turn being something line, 'What do you say to that Mr Pinnock?' This would pick up the wife's direct offer and allocate the next turn to Mr Pinnock to reply. But the turn is given back to Mrs Pinnock and the focus only comes back to her husband at lines 28–9 when the mediator is trying to emphasize again to the wife that he has already agreed to the divorce.

There appear to be two possible ways of analysing lines 22–7. One would be to treat it as a checking out exercise by the mediator. In small civil disputes, the parties are often uncertain what they would settle for

EXTRACT 5

```
1   W   I mean as the children say now (0.1) granted they're willing
2   W   to admit that he's always given them plenty of presents
3   W   expensive presents
4   M                 Mm
5   W                     But they've never 'ad a father, he's never
6   W   been a proper father
7   M                 Mm
8   W                     He's never been interested in anything
9   W   they've done
10  H               No because they was always watchin telly that's
11  H   why
12  W     Oh we always get back to thⸯat Iⸯ'm ever so sorry it's just
13  M                             ⌊Heh ⌊Heh
14  W   an hopeless question
15  M               ↑I think the telly is responsible for a↑lot of
                                                         [
16  H                                                     (
17  M   arguments ⌉in a lot of f⌈amilies, isn't it
18  H            ⌋)            ⌊(        )
19  W                                         Put the
20  W   house aside never mind about the house you give me the divorce
21      (0.1)
22  M   Well he said he ↑ would
23  W   Well if heˉll give me the divorce he can do what he likes with
24  W   the house
25      (2.0)
26  M   Do you ↓ really mean that Mrs Pinnock
27  W   I want a divorce
28  M   We:ll (0.5) now (.) let me, let me ask Mr Pinnock again Y:ou
29  M   are saying that you feel the marriage has ended
```

and part of the orchestration work involves getting them to formulate precise demands and offers as a preliminary to bargaining. Against this, Mrs Pinnock's offer is very clear and specific. If the mediator had any reason to be uncertain, it is surely removed by lines 23–4. Yet she still does not put the offer to Mr Pinnock.

We might, then, prefer an alternative interpretation which hears lines 22–7 as an enquiry into Mrs Pinnock's competence to bargain. Is her mental state such that she actually means what she says? There are two unusual features about lines 19–20. First, it is only the second time that Mrs Pinnock has spoken directly to her husband. All her other utterances have been addressed through the mediator, referring to Mr Pinnock in the third person. The previous use of the second person 'you' is more like that usage, in that Mrs Pinnock is joining an attempt by the mediator to unsettle her husband's confidence in his claim to the house. The second point is that the mediator has already clearly established that there is no dispute about the principle of the divorce. If Mrs Pinnock believes that there is, it implies that she is not tracking the course of the meeting very closely. On both counts, Mrs Pinnock can be seen as frame-breaching: by cutting out the mediator and by losing her grip on the topical coherence of the interaction. The mediator's next turn (line 22) begins to repair this damage by bringing Mrs Pinnock back to the making of offers through her and by reiterating that there is agreement about the divorce itself. Mrs Pinnock's offer at lines 19–20 is discounted by its out-of-frame character and made into evidence of her shaky grip on the bargaining. The mediator's control of the frame takes the session off into other directions.

This fragment alone does not allow us to decide between these interpretations if, indeed, they are in direct competition. It may well be that offers are only checked out when they sound at odds with the framing of the session. Some further evidence can, however, be found later in the interview.

The house disappears from the discussion for a while after this extract as the mediator tries, with some success, to deal with the subsidiary dispute about the sons' contribution to the rent. Having done this, she returns to the property dispute (lines 1–2, extract 6). Mrs Pinnock aligns herself with the mediator (line 3) to the extent of echoing her phrasing and this seems to encourage the mediator into another attempt to get an agreement. She begins with a standard counselling technique of bracketing the subsequent interaction (lines 7 and 10).[4] Whatever is talked about from this point is within a new, special frame of fantasy and supposition. Mrs Pinnock again aligns herself with this (line 8). Despite

EXTRACT 6

```
 1    M    And I hope it won't be long before you can actually resolve
 2    M    what is goin to happen about┌the house
 3    W                                └I hope so
 4         (1.2)
 5    M    Right
 6         (1.0)
 7    M    Let's just sort of be, er fantasize a little bit
 8    W    Yes
 9         (1.5)
10    M    Supposing
11         (2.2)
12    M    you, you come to a crunch (.) and one of you has to go
13         (1.0)
14    M    now
15         (0.7)
16    M    could you find (.) a flat┌↑I know you don't want to
17    H                             └ (Well now that's)      Well
18    H    that'd be up to the council my┌ love
19    M                                  └Well then
20         (0.7)
21    M    do you think you could (.) get
22         (1.0)
23    M    ┌somewhere that would suit you
24    H    └(I shall have to)
25         (0.4)
26    M    by yourself
27         (0.2)
28    M    ┌because I ↑ know ↓ you said you wanted to stay in the same
29    H    └(        )
30    M    area
31         (0.3)
32    H    Yes my love┌I (its up to the council)
33    W               └There's even one-bedroomed flats in our ro:ad
34    M    Are there
35    W    Ye:s
36         (1.0)
37    M    What would you┌ feel
38    H                  └ Well at present the council as I
39    H    told you will not (let me have one of┌ em)
40    M                                         └ No
41         [in-breath by the conciliator as if to go on]
42         (0.2)
43    H    so
44         (1.2)
45    H    you can cut that, you can forget that ┌now
46    M                                          └Well I'm, I'm
47    M    asking you sort of
48         (0.4)
49    M    pretend
50         (0.6)
51    M    really because I you know I think as long as you both
52    M    dig your heels in then nobody's going to get anywhere
53    M    are they?
54    H    (Erh)
55    M    The court's goin to decide for you
56    H    I know tha:at I know ┌tha:at
57    M                         └But (.) that's going ter cost money.
58    M    it's going to take ┌time.  Is  t h e r e   n o  w a y
59    H                       └Well we're never gonna get anywhere here
```

```
60   H      ┌ are we)
61   M      │ in which you could
62   W      └ ↑ I want a way that gets it over quicker get the
63   W        divorce over an settled
64   M        Hmm
65   W        As quick ┌as I can
66   M               └Well    what happens with a divorce is, i:f
67   M        it goes through you get the first bit of it which is
                                                    [continues]
```

the fact that she only has the wife's agreement on this new framing, the mediator presses the first part of the 'game' on Mr Pinnock in the form of a question (lines 10–16). I think we must infer some non-verbal work which moves from the general 'you' of line 12 to the specific 'you' of line 16. Mr Pinnock, however, refuses to involve himself (lines 17 and 18). This is done with a courteous form in his local dialect 'my love' and an indirect disagreement. His willingness to act is not on the line: matters depend on third-party decisions over which he has no influence.

In this sequence, then, the mediator uses her control of the frame to put Mr Pinnock into a circumscribed position by her question of lines 10–16. If he agrees, this amounts to giving ground in the negotiation. If he refuses, he can be heard as breaking frame by not joining in the game of supposition. He tries to avoid this fork by building an indirect rejection, pointing to his lack of power (lines 17–18). But, by virtue of having posed the question, the mediator has acquired an entitlement to decide whether it has been properly answered. She clearly does not hear Mr Pinnock's reply as acceptable, since she recycles the question in a more direct form (lines 19–30). By making the question more explicit, we may infer that she is trying to give him an opportunity to excuse his response to the first version as a misunderstanding. But Mr Pinnock does not take up this offer and repeats his original rejection (line 32). The third version of the question (line 37) accepts this by its highly elliptical form, which now assumes that he has heard and understood both of the previous versions. His refusal to produce an expected response is established as intentional.

One feature which may be worth noting is her apparent reluctance to give way when he tries to speak. Mr Pinnock attempts to get in at three possible completion points (lines 17, 24, and 29). On the first and last occasions the mediator perceptibly raises her voice to talk across him. He gets his turn only when she has completed her acknowledgement of his feelings (lines 16 and 28–30). I think this may have something to do with an attempt to display her neutrality and indicate that she does know that she is asking him to forgo something he wants. Nevertheless she is indicating that she considers his finding a flat as a reasonable and discussable option, and asserting her pre-emptive right to speak as the orchestrator.

By line 37 Mr Pinnock is plainly getting impatient and in line 45 comes close to departing from the sullen courtesy he has displayed towards the mediator as he starts on something like 'you can cut that out' and self-corrects to the politer 'you can forget that'. The mediator's response is to reinvoke the frame from lines 7 to 10 and underline his breach. This is only pretence in which everybody is supposed to be good humoured about an unacceptable proposition just to see if it really is so bad. The mediator goes from this to put him under increasing pressure in lines 51–61.

First she points up his intransigence. Although this is done in a superficially even-handed way it is built out of criticism of Mr Pinnock and (line 54) he identifies himself as the recipient. Mrs Pinnock's interventions have all been in alignment with the mediator (lines 3, 8, 33, and 35). She has agreed to play the game and even contributed to it. Moreover, the mediator then introduces what seems to be the nearest thing to a threat that mediators use—we can do this the easy way here or the hard way in court. As William Felstiner and Austin Sarat's paper also shows, litigation seems invariably to be depicted as expensive, time-consuming, and emotionally painful. All of these statements may well be true but what is interesting is the way in which they are used to attack the seriousness of Mr Pinnock's attachment to the framing of this session, giving the mediator a similar leverage to that of the divorce lawyer facing a client reluctant to settle.

We can, then, argue from these data that the mediator is using her control of the encounter frame to push for an agreement which leaves Mrs Pinnock in possession of the house. She has put Mr Pinnock into a position where he can only prove his compliance for the framing of his character by giving way on this point. The final piece of evidence which I want to offer underlines Mr Pinnock's frustration (extract 7). It begins (lines 1–20) with some strongly affiliative talk between the mediator and Mrs Pinnock. Mrs Pinnock is grateful (line 4) and underlines her concession over the disputed rent (lines 7–11). The mediator stresses that she has got her husband's agreement to the divorce (lines 15–20), although it is hard to find unequivocal evidence for this on tape. In acknowledging this, however, Mrs Pinnock lets slip the apparent offer about the house again (line 22). Mr Pinnock boils over as Mrs Pinnock desperately retracts with the mediator's endorsement, as she laughs at Mr Pinnock (line 25) and echoes the wife's strong claim to the house (line 32). Mr Pinnock's attack (lines 23 and 24) seems to be directed at both his wife and at the mediator.

EXTRACT 7

```
 1    M    Right so we'll leave it at that ⌈ ↓shall we
 2    W                                   ⌊   Yes
 3         (1.0)
 4    W    Yes thank you for trying        ⌈(      )
 5    M                                    ⌊Hmn
 6         (7.0)
 7    W    We are much clearer really except I'll give im the money
 8    W    for the rent
 9         (0.4)
10    M    I ⌈ think you        (and I've said)              ⌈
11    W      ⌊ I'll give im ↑ five pounds it won't get very far↑  anyway
12    M    I think you're clear about your divorce ↓ you know ⌈don't you
13    W                                                       ⌊definitely
14    W    clear about the divorce definite
15    M    But I think you are clearer together I know ⌈you've got to
16    W                                                ⌊Hm
17    M    set it right with Mr⌈ Ritz
18    W                        ⌊ Hmm
19         (0.6)
20    M    but your husband is saying ⌈yesss (.) (he does seem to be)
21    W                               ⌊ Yes as long as he'll say yes
22    W    he can I said he can take the house
23    H    There you ↑ are she says ↑I can take the house now then
24    H    Just a minute ago ⌈she says I couldn't    what's she want?
25    M                      ⌊Huhuh
26    W                                      ↓  Yeh but I mean if he wants to
27    W    just ↓No ⌈I don't mean it like ↓ th:at.   I mean if he's only
28    H         ⌊(          )
29    W    gonna hang out for the sake of havin the house I don wan him
30    W    to take the house definitely not⌈
31    H                             [door open]⌈(↓That's it then)[door slams]
32    M                                        ↓No
33         (18.0 with sobs in pause)
```

He tries to appeal to the mediator ('There you *are* then') to recognize his wife as confused and indecisive but the mediator's laughter (line 25) seems to reject this. The floor is left for his wife's attack on him as obstinate and unreasonable and he can find no other exit but the door.

The mediator, then, seems to be trying to dissuade one party from offering an agreement which the other would accept and to persuade the other to a different agreement. No doubt many people would think the mediator had acted quite properly in this case. Mrs Pinnock was audibly in a state of emotional arousal and a settlement on the terms she offered would, by most possible criteria, have been against her own interests. Through her interventions, the mediator could be seen merely to have equalized the bargaining position between a woman who was desperate for a divorce and a man who did not care greatly either way but was capable of setting a price on his co-operation. On the other hand, if mediation is about client-determined agreements, the mediator had clearly obstructed an agreement that the parties could have reached with her help. With the possible exception of extract 7 line 25, where the mediator is heard by Mr Pinnock as laughing at him, her actions cannot simply be dismissed as an example of bad practice. These data show ample evidence of textbook skills. The mediator maintains her neutrality, sustains the focus of the interview, and employs a variety of techniques in the hope of producing agreement. But it will be an agreement on her terms.

The Implications of Orchestration

Even on this limited presentation and analysis, it should be clear that mediators can play a very active role in orchestrating these encounters in ways which seem inconsistent with the aspiration to party control. In this case, it is clear that the mediator has her own view of what will constitute an acceptable outcome and is able to make use of her control of the encounter frame to push for this.

The question though, is whether it could ever be any different. A firm answer to that must await further detailed empirical studies, but such data as we have certainly encourages a negative answer. Silbey and Merry (1986), for instance, examined 40 mediators conducting 175 sessions in three programmes from the North Eastern United States. They show that mediators tended to operate with one or other of two distinctive styles, 'bargaining' or 'therapeutic'. The choice was related less to the nature of the dispute or the clients than to the mediators' own preferences and work setting.

This conclusion can also be reached on purely theoretical grounds. A mediator's influence derives from the triadic structure of these encounters.[5] As Simmel observed almost eighty years ago,

. . . there is no triad . . . in which the third member does not play a mediating role. This happens innumerable times in a very rudimentary and inarticulate manner, mixed with other actions and interactions from which the mediating function cannot be isolated. Such mediations do not even have to be performed by means of words. A gesture, a way of listening, the mood that radiates from a particular person are enough to change the difference between two individuals . . . (Simmel in Wolff 1950: 148–9).

Two of the participants in a formal mediation encounter would not have come together if it were not for the frame created by the third. They are there because their dyadic relationship has failed. But, in joining this encounter, their dispute is modified. In consequence the ownership of any agreement becomes problematic.

> . . . the universe of meaning and values within which the process takes place is necessarily extended and changed . . . As a result, some control over the process of decision-making and the outcomes is 'lost' by the disputants once the assistance of a mediator is invoked or imposed . . . the configuration of power as between the disputants themselves may (also) be altered by the mediator's presence. (Roberts 1983: 549.)

The dispute is no longer a private matter but one which involves their standing in the eyes of an outsider, who is defining what will count as acceptable, in-character behaviour. Given this, the element of enforcement seems ineradicable from mediation.

It does not, of course, necessarily follow from this that mediation should be abandoned as postulating an unattainable ideal of party-controlled dispute resolution. There are other policy arguments in its favour. In particular, the active involvement of parties possessing fuller information about their individual circumstances than any adjudicator may still lead to qualitatively better settlements, particularly if the mediator is also seen as an active contributor of ideas and information. These may not be available to either party as a one-shot player of the divorce game but are part of the professionals' stock-in-trade.

But to acknowledge this makes the regulation of mediation into the key policy issue. If mediation is to substitute for adjudication, then, unless we are to abandon the ideals of equity and child protection that persist in the latter, some means must be devised for ensuring that they are maintained in the former. The case presented here suggests that some of the worst fears of feminist critics like Bottomley (1984) may not necessarily be realized. Nevertheless, if a woman mediator can impose one set of values, a man can impose another. Our efforts must be devoted not only to mediation techniques but also to the development of clear statements about the values which we wish to see expressed in divorce settlements, of training and credentialling programmes that will ensure mediators are fully aware of the implications of these and to the design of organizations which will make adequate monitoring and supervision possible, to maintain compliance. This suggests the need for clearer legislative guidance, modelled on, if not copied from, the Californian attempt to stipulate preferred outcomes; for certification of mediators; and for the institutionalized review of mediated settlements. But the first step must be to acknowledge the power of mediators and to accept that its existence creates a potential for abuse which may be different from but is no less real than the dangers of adversarial dispute proceedings.

Notes

1. The origins of this ambiguous message lie in the fundamental dilemma of all organized service occupations which are constrained to make private promises of a highly personalized form of work, to generate a clientele, and public protestations of a commitment to wider civic values, to sustain their claims to social legitimacy (Murray *et al.* 1983: 196–200).

2. One of the agency's annual reports sums up the difficulty: 'As one of the main aims of the service is to be available early on in the divorcing process, it has to balance easy accessibility to the public with maintaining a neutral non-partisan position with the person who first approaches us . . . Too great an involvement with one half of the couple at this stage can easily jeopardize the service's neutrality'.

3. The conventions used in this and the following transcripts are based on a system devised by Gail Jefferson and described fully in Atkinson and Heritage (1984: ix–xvi). The main symbols used here are:

   [ ] Square brackets mark the beginning and end of simultaneous or overlapping utterances.

   (0.2) Intervals in the talk are timed in tenths of a second.

   (.) Interval hearable but too short to time.

   : An extension of the preceding syllable

   di<u>vor</u>ce Underlining indicates unusual emphasis on a syllable or word.

   ( ) Empty brackets indicate undecipherable talk. Speech transcribed in brackets is uncertain.

   ↑↓ Marked rising and falling shifts in intonation.

4. Variations on this can be found in Lemmon's (1985: 62–9) discussion of related techniques from psychodrama and Folberg and Taylor's (1984: 49–53) exposition of ways to create new options in negotiation.

5. In analytic terms, the presence of a second mediator, in co-mediation techniques, is not of great significance. Either the two mediators act together, in which case they function as a single third party, or they split in alliance with each participant, in which case the whole encounter is likely to collapse.

11.   A Wider Vision

ROBERT DINGWALL AND JOHN EEKELAAR

As we noted in the Preface to this collection, the contributors do not subscribe to any particular position on the use of alternative means of dispute resolution in divorce cases. Some are clearly more sympathetic to the concept of mediation than others. Yet there are a number of common themes. One is a pervasive dissatisfaction with the way previous discussions have treated the relationship between the legal system and its competitors. All too often mediation has been seen as something which can simply be tacked onto or inserted into a legal process which remains essentially unchanged. The contributors to this volume demonstrate repeatedly that the work of mediators cannot be understood without examining the whole role of the legal system in divorce cases and its implications for the practice of both traditional and alternative methods for settling disputes. Another theme is the concern over the extent to which mediation can deliver the benefits claimed for it. In the absence of regulation, it may become an arena for the free play of unequal social and economic forces or of maverick mediators. There are glimpses of outcomes which could be as oppressive as those imposed by the courts, even if reached by more subtle means. Finally, and to some extent underlying both of the other themes, there rumbles a discontent with the narrow research traditions of programme evaluation that have dominated mediation studies and obscured the critical value problems which are posed by the whole movement.

Rein (1983) has outlined three approaches to the study of social policy. The value-critical method examines the assumptions that frame social problems and policy responses. What value judgments lead us to perceive some set of events as a problem which requires a social response and to define some policy measures as legitimate and others as illegitimate? Divorce becomes a matter for concern as a result of the way we value family life: policies for the divorced are shaped by the relative values of work incentives and the relief of poverty. The analytic method of policy research takes the problem as given and breaks it into small components. It starts from an expression of intent and tries to design programmes which will realize this in a way which is both efficient and effective. A desire to reduce public expenditure on court costs, for example, may be translated into a number of different packages which can be evaluated for their success in achieving that objective. In so doing, however, the analytic method is likely to disregard other possible outcome measures like the balance between private and social costs or the quality of the court experience for the parties. Finally, Rein describes a value-committed approach of the sort exemplified by much of the mediation literature (e.g. Haynes 1981; Folberg and Taylor 1984; Lemmon 1985; Fisher and Ury 1981; Parkinson 1986*b*). This starts from an ideal and works out its implications for identifying and explaining deficiencies in the present state of affairs and for prescribing remedies. The assumptions underlying the ideal are not themselves subject to review.

In our joint contribution, we demonstrated that one of the major problems with mediation in the United Kingdom was the way in which three diverse interests had become joined in a movement for reform. Their priorities were quite different and, to some extent, even contradictory. One was concerned with cost-saving, another with the extension of welfare paternalism, and a third with the encouragement of self-reliant dispute resolution. We have no reason to suppose that the United Kingdom is exceptional in this regard, although the balance between these interests is likely to vary under different cultural and institutional conditions. But the existence of these divergent interests raises serious problems for any sort of programme evaluation study. As Rein points out, the definition of success is a contestable matter. It embodies one set of values in preference to others, which may be equally valid but have less power or legitimacy in the particular setting.

In the same way, criticism also derives from a set of prior values. The chapters by Felstiner and Sarat, and by Ingleby address the mediators' challenge to the legal system. One of the problems of evaluation research is often the lack of data on the baseline system. The funds are to study the innovation not the tradition. Yet these data are of great importance to any assessment of the case for change. Without them we cannot tell whether alternative methods of dispute processing really make any difference, let alone judge whether they are an improvement (cf. Bradshaw 1986). The mediators' assertions about the role of the legal system in stimulating conflict, for instance, sit uneasily beside the well-established preference for negotiated settlements in most civil cases discussed by both those contributions and the English evidence that actively pursued contests on custody and access probably occur in no more than 10 per cent of divorce cases (Eekelaar and Clive 1977; Maidment 1976; Priest and Whybrow 1986). While we do not know how many reluctant consents are given in the remaining cases, such figures hardly suggest that conflict is endemic. If mediators are tapping that larger pool to any great extent, a significant number of their cases could be expected to settle anyway, regardless of the mode of intervention.

There are, of course, differences between a settlement negotiated with the help of lawyers and one reached through mediation. The parties may be more detached from the outcome reached by the former process than the latter. On the other hand both contributions point to the *similarities* in the interactional relationship between solicitors or mediators and their clients. And Ingleby's paper firmly reminds us of the occasions where the greater detachment of the legal process might hold advantages, although he may understate the ability of mediators to contain highly-charged situations. Nevertheless, what is possible for the skilled pioneer may be less readily achieved by her routine successors in a mass service.

The discussion of existing services was extended by Adrian James in his analysis of civil work in the English Probation Service. Although probation staff have been involved in providing court-based social work support and investigation in family cases since the nineteen thirties, this area of their practice has suffered from official neglect. There has been little effort to resolve the policy conflicts we identify or even to produce good descriptions of existing practices which might serve as a basis for professional or public debate. The whole area has been labelled as low-priority by the government department responsible for it. Yet, from the point of view of family law reform, existing court-based social work services are of great importance. They are the agencies in place, providing a variety of facilities to both courts and families. Given the problems in constructing any national family court social work service from scratch, these agencies must be investigated and considered in any policy discussion.

Part I concludes with a review by Jessica Pearson and Nancy Thoeness of what evaluation studies have established in the United States. The early experience of the United States with alternative means of dispute resolution in general and family mediation in particular has generated a large national literature attempting to evaluate these innovations. Almost without exception the results appear to be disappointing for the proponents of mediation. The clients' reactions were not markedly more positive than to the litigation process, with the exception of their strong dislike of a public court hearing. Five years on from the divorce there appear to be no major differences in compliance with settlements or re-litigation rates. The method of dispute resolution seems to be less important than the dynamics of a family in accounting for children's adjustment to a divorce. There seem to be some short-term psychological benefits to the adults and some elements of the process were regarded as helpful but it is hardly an overwhelming vote of confidence.

Pearson and Thoeness, however, underline the deficiencies of the existing literature. There is a lack of clarity in defining what constitutes mediation so that the commensurability of findings cannot be established. Just as in the United Kingdom there is uncertainty about the outcomes to be measured. Is the main goal court avoidance or dispute resolution? They also raise the important question of public perceptions. What do clients want from divorce procedures? Satisfaction measures can only be understood with some reference to expectations, to the sheer distress of the breakdown itself, and, we would add, to what is socially possible. As we suggest below, there may be reasons why client satisfaction should not be an overriding objective of any procedure in divorce cases. What Pearson and Thoeness present is not a case *against* mediation but a case *for* caution and for more sophisticated, fundamental, and wide-ranging research.

The five remaining contributors draw on case studies in different types of mediation. Davis and Minamikata both discuss court-based mediation. In the British context, they represent a particular challenge to the proposals of the Booth Committee on procedural reform in divorce cases. The authors describe systems which are founded on assumptions about the desirability of avoiding trial, whether for economic or cultural reasons. Each underlines the pressure that may be applied to parties in such circumstances, pressure which may reflect the shadow of the law rather than its substance. As in other areas of law, the party who 'stood on their rights' was liable to be discredited (cf. Dingwall *et al.* 1983: 92–6; Piliavin and Briar 1964; Emerson 1969; Hawkins 1983). Minamikata also makes some telling observations on a routinized family court system. Forty years after its foundation, the Japanese family court finds itself struggling for resources and staffed by bored judges serving an unavoidable term as part of their career progression, assisted by the local equivalent of retired colonels and well-meaning ladies in flowered hats. It is not an encouraging picture either for families or for the administration of civil justice.

Griffiths discusses matrimonial dispute resolution in a third-world setting. The growing literature of legal anthropology has attracted considerable attention from advocates of mediation who, rightly, recognize that it illustrates ways in which the resolution of disputes can occur without an elaborate institutional apparatus. What is less well recognized, however, is that modern societies might have good reasons for finding such methods inadequate or inappropriate. The general case was put some years ago by Merry (1982) and Griffiths provides further documentation of the openness of mediation to extrinsic social inequalities. In the end Mrs Busang loses not because she has a bad case but because of the low status of women among the Bakwena. As Atkinson (1982) observed, formality exists in courts because it contributes to the achievement of some of their practical goals. He focused on the problems of sustaining joint attention to the task in hand but one can also argue that formality serves wider organizational purposes. In particular, it is a way of framing the encounter and defining certain attributes of the parties as irrelevant to the outcome. Formal divorce procedures are part of the aspiration to treat each case on its own merits, regardless of the social or economic status of the parties involved. They may not be very effective in this but their removal eliminates whatever restraint they do constitute on the naked oppression of particular groups. The court system can always be challenged for its failure to achieve its ideal of impersonal justice: in mediation justice is by definition personal and the failure to achieve it is an individual weakness not a structural one.

This observation has been picked up by feminist critics like Bottomley (1984) who see mediation as a way of rolling back gains made by women from the demand that courts deliver impersonal justice. Dingwall's contribution qualifies this by showing that the power of a woman mediator can equally be used to deny an advantage to a male client. The wider significance of this paper, however, is in its contrast with Roberts's arguments about the possibility of a minimalist approach to mediation.

Roberts describes three ideal types of divorce mediation. An ideal type is an analytic construct and it is not argued that these models exist empirically in a pure form. Nevertheless, it is a convenient device for summarizing the variety of real-world experiences in a manner which allows the basic range of social organizational solutions to be identified and discussed and for actual agencies to be evaluated in terms of the practical compromises they have adopted as an attempt to combine the strengths or mitigate the weaknesses of each theoretical possibility. From his comparison of these ideal types, Roberts argues that the minimalist version leads to a type of practice which is more in correspondence with certain social values of justice and self-determination, although he concedes that it may be less effective in dealing with the problems of third-party interests and transactional incapacity.

Dingwall, however, adopts an alternative approach from his starting point in data on one agency's practice. Rather than setting up a model with which to contrast this, his interest lies much more in understanding why events happen this way at all. Thus his use of the ideal types developed from the empirical study of social interaction is rather different. Here, they are used to identify mediation sessions as members of a class of social situations with certain established properties and bound in a particular fashion to the constraints of the context in which they occur. From this Dingwall's analysis challenges Roberts's argument on the possibility of minimalism. In effect, Dingwall suggests, it is an error to suppose that social interaction of this kind could ever be so purified that mediators would cease to possess and use power, wittingly or unwittingly. The power exists by virtue of the sort of occasions that these are. It is simply *there*. If it cannot be abolished, then the correct policy may be to discuss its regulation rather than to engage in fruitless attempts to wish it away. Any discussion of its regulation will, however, inevitably involve an examination of the issues identified by Roberts, of the values which our societies wish to see embedded in and governing the process of resolving family disputes.

Policy and Practice

We have insisted on the necessity of value-critical research on divorce mediation and tried to illustrate its contribution. In closing this book, however, we believe that it is right to go on from the material presented here to outline the terms of debate and policy options that we would consider fundamental to any review of divorce procedure. We should, perhaps, again specifically exempt our contributors from any direct responsibility for what follows.

The problem of consent

Mediation differs from adjudication in that the status of the outcome derives directly from the consent of the parties rather than the authority of the adjudicator, although, as we note below, even that has an indirect basis in consent. But the concept of consent is highly ambiguous. It may mean different things for different purposes (Lee 1987). A participant in plea bargaining, for example, may be said to 'consent' to enter a guilty plea on a lesser charge in order to avoid trial on a serious one. It is, however, hard to say that he has then 'consented' in any real sense to the consequent punishment.

Court avoidance can be achieved in many ways. Costs may be made prohibitive. Litigants thought to be behaving unreasonably may be threatened with adverse consequences. Inducements may be offered to encourage out-of-court settlements. The degree of 'consent' in a party's acquiescence in a specific outcome is not purely a matter of individual judgment but of judgment in a social context which constructs a particular matrix of incentives and sanctions. Many of these will, obviously, feature in any bargaining process. What is important in the present debate is the propriety of a *calculated systematic intervention* which so structures the context of bargaining as to impose prohibitive costs on the option of litigation. We believe that the constitutional arguments against such procedures must be conclusive. The principle of access to justice is fundamental to the Rule of Law. This cannot be reconciled with the erection of institutional mechanisms within the legal system itself which intend or have the direct effect of deterring people from the legitimate use of that system.

The problem of supervision

This leaves the problem of the conflict between the promotion of private ordering and the supervision of settlements to protect third-party interests.

Eekelaar (1986) has underlined the artificiality of separating the discussions of divorce procedures from discussion of the substantive law. Many of the cumbersome aspects of divorce procedures derive from the political difficulty of introducing divorce by consent.

The present system has worked because it *appears* to retain moral scrutiny over the legal dissolution of marriage while in practice satisfying demand for consensual divorce at the price of requiring the submission of allegations to a tribunal which is denied the means of verifying them. (Eekelaar 1986: 228.)

The price of this 'shabby compromise' is paid by divorcing couples in the petty humiliations of the process. It is a price they will continue to pay until the substantive law is reformed, whatever procedure is adopted. This could be avoided by reducing the granting of divorce to a purely administrative act of registration on the joint application of the parties. But this does not imply that all the arrangements connected with the divorce should be treated in the same way, although that would, presumably, have its attractions to minimalists for it would give the greatest opportunity for self-determination. It would also be a most effective way to save costs.

We could envisage three theoretical objections to doing this and one practical limitation. The first objection relates mainly to making the grant of divorce an administrative act. It is simply the political one that neither public opinion nor the state's interest in the institution of marriage would permit such a step. The alleged views of the public, it must be said, owe more to the assertions of lobbyists than to reliable survey data. Small attention is paid to the causal relationship between procedural niceties and the social phenomenon of family breakdown, and the nature of the state's interest is seldom closely examined. While there are good liberal arguments for encouraging the integrity of families as a check on the abusive potential of state power, the reality more often seems to be concerned with maintaining private relationships of economic dependency and rationing public welfare expenditures.

The two other objections concern the arrangements necessitated by the divorce. One follows from the view that a special regime of family law is the need to ensure separate consideration of the interests and welfare of children (Eekelaar 1984), and the substantive law requirement that the interests of children should be given first consideration. Since they are unrepresented third parties in divorce cases and may be considered too young to speak on their own behalf, the state has a duty to ensure that parents take account of their needs and, if necessary, to prevent parents from reaching settlements which may be convenient for the adults but detrimental to the children. This objection, of course, only applies where there are children and it may be arguable that separate divorce regimes could operate for couples with and without dependants.

The other objection is that a wholly administrative divorce process may selectively disadvantage certain groups who are less competent or effective bargainers. Formal systems, as we have suggested, may incorporate procedural safeguards which inhibit exploitative or oppressive behaviour. The more power that is conceded to the parties, the less opportunity there is for that power to be regulated.

Finally, the limitation on any administrative system, as Minamikata shows, is that it does not eliminate conflict. Disputes are displaced from the courts but the society must find ways of resolving them. Even if it were conceded that a wholly administrative divorce process were acceptable where only adults are affected, leaving issues of dependency to the social security system and accepting some risk of abuse arising from pre-existing inequalities, some institutional means of imposing closure on disagreements would continue to be necessary.

This is the traditional role of courts in Anglo-American societies. They are the last resort where other means of dispute resolution fail (Atkinson and Drew 1979). Judges, then, tend to be characterized as officials who are primarily concerned by *decide* cases (e.g. Holmes 1897: 457–78; Cardozo 1921; Llewellyn 1962; Hart 1961; Jaffe 1969; Dworkin 1986).

As Bell (1987) points out, though, such a narrow focus gives a misleading impression of judicial work. He identifies eight quite distinct functions which judges, or similar officials like registrars or referees, may perform: dispute settlements by adjudication; conciliation, as in plea bargaining, in 'Children's Appointments' of the kind described earlier by Davis, or, by force of authority, in promoting 'door of the court' agreements; rule determination, giving an authoritative interpretation of statutes or regulations; enunciation of publicly acceptable standards of behaviour; legal authentication, as in uncontested divorces, guilty criminal pleas and undefended debt actions; supervision, as in taking children into the care of the state, winding up a company, varying trusts, or authorizing warrants; constitutional control over the behaviour of other organs of the state; and social engineering, as in anti-discrimination cases. Courts, then, can perform a wide range of functions: the challenge is to discover the correct mix for a particular set of issues.

The problem about any single-function solution to the reform of divorce procedures is the way in which it can only address one of these roles and that often at the expense of the complex relationships between them. Shapiro (1981), for instance, points to the way in which both adjudication and mediation are influenced by the constraints of organizational legitimacy. To maintain social support, a system of dispute resolution, like any other social organization, must generate some measure of satisfaction with its work and be capable of demonstrating its effectiveness in achieving its supposed goals. Shapiro argues that the former concern leads most court systems to incorporate some elements of mediation in an attempt to win a degree of consent from the 'losers'. Conversely, Silbey and Merry (1986) show that mediators may sometimes be pushed towards adjudication by the need to deliver settlements. The pressures of legitimacy are a constraint on both systems, but they are also what distinguishes them from other possibilities like coercion, the illegitimate alternative noted by Ingleby.

In assessing any proposal for change, it is essential to ask how it will affect the whole system of family justice not just those parts to which a would-be reformer has taken particular exception. Some of those may reflect essential institutional compromises, such as between administrative and supervised divorce, which reflect the history and traditions of a society. It is no simple matter to create, or dismantle, respected, complex organizations attempting to deliver a common standard of service throughout a particular geographical area. Moreover, the administration of justice cannot be viewed solely in terms of a utilitarian calculus. Procedures which defy the cost–benefit justification of rational policy evaluation may none the less be defensible for their symbolic importance as statements about the ultimate values of a society. Thus the supervisory elements of family law have a significance beyond the facts of any individual case in their statement of the desirability of child protection and of substantive equity. In practice the system may fail to achieve these goals but that is not necessarily a reason for abandoning them. What is important is that these are public statements whose propriety may legitimately be challenged, on appeal or through the legislature. If divorce court judges agonize about giving child custody to lesbian mothers, the issue is at least in the public arena for debate and investigation.

The supervisory aspirations of family law lie at the heart of its current procedural troubles. They are costly to administer and vulnerable to criticism both for their ineffectiveness and their intrusiveness. This disarray is most marked in the treatment of arrangements for children. In England, for example, Davis *et al.* (1983) show how perfunctory is the scrutiny of arrangements for children in undefended cases. The only way for courts to generate evidence independent of the parties is to commission a welfare investigation. But Eekelaar (1982) has shown that this occurs in only about 10 per cent of undefended divorces. Any attempt to raise this would be faced with the libertarian objection that, in an age of mass divorce, it is no longer right that courts and welfare agencies should have a free rein to examine families simply because a marital relationship has broken down. The failure of a marriage has ceased to be a token of social deviance which may cause wider damage to the reputation and moral character of the parties. It is simply a normal hazard of life. If the parents' character remains unblemished, the argument goes, there are no justifications for investigating their fitness to take decisions about their children's welfare (Murch 1980; cf. Dingwall *et al.* 1983: 79–89).

Recent developments in England have attempted to revitalize the process of supervision. The Booth Committee suggested that parents should be required to submit a more detailed Statement of Arrangements for children, going into details about accommodation, child care, and health status. But even if the future could be fixed by the provision of extra information, when the reality is that all such matters are likely to be subject to a high degree of change and uncertainty following a divorce, the court is still no better placed to investigate its veracity. If the court is dissatisfied, it is hard to see what can be done to influence the actual arrangements devised between parents. The refusal of a decree does not correct the situation but merely imposes extra costs and possible sources of conflict on the parties as they seek to devise a more acceptable paper representation of their intentions. The court's power to place children in the care of the state is too draconian to be appropriate as a lever in the bargaining. Parents can be forced to present their proposals in a different form: they cannot be forced to adhere to them where both prefer an alternative.

In contrast to arrangements for child custody, courts would seem to have more control over financial agreements. Both parties have an incentive to submit full and accurate information if they are genuinely seeking a settlement. If they fail to do so, any court order will generally be overturned. Moreover, the court can actually control outcomes through its orders, although this power is limited by the problems of enforcement. No jurisdiction has yet satisfactorily resolved the difficulty of ensuring continuing compliance with support orders, even where these were originally agreed between the parties.

But supervision does increase the transaction costs to the parties in the preparation of information and it also raises questions about the responsibility of the court. Is it right, for example, to use divorce courts as a way of attempting to prevent husbands from transferring to the state the costs of support for their former wives and children? If social security law does not regard a former spouse as liable to reimburse the state for expenditure on the support of the other former spouse (although Ingleby notes that practice may be different) should private law incorporate this objective? On the other hand, supervision may be defended by reference to what Mnookin (1984) calls the 'transactional incapacities' of people involved in divorce. Under conditions of economic and emotional stress, people may reach agreements which are contrary to their long-run interests, as they subsequently recognize these, but which are not easily reversible in the absence of obvious exploitation or duress by the other party. As in child custody, it could also be argued that the court does have a proper supervisory role in relation to the economic position of children following a divorce.

Nevertheless, the potential role of legal proceedings in imposing reflection on the prospective parties should not be underestimated. As we showed in an earlier study of decision-making in child-abuse cases, the requirement to present a case which meets certain criteria of adequacy and defensibility may 'reach back' and influence events well before any possible court hearing (Dingwall *et al.* 1983). But divorce is different in that most of the information which forms the basis of an uncontested application is actually controlled by parties who have a joint interest in discouraging its scrutiny. It seems implausible to suppose that, in practice, supervisory provisions do much to concentrate the minds of the parties on the implications of a divorce for their children or, in some cases, their own economic circumstances rather than on how arrangements can best be presented to the courts.

The supervisory aspiration could, however, give grounds for concern in family court or mediation-based systems which incorporate therapeutic aspirations alongside the process of dispute resolution. Welfare can be a more insidious form of social control than law, although it is always a fine judgment as to whether its enticements to conformity may not be preferable to outright coercion. It is not our contention that supervision has *no* part to play in the divorce process, but that part must always be tempered by a recognition of the information available to the supervisors, their ability to evaluate it, and their capacity to influence events.

A mixed system

Ultimately, the movement for alternative dispute resolution in divorce must confront this problem: should supervision be retained? In our view, the answers could be different for different types of divorce. Where agreements do not have implications for dependants, we see no good reason why court supervision should be retained, provided each party has received independent legal advice. Any criteria which the court might apply to evaluate the agreement seem so uncertain that we doubt whether active judicial involvement serves any useful purpose. If the enforcement advantages of a court order are thought to be desirable, then it should simply be possible to register an agreement. Where this agreement may have tax, social security, or housing implications, the responsibility for pursuing these should rest between the parties and those agencies rather than occupying the attention of courts operating family law. If costs are a significant concern, then administrative divorce by consent seems capable of making a more substantial contribution than any procedural tinkering.

Where dependants, especially children, are involved, however, we think that the arguments are very different. We do not accept that parents are invariably the best judges of their children's interests, although their unique access to information about their own children's needs must mean that their views should carry considerable weight. Nevertheless, the principle that children should not be avoidably prejudiced in their life-chances by the behaviour of their parents compels us towards endorsing some measure of supervision (cf. Dingwall *et al.* 1983, Dingwall and Eekelaar 1984, Eekelaar and Maclean 1986). On the other hand, such supervision in divorce cases should be confined to those matters where the court's intervention has some chance of being effective. These would include the distribution of legally recognized parental authority, the general basis of access or visitation rights, and the settlement of finance and property for the support of the child.

But if all these matters are subject to court supervision, then we believe that there are important implications for divorce mediation. Our argument would be that the explicit criteria used by supervisors to assess settlements should be the incentives to agreement rather than any other institutional pressure. In effect, the pressure on a recalcitrant parent should take the form, 'it is no use holding out for X; even if you were to achieve this, the court would strike it down as contrary to a statutory definition of children's interests' rather than 'it is no use holding out for X; you are unlikely to achieve it, your costs will pile up, and the judge is likely to be hostile to you because he will think you are being obstructive'.

The supervisory criteria expressed in statute or case law would constitute the framework for pre-litigation discussions. In this respect there would be no difference between negotiation through lawyers or mediation. The roles of negotiators and mediators would be similar: explaining and interpreting the supervisory criteria and exploring the means by which these can be reconciled with the wishes of parents. The parties, however, would retain their choice of forum. Some may cling to their own perception of the criteria or maintain that there are exceptional grounds why they should not apply in the particular case. We cannot believe that they should be aggressively deterred from arguing their position in a formal hearing before a judge. Nevertheless, mediation may still succeed where negotiation fails to persuade a party of their misapprehension of the supervisor's expectations.

A central and open part of the mediation process would consist of *informing* the parties about the options available to them and the means by which their choice will be evaluated. There is no particular reason why this should be inserted between the lawyers' office and the court. Such a service could reasonably function alongside other public community advice agencies or private lawyers as an open door for people embarking on a divorce. We are, in effect, advocating a 'mixed economy' in which lawyers and mediators are able to compete on equal terms offering a variety of means to ends defined by a set of statutory parameters. What is important is that clients retain a degree of choice which recognizes the variation in their needs and circumstances. The issue of public funding is a separate one. The logic of our proposals may point towards some kind of system of vouchers, which clients may exchange for the services of whichever professionals, or mix of professional services, they find most helpful. They may also imply some form of certification, although not licensing, for mediators given the asymmetry of information between professionals and clients about service quality (Dingwall and Fenn 1987). What seems wholly unacceptable is a monolithic state service operating in a market rigged to guarantee it a monopoly position by imposing penal costs on those who would prefer alternatives.

A system of the kind we envisage is nowhere wholly in operation but it combines elements from several jurisdictions. California, for example, incorporates in its divorce law a statutory preference for joint custody except where a judge is persuaded that this is undesirable. Disputes over child custody take place in the knowledge that a court will order it to be held jointly unless there is a strong evidence of, say, child abuse or parental drug addiction which incapacitates the claimant. We would not wish to argue for any particular standards at this stage: merely endorse the principle of a democratically elected legislature explicitly defining the parameters of negotiation. For reasons already cited, we would not favour the Californian policy of compulsory mediation. On the other hand, at least some counties appear to operate an effective chain of supervision from family judges to publicly funded mediation staff. The mediators are aware that their documentation will be subject to review and that they may be asked to account for unusual-seeming outcomes. Thus, the opportunity for mediators to introduce idiosyncratic values would be restricted.

Some Australian registries have explored the possibility of community-based divorce mediation services. It would be necessary in such circumstances to ensure that the line of supervision was not diluted. On the other hand, these offer genuine possibilities for both reducing costs and enhancing access. The problem of supervision is well recognized in the organization of public social-work agencies and does not seem insuperable. Alongside such developments, however, our arguments tend to insist that the court itself should retain its formal, legal character. This does not necessarily imply the maintenance of every last robe and wig: rather that the court will still be asked to fulfil its unique function of adjudicating on contested matters by consideration of substantial evidence or of clarifying points of law to permit negotiations to continue. In Dingwall's observations of a Californian court, for instance, the judge was called upon to determine matters like the extent to which certain inherited assets were community or separate property or the means by which stock options in a high-tech company should be valued. These are problems which no mediator or negotiator can *decide*, but once resolved set the framework for further bargaining.

If there is one lesson which social scientists have struggled to teach over the last forty or fifty years, it is that social policies always have unforeseen consequences. The movement for divorce mediation has gripped the imagination of a section of the policy community. If this collection has achieved anything, however, we hope that it is to temper their enthusiasm with a note of caution. There are serious and substantial problems about the values, practice, and organization of divorce mediation. As yet these have only received limited research attention. The work that has been done has all too often been the narrowest kind of programme evaluation. This collection has tried to offer a wider vision, a glimpse both of research agenda and of the variety of means by which it might be pursued. In our Preface we promised no answers: we hope to have established that there are questions worth asking.

References

Abel, R. L. (1982a) 'The contradictions of informal justice', in Abel (1982b), vol. i.
—— (1982b), *The politics of informal justice* (2 vols.) (New York: Academic Press).
Achenbach, T., and C. Edelbrock (1980), 'A typology of child behavior profile patterns: distribution and correlates for disturbed children aged 6–16', *Journal of Abnormal Child Psychology*, 8: 441–70.
Archbishop's Commission (1966), *Putting asunder: a divorce law for contemporary society* (London: SPCK).
Asahi-Shimbunsha (1985) *Asahinenkan 1985* (Tokyo: Asahishimbunsha).
Association of Chief Officers of Probation (ACOP) (1985), Survey of conciliation work, Civil Work Sub-Committee (April).
Association of Chief Officers of Probation (1986), *Information Bulletin*, 93, (July).
Atkins, S., and B. Hoggett (1984), *Women and the law* (Oxford: Basil Blackwell).
Atkinson, J. M., and P. Drew (1979), *Order in court* (London: Macmillan).
Atkinson, J. M. and J. Heritage, eds. (1984) *Structures of social action: Studies in conversation analysis* (Cambridge: Cambridge University Press).
Baldwin, J., and M. McConville (1977), *Negotiated justice* (London: Martin Robertson).
BASW (1985), *Family courts* (Birmingham: British Association of Social Workers).
Bell, J. (1987), 'The judge as bureaucrat', in J. M. Eekelaar and J. Bell (eds.), *Oxford essays in jurisprudence*, 3rd ser. (Oxford: Oxford University Press).
Berends, M. (1981), 'Modes of lawyer–client interaction: translation, transformation and social control', Paper read at Law and Society Association Annual Meeting, at Amherst, Mass.
Bienenfeld, F. (1983), *Child custody mediation* (Palo Alto: Science and Behavior Books).
Block, J., and B. Kreger (1982), *Mediation: an alternative for PINS*, research report of the Children's Aid Society, PINS Mediation Project, New York.
Blumberg, A. S. (1967), 'The practice of law as confidence game', *Law and Society Review*, 1, 2: 15–39.
Bochel, D. (1976), *Probation and after-care: its development in England and Wales* (Edinburgh: Scottish Academic Press).
Bogoch, B., and B. Danet (1984), 'Challenge and control in lawyer–client interaction', unpublished paper.
Booth Committee (1983), *Committee on matrimonial causes procedure: consultation paper* (London: Lord Chancellor's Department).
—— (1985), *Report of the committee on matrimonial causes procedure* (London: HMSO).
Borkowski, M., M. Murch, and V. Walker (1983), *Marital violence* (London: Tavistock).

Boswell, G. R. (1982), 'Goals in the probation and after-care service', unpublished Ph.D. thesis: University of Liverpool.

Bottomley, A. (1984), 'Resolving family disputes: a critical view', in M. D. A. Freeman (ed.), *State, law and the family* (London: Tavistock).

—— (1985), 'What is happening to family law? A feminist critique of conciliation', in J. Brophy and C. Smart (eds.), *Women in law* (London: Routledge and Kegan Paul).

Bradshaw, A. (1986) 'Conciliation in Cleveland monitored' *Journal of Social Welfare Law*, 3–13.

Brandeis, L. (1933), 'The opportunity in law', in *Business—a profession* (Boston: Hale, Cushman, and Flint).

Bristol Trustees (1984), 'Conciliation: the interdepartmental report examined', *Family Law*, 14: 48–53.

Brown, D. (1982), 'Divorce and family mediation: history, review and future directions', *Conciliation Courts Review*, 20: 1–40.

Bryan, M. (1984), 'Domestic violence: a question of housing', *Journal of Social Welfare Law*: 195–207.

Burgoyne, J., R. Ormrod, and M. Richards (1987), *Divorce Matters* (Harmondsworth: Penguin).

Caesar-Wolf, B. (1984), 'Professionalized lawyer–client interaction: an exemplary case study of a divorce consultation', paper read at Workshop on the Study of the Interaction Between Lawyer and Client, at Groningen, the Netherlands.

Cain, M. (1983), 'The general practice lawyer and the client', in R. Dingwall and P. S. C. Lewis (eds.), *The sociology of the professions: lawyers, doctors and others* (London: Macmillan).

Cardozo, B. N. (1921), *The nature of the judicial process* (New Haven: New York University Press).

Cauble, A. E., N. Thoeness, J. Pearson, and R. Appleford (1983), 'A case study: custody resolution counseling in Hennepin County, Minnesota', *Conciliation Courts Review*, 23: 27–36.

Chess, T., A. Thomas, S. Korn, M. Mittleman, and J. Cohn (1983), 'Early parental attitudes, divorce and separation and young adult outcome: findings of a longitudinal study', *Journal of the American Academy of Child Psychiatry*, 22: 47–51.

Cohen, S. (1981), 'The diversion study: a preliminary report', unpublished (Oregon City: Clackamas County Circuit Court).

Comaroff, J., and S. Roberts (1981), *Rules and processes* (London: University of Chicago Press).

Comeaux, E. (1983), 'A guide to implementing divorce mediation services in the public sector', *Conciliation Courts Review*, 21: 1–25.

Conference of Chief Probation Officers (1982), 'Models for civil work within the probation and after-care service', Policy Document (July).

Coogler, O. J. (1978), *Structured mediation in divorce settlement* (Lexington, Mass.: Lexington Books).

Coogler, O. J., R. Weber, and P. McKenry (1979), 'Divorce mediation: a means of facilitating divorce and adjustment', *The Family Coordinator*, 26: 255–9.

Cretney, S. (1984), *Principles of family law*, 4th edn. (London: Sweet and Maxwell).

Curran, B. (1977), *The legal needs of the public* (Chicago: American Bar Foundation).

Danet, B., K. B. Hoffman, and N. C. Kermish (1980), 'Obstacles to the study of lawyer–client interaction: the biography of a failure', *Law and Society Review*, 14: 905–22.

Davis, G. (1980), 'A report on the Bristol Courts' Family Conciliation Service', *Legal Aid Annual Reports, 1979–80*, Appendix D.

—— (1982*a*), 'Conciliation: a dilemma for the divorce court welfare service' *Probation Journal*, 29: 123–8.

—— (1982*b*), 'Settlement-seeking in divorce', *New Law Journal*, 132: 355–6.

—— (1982*c*), 'Conciliation or litigation', *LAG Bulletin*, April: 11–13.

—— (1983*a*), 'Conciliation and the professions', *Family Law*, 13: 6–13.

—— (1983*b*), 'Mediation in divorce: a theoretical perspective', *Journal of Social Welfare Law*: 131–40.

—— (1985), 'The theft of conciliation', *Probation Journal*, 32: 7–10.

Davis, G., with K. Bader (1982) 'Research report on in-court mediation in custody and access disputes' (Bristol: mimeo).

Davis, G., and K. Bader (1983*a*), 'In-court mediation observed', *New Law Journal*, 133: 355–7, 403–5.

—— (1983*b*), 'Can in-court mediation work?' *LAG Bulletin*, July: 10–14.

—— (1985), 'In-court mediation: the consumer view', *Family Law*, 15: 42–9, 82–6.

Davis, G., and J. Westcott (1984), 'Report of the Interdepartmental Committee on Conciliation', *Modern Law Review*, 47: 215–22.

Davis, G., A. Macleod, and M. Murch (1982), 'Divorce and the resolution of conflict', *Law Society's Gazette*: 40–1.

—— (1983), 'Undefended divorces: should Section 41 of the Matrimonial Causes Act 1973 be repealed?', *Modern Law Review*, 46: 121–46.

Delaware Revised Court Rule 151 Connecticut Special Act No. 84–74 (1980), *Dispute resolution.*

Denning Committee (1947), *Final report of the committee on procedure in matrimonial causes*, Cmnd. 7024 (London: HMSO).

Dingwall, R. (1980), 'Orchestrated encounters: an essay in the comparative analysis of speech-exchange systems', *Sociology of Health and Illness*, 2: 151–73.

—— (1986), 'Some observations on divorce mediation in Britain and the United States', *Mediation Quarterly*, 11: 5–23.

Dingwall, R., and J. M. Eekelaar (1984), 'Rethinking child protection', in M. D. A. Freeman (ed.), *State, law and the family* (London: Tavistock).

—— (1987), 'Judgements of Solomon: psychology and family law', in M. P. M. Richards and P. Light (eds.), *Children of social worlds* (Cambridge: Polity Press).

Dingwall, R., and P. Fenn (1987), 'A respectable profession? Sociological and economic perspectives on the regulation of professional services', *International Review of Law and Economics*, 7: 51–64.

Dingwall, R., J. M. Eekelaar, and T. Murray (1983), *The protection of children* (Oxford: Basil Blackwell).

Donohoe, W. A., M. Allen, and N. Burrell (1985), 'How and when do mediators intervene when disputants attack each other verbally?' *Mediation Quarterly*, 10: 75–89.

Dworkin, R. (1986), *Law's empire* (London: Fontana Press).

Economic Planning Agency (1983) *Kokumin seikatsu hakusho (White paper on living standards)* (Tokyo: Ookurashoinsatsukyoku).

Eekelaar, J. (1982), 'Children and divorce: some further data', *Oxford Journal of Legal Studies*, 2: 63–85.

—— (1984), *Family law and social policy*, 2nd edn. (London: Weidenfeld and Nicolson).

—— (1986), 'Divorce English style—a new way forward', *Journal of Social Welfare Law*: 226–36.

Eekelaar, J., and E. Clive (1977), *Custody after divorce* (Oxford: SSRC Centre for Socio-Legal Studies).

Eekelaar, J., and M. Maclean (1986), *Maintenance after divorce* (Oxford: Oxford University Press).

Emerson, R. (1969), *Judging delinquents* (Chicago: Aldine).

Emery, R. (1982), 'Interparental conflict and the children of discord and divorce', *Psychological Bulletin*, 92: 310–30.

Emery, R., M. Hetherington, and L. Fisher (1983), 'Divorce, children and social policy', in H. Stevenson and A. Seigel (eds.), *Child development and social policy* (Chicago: University of Chicago Press).

Epstein, A. L. (1971), 'Dispute settlement among the Tolai', *Oceania*, 51: 157–70.

Erlanger, H. S., E. Chambliss, and M. S. Melli (1986), 'Cooperation or coercion? Informal settlement in the divorce context', Disputes Processing Research Program: Institute for Legal Studies, University of Wisconsin, Madison.

Family Bureau (1986), 'Kateisaibanshojiken no gaiyo: Kajijiken' ('An overview of family affairs cases in 1984') *Kateisaibangeppo* 38: 1–128.

Felstiner, W. L. F., R. L. Abel, and A. Sarat (1981), 'The emergence and transformation of disputes: naming, blaming and claiming', *Law and Society Review*, 15: 631–54.

Ferguson, S., and H. Fitzgerald (1954), *Studies in the social services* (London: HMSO/Longmans).

Finer Committee (1974), *Report of the committee on one-parent families*, Cmnd. 5629 (London: HMSO).

Fisher, R., and W. Ury (1981), *Getting to yes* (Boston: Houghton Mifflin).

Fletcher, R. (1968), *The family and marriage in Britain* (Harmondsworth: Penguin) [Revised edition: first published as *Britain in the sixties: family and marriage* (Harmondsworth: Penguin, 1962)].

Folberg, J., and A. Taylor (1984), *Mediation: a comprehensive guide to resolving disputes without litigation* (San Francisco: Jossey Bass).

Forum (1979) 'Kateisaibansho wa ikani kino shiuruka' ('How can the family court accomplish its functions?') in The Hogaku Seminar *Special Issue: nikon no kazoku (The family in Japan)* (Tokyo: Nihonhyoronsha).

—— (1983) 'Kaji hiotei wo kangderu' ('Considering family mediation') *Case Kenkyu*, 197: 39–74.

Frank, J. (1950), *Courts on Trial* (Princeton: Princeton University Press).

Freeman, M. D. A. (1984), 'Questioning the delegalization movement in family law', in J. M. Eekelaar and S. N. Katz (eds.), *The resolution of family conflict: comparative perspectives* (Toronto: Butterworth).

Fukaya, M. (1983), *Gendai kazoku ho (Current Family Law)* (Tokyo: Seirinshoin-shinsha).

Fukutake, T. (1982), *The Japanese social structure* (Tokyo: University of Tokyo Press).

Gabel, P. (1980), 'Reification in legal reasoning', *Research in Law and Sociology*, 3: 25–51.

Galanter, M. (1984), 'World of deals: using negotiation to teach about legal process', *Journal of Legal Education*, 34: 368–76.

General Secretariat (1976), *Kaji Chotei no Tebiki (A manual for family mediation)* (Tokyo: General Secretariat of the Supreme Court).

Genn, H. (1987), *Hard bargaining* (Oxford: Oxford University Press).

Gibson, C. (1980), 'Divorce and the recourse to legal aid', *Modern Law Review*, 43: 609–25.

Goffman, E. (1972), *Encounters* (Harmondsworth: Penguin).

—— (1983) 'Felicity's Condition', *American Journal of Sociology*, 89: 1–53.

Gordon, R. (1982), 'New development in legal theory', in D. Kairys (ed.), *The politics of law* (New York: Pantheon).

Gough, D. M. (1982), 'Comparison of costs between cases dealt with under the conciliation scheme and the preparation of divorce court welfare reports', unpublished project report: Brighton Polytechnic.

Griffiths, A. (1984), 'Support for women with dependent children under the customary system of the Bakwena and the Roman-Dutch common and statutory law of Botswana', *Journal of Legal Pluralism and Unofficial Law*, 23: 1–15.

Griffiths, J. (1986), 'What do Dutch lawyers actually do?' *Law and Society Review*, 20: 135–75.

Gulliver, P. H. (1979), *Disputes and negotiations* (New York: Academic Press).

Haley, J. (1982), 'The politics of informal justice: the Japanese experience 1922–1942', in Abel (1982*b*), vol. ii.

Hall, J., and D. F. Martin (1983), 'Towards a unified family court: the cost factor', *Civil Justice Quarterly*, July: 223–43.

Hart, H. L. A. (1961), *The concept of law* (Oxford: Clarendon Press).

Hart, N. (1976), *When marriage ends: a study in status passage* (London: Tavistock).

Harvey, C. P. (1953), 'On the state of the divorce market', *Modern Law Review*, 16: 129–39.

Hawkins, K. (1983), *Environment and enforcement: regulation and the social definition of pollution* (Oxford: Oxford University Press).

Haxby, D. (1978), *Probation: a changing service* (London: Constable).

Haynes, J. (1978), 'Divorce mediation: theory and practice of a new social work role', unpublished doctoral dissertation, Union Graduate School, New York.

Haynes, J. M. (1981), *Divorce mediation* (New York: Springer).

Hetherington, M., M. Cox, and R. Cox (1979), 'Play and social interaction in children following divorce', *Journal of Social Issues*, 35: 26–49.

Hiraga, K. (1974), *Kateisaibansho (Family Court)* in Z. Nagakawa (ed.), *Kazoku mondai to Kazokuho VII: kaji saiban (Family problems and family law VII: family court)* (Tokyo: Sakaishoten).

Hoggett, B., and D. Pearl (1983), *The family, law and society* (London: Butterworth).

Holmes, O. W. (1897), 'The path of the law', *Harvard Law Review*, 10: 457–78.

Home Office (1966), *Report of the work of the Probation and After-Care Department, 1962–1965)*, Cmnd. 3107 (London: HMSO).

—— (1972), *Report of the work of the Probation and After-Care Department 1969–1971*, Cmnd. 5158 (London: HMSO).

—— (1976), *Report of the work of the Probation and After-Care Department 1972–1975*, Cmnd. 6590 (London: HMSO).

—— (1979), *An index of probation service research and experimental projects*, 3rd edn. (London: HORU).

—— (1980), *Review body on the management structure in the probation and after-care service: report of the Working Party* (London: Home Office).

—— (1984a), *Probation statistics, England and Wales 1983* (London: Home Office).

—— (1984b), *Statement of national objectives and priorities for the probation service in England and Wales* (London: Home Office).

—— (1986), *Probation statistics, England and Wales 1984* (London: Home Office).

Home Office Research and Planning Unit (1985), *Research Programme* (London: HORU).

Home Office Working Party (1979), *Marriage matters* (London: HMSO).

Hosticka, C. (1979), 'We don't care about what happened, we only care about what is going to happen', *Social Problems*, 26: 599–610.

House of Commons Expenditure Committee (1972), *First report of the expenditure committee of the House of Commons, session 1971–1972: probation and after-care, 1971* (London: HMSO).

Illich, I. (1977), *Toward a history of needs* (New York: Pantheon).

Ingleby, R. (1984), 'Consent orders', *New Law Journal*, 134: 1023–4.

—— (1985) 'Consent orders: disclosure requirements', *Cambridge Law Journal*, 44: 202–4.

—— (1986a), 'Out of court settlements: policy, principle and practice, procedure', *Mediation Quarterly*, 11: 57–68.

—— (1986b), 'The clean break—allusions to illusions and the welfare of the child', *Journal of Social Welfare Law*: 257–66.

Irving, H. H. (1980), *Divorce mediation* (Toronto: Personal Library Publishers).

Isono, S. (1985), *Kaji chotei seido no kenkyu (A study on family mediation)* (Tokyo: Daiichihokishuppan).

Isono, S., and F. Isono (1958), *Kazokuseido (The family system)* (Tokyo: Iwanamishoten).

Jaffe, L. L. (1969), *English and American judges as lawmakers* (Oxford: Oxford University Press).

James, A. L. (1985), 'Training for civil work in the probation service', *Social Work Education*, 4: 15–19.

James, A. L. and K. Wilson (1984*a*), 'Reports for the court: the work of divorce court welfare officers', *Journal of Social Welfare Law*, 89–103.

—— (1984*b*), 'The trouble with access: a study of divorcing families', *British Journal of Social Work*, 14; 487–506.

—— (1986), *Couples, conflict and change: social work with marital relationships* (London: Tavistock).

Kawashima, T. (1976), 'Dispute resolution in contemporary Japan', in H. Tanaka (ed.) assisted by M. Smith, *The Japanese legal system* (Tokyo: University of Tokyo Press).

Kelly, J. B. (1983), 'Mediation and psychotherapy: distinguishing the difference', *Mediation Quarterly*, 1: 33–44.

Kessler, S. (1978), *Creative conflict resolution: mediation* (Fountain Valley, Cal.: National Institute for Professional Training).

King, M. (1984), 'Child protection and the search for justice for parents and families in England and France', in M. D. A. Freeman (ed.), *State, law and the family* (London: Tavistock).

Kobayashi, K. (1984), *Kateisaibansho dewa Ima (Family court today)* in The Hogaku Seminar, *Special Issue: Josei to ho (Women and the Law)* (Tokyo: Nihonhyoron-sha).

Kressel, K. (1986), 'Research on divorce mediation: a summary and critique of the literature', *Vermont Law Review* (in press).

Kressel, K., M. Lopez-Morillas, J. Weinglass, and M. Deutsch (1979), 'Professional intervention in divorce: the views of lawyers, psychotherapists and clergy', in G. Leving and O. C. Moles (eds.), *Divorce and separation* (New York: Basic Books).

Law Commission (1966), *Reform of the grounds of divorce: the field of choice*, Cmnd. 3123 (London HMSO).

—— (1981), *The financial consequences of divorce*, Working Paper 112 (London: HMSO).

Law Society (1985), *A family court—consultation paper* (London: Law Society).

Lee, B. H. (1974), *Divorce law reform in England* (London: Peter Owen).

Lee, S. (1987), 'Towards a jurisprudence of consent', in J. M. Eekelaar and J. Bell (eds.), *Oxford essays in jurisprudence*, 3rd ser. (Oxford: Oxford University Press).

Lemmon, J. A. (1985), *Family mediation practice* (New York: Free Press).

Lewis, J. (1980), *The politics of motherhood* (London: Croom Helm).

Llewellyn, L. K. (1962), *Jurisprudence: legalism in theory and practice* (Chicago: University of Chicago Press).

Lohman, M. (1981), *Comprehensive mediation: a new approach to the settlement of divorce disputes* (Falls Church, Va.: mimeo).

Lord Chancellor's Department (1986), *Legal aid efficiency scrutiny* (London: Lord Chancellor's Department).

—— (1986), *Judicial statistics annual report 1985*, Cmnd. 9864 (London: HMSO).

Lyon, E., N. Thoeness, J. Pearson, and R. Appleford (1985), 'A case study: the custody mediation services of the family division, Connecticut Superior Court', *Conciliation Courts Review*, 23: 15–26.

Macaulay, S. (1979), 'Lawyers and consumer protection cases', *Law and Society Review*, 14: 115–71.

McEwen, C., and R. Maiman (1982), 'Mediation and arbitration: their promise and performance as alternatives to court', in P. Dubois (ed.), *The analysis of judicial reform* (Lexington, Mass.: D. C. Heath).

McGregor, O. R. (1957), *Divorce in England* (London: Heinemann).

McGregor, O. R., L. Blom-Cooper, and C. Gibson (1970), *Separated spouses: a study of the matrimonial jurisdiction of magistrates' courts* (London: Duckworth).

McIntosh, J. (1974), 'Processes of communication, information seeking and control associated with cancer', *Social Science and Medicine*, 8: 167–87.

McIsaac, H. (1981), 'Mandatory conciliation custody/visitation matters: California's bold stroke', *Conciliation Courts Review*, 19: 43–51.

Maidment, S. (1976), 'A study in child custody', *Family Law*, 6: 195–200; 236–41.

Manchester, A. H., and J. M. Whetton (1974), 'Marital conciliation in England and Wales', *International and Comparative Law Quarterly*, 23: 339–82.

Marshall, L. C. and G. May (1932), *The divorce court*, vol. i (Baltimore: The Johns Hopkins Press).

Mather, L., and B. Yngvesson (1981), 'Language, audience and the transformation of disputes', *Law and Society Review*, 15: 775–821.

Melli, M. S., H. S. Erlanger, and E. Chambliss (1985), *The process of negotiation: an exploratory investigation in the divorce context*, Disputes Processing Research Program, Institute for Legal Studies, University of Wisconsin, Madison.

Merry, S. (1982), 'The social organization of mediation in non-industrial societies', in Abel (1982*b*), vol. ii.

Merry, S. E., and A. Rocheleau (1985), *Mediation in families: a further study of the children's hearing project* (Cambridge, Mass.: mimeo).

Mikazuki, A. (1976), 'Saibansho seido' ('The judicial system') in H. Tanaka (ed.) assisted by M. Smith, *The Japanese legal system* (Tokyo: University of Tokyo Press).

Miller, R., and A. Sarat (1981), 'Grievances, claims and disputes', *Law and Society Review*, 15: 525–66.

Ministry of Health (1984), *Vital Statistics special report: divorce* (Tokyo: Koseitokeikyokai).

Mitchell, J. C. (1983), 'Case and situation analysis', *Sociological Review*, 31: 187–211.

Mnookin, R. (1975), 'Child custody adjudication: judicial functions in the face of indeterminacy', *Law and Contemporary Problems*, 39: 226–9.

—— (1984), 'Divorce bargaining: the limits of private ordering', in J. M.

Eekelaar and S. N. Katz (eds.), *The resolution of family conflict: comparative legal perspectives* (Toronto: Butterworth).

Mnookin, R. H., and L. Kornhauser (1979), 'Bargaining in the shadow of the law: The case of divorce', *Yale Law Journal*, 88: 950–97.

Mortimer, J. (1982), *Clinging to the wreckage* (London: Weidenfeld and Nicolson).

Murch, M. (1980), *Justice and welfare in divorce* (London: Sweet and Maxwell).

Murray, T., R. Dingwall, and J. M. Eekelaar (1983), 'Professionals in bureaucracies: solicitors in private practice and local government', in R. Dingwall and P. S. C. Lewis (eds.), *The sociology of the professions: lawyers, doctors and others* (London: Macmillan).

Naito, Y. (1974), 'Kateisaibansho no enkaku' ('A history of the family court'), in Z. Nakagawa (ed.), *Kazoku mondai to Kazokuho VII: kaji saiban (Family problems and family law VII: family court)* (Tokyo: Sakaishoten).

NAPO (1984), *Discussion paper on conciliation*, National Association of Probation Officers, Probation Practice Committee, February.

National Probation Research and Information Exchange (1984), *An index of probation projects, 1983/94: information about developing probation practice and projects* (London: NPRIE).

Numabe, A. (1977), *Kaji chotei biboroku (A memorandum for family mediation)* (Tokyo: Nihonchoteikyokairengokai).

O'Donovan, K. (1985), *Sexual divisions in law* (London: Weidenfeld and Nicolson).

Olsen, D., M. Cleveland, P. Doyle, R. Reimer, B. Robinson, and M. Rockcastle (1979), *Child custody research project* (Minneapolis, Minn.: unpublished report).

Ormerod. R. (1973), 'The role of the courts in relation to children', Sixth Hilda Lewis Memorial Lecture, London.

Osaka Women Lawyers (1983), *Kasai chotei (Chotei in the family court)* (Osaka: Osaka Branch of the Women Lawyers' Association).

Pahl, J. (1985), *Private violence and public policy: the needs of battered women and the response of the public services* (London: Routledge and Kegan Paul).

Palazzoli, M. S. (1985), 'The emergence of a comprehensive systems approach', *Journal of Family Therapy*, 7: 135–46.

Palazzoli, M. S., L. Goscolo, and G. Prata (1978), *Paradox and counter-paradox* (New York: Aronson).

Parmiter, G. (1981), 'Bristol in-court conciliation procedure', *Law Society's Gazette*, 25 February: 196.

Parker, R. A. (1975) 'Social administration and scarcity', in E. Butterworth and R. Holman (eds.) *Social welfare in modern Britain* (London: Fontana/Collins).

Parkinson, L. (1983a), 'Conciliation: pros and cons (I)', *Family Law*, 13: 22–5.

—— (1983b), 'Conciliation: a new approach to family conflict resolution', *British Journal of Social Work*, 13, 19–37.

—— (1986a), 'Conciliation in Britain', *Mediation Quarterly*, 11: 69–82.

—— (1986b), *Conciliation in separation and divorce* (London: Croom Helm).

Parsons, T. (1954), 'A sociologist looks at the legal profession', in T. Parsons (ed.), *Essays in sociological theory* (Glencoe, Ill.: Free Press).

Pearson, J. (1982), 'An evaluation of alternatives to court adjudication', *Justice System Journal*, 7: 420–44.

Pearson, J., and N. Thoeness (1982), 'Mediation of contested child custody disputes', *The Colorado Lawyer*, 11: 337–55.

—— (1984*a*), 'A preliminary portrait of client reactions to three court mediation programs', *Mediation Quarterly*, 3: 21–40.

—— (1984*b*), 'Mediating and litigating custody disputes, a longitudinal evaluation', *Family Law Quarterly*, 17: 497–524.

Pearson, J., N. Thoeness, and A. Milne (1982), *Directory of mediation services* (Denver: AFCC Research Unit).

Pearson, J., M. Ring, and A. Milne (1983), 'A portrait of divorce mediation services in the public and private sector', *Conciliation Courts Review*, 21: 1–24.

Piliavin, I., and S. Briar (1964), 'Police encounters with juveniles', *American Journal of Sociology*, 69: 206–14.

Practice Direction (1986) *Family Law* 16: 286.

Priest, J. A., and J. C. Whybrow (1986), *Custody law in practice in the divorce and domestic courts: supplement to Law Commission Working Paper No. 96, review of child law: custody* (London: HMSO).

Pruitt, D., and K. Kressel (1985), 'Mediation in social conflict: an introduction', *Journal of Social Issues*, 41: 1–10.

Rein, M. (1983), *From policy to practice* (London: Macmillan).

Report of the departmental committee on social services in the courts of summary jurisdiction (1936), Cmnd. 5122 (London: HMSO).

Rheinstein, M. (1972), *Marriage stability, divorce and the law* (Chicago: University of Chicago Press).

Roberts, S. (1983), 'Mediation in family disputes', *Modern Law Review*, 46: 537–57.

—— (1986), 'Toward a minimal form of alternative intervention', *Mediation Quarterly*, 11: 25–41.

Robinson Committee (1983), *Report of the interdepartmental committee on conciliation* (London: HMSO).

Robson, P., and P. Watchman (1981), 'The homeless person's obstacle race', *Journal of Social Welfare Law*, 1–15.

Ross, H. L. (1970), *Settled out of court: the social process of insurance claims* (Chicago: Aldine).

Royal Commission on Marriage and Divorce (1956), *Report of the royal commission on marriage and divorce*, Cmnd. 9678 (London: HMSO).

Rutter, M., and H. Giller (1983), *Juvenile delinquency: trends and perspectives* (Harmondsworth: Penguin).

Sander, F. E. A. (1976), 'Varieties of dispute processing', *Federal Rules Decisions*, 70: 111–33.

—— (1985), 'Alternative dispute resolution in the United States: an overview', *Justice for a Generation* (St Paul: West Publishing Co.).

Sarat, A. (1977), 'Studying American legal culture', *Law and Society Review*, 11: 427–88.

Sarat, A., and W. L. F. Felstiner (1986), 'Law and strategy in the divorce lawyers office', *Law and Society Review*, 20: 93–134.

Schapera, I. (1955), *A handbook of Tswana law and custom*, vol. i (London: Oxford University Press).

Shapiro, M. (1981), *Courts: a comparative and political analysis* (Chicago: University of Chicago Press).

Shepherd, G., and J. Howard (1985), 'Theft of conciliation? The thieves reply', *Probation Journal*, 32: 59–60.

Shepherd, G., J. Howard, and J. Tonkinson (1984), 'Conciliation: taking it seriously?' *Probation Journal*, 31: 21–4.

Silbey, S. (1981), 'Making sense of the lower courts', *The Justice System Journal*, 6: 13–27.

Silbey, S., and S. Merry (1986), 'Mediator settlement strategies', *Law and Policy*, 8: 7–32.

Simon W. (1978), 'The ideology of advocacy', *Wisconsin Law Review*, 30: 29–144.

Skolnick, J. (1966), *Justice without trial: law enforcement in democratic society* (New York: Wiley).

Strong, P. M. (1979), *The ceremonial order of the clinic* (London: Routledge and Kegan Paul).

Tanaka, H. (1976), 'Jittei hogaku nyumon' ('Introduction to the study of positive law') in H. Tanaka (ed.) assisted by M. Smith, *The Japanese legal system* (Tokyo: University of Tokyo Press).

Titmuss, R. M. (1950), *Problems of social policy* (London: HMSO).

Unger, R. (1975), *Knowledge and politics* (New York: Free Press).

Vanderkooi, L., and J. Pearson (1983), 'Mediating divorce disputes: mediator behaviors, styles and roles', *Family Relations*, 32: 557–66.

Wallerstein, J. S., and J. B. Kelly (1980), *Surviving the break-up: how children and parents cope with divorce* (London: Grant McIntyre).

Weitzman, L. (1984), 'No fault divorce and the transformation of marriage', paper read at the Law and Society Association Annual Meeting, Boston, Mass.

Westcott, J. (1983), 'Report of the interdepartmental committee on conciliation: a review', *Law Society'e Gazette*, 12 October: 2509–10.

Wolff, K. (1950), *The sociology of Georg Simmel* (New York: Free Press).

Yates, C. (1983a), 'Out of court conciliation services: the tolling bell that dropped a clanger', *New Law Journal*, 133: 993–4.

—— (1983b), 'The interdepartmental committee: a step backwards', *Journal of Social Welfare Law*, 335–41.

Acts

Children and Young Persons Act 1969
Courts Act 1971
Criminal Justice Act 1972
Divorce Reform Act 1969
Housing (Homeless Persons) Act 1977
Legal Aid Act 1960
Matrimonial Causes Act 1937
Matrimonial Causes Act 1963
Matrimonial Causes Act 1973
Supplementary Benefit Act 1976
Summary Procedure (Domestic Proceedings) Act 1937

Cases

Brown *v.* Brown [1967] P 105
Edgar *v.* Edgar [1980] 1 WLR 1410
Edwards *v.* Edwards [1986] 1 FLR 187
Emanuel *v.* Emanuel [1946] P 115
Godfrey *v.* Godfrey [1965] AC 444.
Hulley *v.* Thompson [1981] 1 WLR 159
Morley-Clarke *v.* Jones [1986] Ch 311; [1986] 1 WLR 978
Nash *v.* Nash [1965] P 266
Re H (a Minor) [1986] 1 FLR 476
Re W (a Minor), *The Times*, 27 October 1982
Scott *v.* Scott [1986] 2 FLR 320
Sherdley *v.* Sherdley [1986] 1 WLR 732

Index

Abel, R. L. 30, 111, 114–15, 136, 138, 150
Abse, Leo 9
Achenbach, T. 83
Archbishop of Canterbury 9
Arnold, Sir J. 62
Atkins, S. 52
Atkinson, J. M. 167, 172, 175

Bader, K. 95, 98–9, 105
Baldwin, J. 8
Bell, J. S. 176
Berends, M. 23
Bienenfeld, F. 71
Block, J. 87
Blumberg, A. S. 28, 32, 35, 38
Bochel, D. 56–7
Bogoch, B. 23
Booth, Mrs. Justice 6, 20–1, 51–2, 54, 64, 70, 95, 109, 111, 147, 171, 177
Borkowski, M. 53
Boswell, G. R. 68
Bottomley, A. 111, 141–2, 166, 172
Bradshaw, A. 169
Brandeis, L. 23
Briar, S. 171
Bristol, conciliation schemes in 14, 17–18, 95 ff.
Bromley, conciliation scheme in 17
Brown, D. 71
Bryan, M. 50
Burgoyne, J. 9

Caesar-Wolf, B. 23
Cain, M. 9, 23, 37–8
Cardozo, B. N. 175
Cauble, A. E. 86
Chess, T. 88
children 6, 15, 47, 56–7, 62–5, 71, 74, 77, 81, 83–5, 88, 142, 145–6, 149, 151, 175, 177–80
Clive, E. 63, 169
Cohen, S. 86
collusion 7–8
Comaroff, J. 138
Comeaux, E. 71, 73
conciliation, process of 3–22, 51–3, 60–6, 97–115, 150–67
    see also mediation

condonation 7
Connecticut, mediation in 72 ff.
consent 173–4
Coogler, O. J. 71
Cretney, S. M. 45, 49
Curran, B. 23

Danet, B. 23
Davis, G. 15, 18, 64, 66, 95–9, 105, 110, 171, 176–7
Denning, Mr. Justice (Lord) 5–6, 8, 56
Dingwall, R. 13, 14, 17, 43, 53, 110–11, 152, 171–3, 177–9, 180–1
divorce, grounds 4, 7, 10
    incidence 4–7, 10
    in Japan 116–20
Donohoe, W. A. 75
Drew, P. 175
Dworkin, R. 175

Edelbrock, C. 83
Eekelaar, J. 10, 17, 63, 111, 169, 174–5, 177, 179
Emerson, R. 171
Emery, R. 71, 88
Epstein, A. L. 113
Erlanger, H. S. 8
Ewbank, Mr. Justice 61

family court 11, 69, 122–6, 147, 170–1
Felstiner, W. 24, 30, 38, 40, 46, 169
Fenn, P. 181
Ferguson, S. 5
Finer, Sir M. 11, 57, 61, 69, 147
Fisher, R. 169
Fitzgerald, H. 5
Fletcher, R. 7, 10
Folberg, J. 44, 51, 53–4, 167, 169
Frank, J. 30
Freeman, M. 53–4
Fukaya, M. 120
Fukutake, T. 118

Gabel, P. 32, 41
Galanter, M. 48
Genn, H. 8, 47
Gibson, C. 11
Giller, H. 57

Goffman, E. 152
Gordon, R. 41
Gough, D. M. 63
Griffiths, A. 171–2
Griffiths, J. 37, 45–6, 49
Gulliver, P. H. 113, 141

Haley, J. 121
Hall, J. 58, 63, 69
Hart, H. L. A. 175
Hart, N. 22, 52
Harvey, C. P. 9
Hawkins, K. 43, 171
Haxby, D. 57
Haynes, J. M. 44, 53–4, 71, 151, 169
Heritage, J. 167
Hennepin County, mediation in 72 ff.
Hetherington, M. 88
Hiraga, K. 122
Hoggett, B. 45, 52
Holmes, O. W. 175
Hosticka, C. 23
Howard, J. 102

Illich, I. 41
Ingleby, R. 8, 43, 51, 54, 169–70, 176, 178
Irving, H. H. 71
Isono, F. 121
Isono, S. 121

Jaffe, L. L. 175
James, A. 60–1, 63–4, 66, 68, 170
Jefferson, G. 167

Kawashima, T. 121
Kelly, J. B. 51–2, 61, 63
Kessler, S. 71
King, M. 113–14
Kornhauser, L. 49–50
Kreger, B. 87
Kressel, K. 72, 88

Lee, B. H. 10
Lee, S. 173
legal aid, 7, 10, 19, 48, 180–1
Lemmon, J. A. 167, 169
Lewis, J. 4
Listowel, Lord 4
Llewellyn, K. 175
Lohman, M. 71
Lord Chancellor's Department 19–20
Los Angeles, mediation in 72 ff.
Lyon, E. 76

Macaulay, S. 38
McConville, M. 8
McEwen, C. 72, 87
McGregor, O. R. 3, 7, 10
McIntosh, J. 23
McIsaac, H. 86
Maclean, M. 179
magistrates' courts 3–4, 6, 111–12
Maidment, S. 169
Maiman, R. 72, 87
Manchester, A. H. 12–14
marriage guidance 4, 13–14
Marshall, L. C. 8
Martin, D. F. 58, 63, 69
Mather, L. 30, 38
May, G. 8
mediation, process of 73–91, 117–19, 144–9, 176
Melli, M. S. 8, 49
Merriman, Lord 6, 8
Merry, S. 87, 165, 172, 176
Mikazuki, A. 125
Miller, R. 23
Minamikata, S. 171, 175
Mitchell, J. C. 130, 152
Mnookin, R. 49–50, 88, 178
Mortimer, John 8
Murch, M. 4, 12, 15, 177
Murray, T. 167

Naito, Y. 122
National Family Conciliation Council 14
Numabe, A. 124

O'Donovan, K. 130
Olsen, D. 83
Ormerod, Sir R. 102

Pahl, J. 53
Palazzoli, M. S. 16
Parkinson, L. 8, 12, 14–15, 43, 48, 63, 95, 109, 151, 169
Parmiter, G. 18, 95
Parsons, T. 23
Pearl, D. 45
Pearson, J. 71–6, 80, 87–8, 108, 170–1
Piliavin, I. 171
Priest, J. A. 169
probation (welfare) service 4, 6, 16, 19, 56–70, 104–6
Pruitt, D. 72

reconciliation 3–12, 79, 119
Rein, M. 21, 168–9

Rheinstein, M. 9
Roberts, S. 97, 104–5, 109–10, 138, 145, 149, 151, 166, 172–3
Robinson Committee 18–21, 142
Robson, P. 50
Rocheleau, A. 87
Ross, H. L. 8, 47
Royal Commission on Marriage and Divorce (1956) 7, 56
Rutter, M. 57

Sander, F. E. A. 147–8
Sarat, A. 23–4, 30, 40, 46, 169
Schapera, I. 139
Shapiro, M. 176
Shepherd, G. 102
Silbey, S. 111–12, 165, 176
Simmel, G. 165
Simon, W. 30
Skolnick, J. 43
Strong, P. 153
supervision 174–9

Tanaka, H. 121

Taylor, A. 44, 51, 53–4, 167, 169
Thoeness, N. 73–4, 76, 80, 88, 108, 170–1
Titmuss, R. 5
Tonkinson, J. 102

Unger, R. 32
Ury, W. 169

Vanderkooi, L. 75
violence, marital 52–3

Wallerstein, J. S. 51–2, 63
Watchman, P. 50
Weitzman, L. 41–2
Westcott, J. 18
Whetton, J. M. 12–14
Westcott, J. 97
Whybrow, J. C. 169
Wilson, K. 60–1, 63–4, 66
Wolff, K. 165

Yates, C. 18
Yngvesson, B. 30, 38